SAVING
EMPATHY

Ryan Harper

SAVING EMPATHY

Na·ture

noun

the phenomena of the physical world collectively, including plants, animals, the landscape, and other features and products of the earth, as opposed to humans or human creations.

CHAPTER ONE
SAVING EMPATHY,
WORKSHOP 1

"Hi Jess."

"Hello Ryan. How are you today?"

"Well...I guess it remains to be seen or heard," I said, smiling.

"Oh lord. So...are you going to tell me?"

"Tell you?"

"Don't do that."

"Do what?"

"Starting out annoying, I see. So that's how it's going to be?"

"No, Jess, I just need a moment to find my in."

"Your in?"

"Yeah, my pivot." I then move back and forth like a basketball player in front of her, trying to find my lane to an imaginary basket.

"Trust me, I'm giving you the entire court," she says.

"It's not easy, Jess."

"What's not easy? You're being strange."

"It's not easy starting."

"Staring what? You know we only have our lunch break, right?"

"Right. Ok. Here I go, ready?"

"Oh god, would you please go? Do you have cancer? Did you win the lottery? Did you invent a sustainable fusion reactor?"

I slap my face on both sides with both hands as fast as possible, getting up the courage. Jess looks at me with frustration but also a tinge of amusement.

I begin. "Alright, Jessica, thank you for letting us meet at your house today. I need your help with a special project."

"A project? So, it is a fusion reactor?" she questions jokingly.

"Ah, not exactly. Think more special. The most special of all special projects. The pinnacle, the crest, the zenith, the apex, the peak of all scientific endeavors."

"Better than a fusion reactor? Well, this sounds interesting."

"Yes, better than fusion but very different. Way more important to humanity, I might add."

"Ok, my curiosity is sparked. What is it?"

"Hmm, ok, first though, I need to tell you a secret."

"A secret?"

"Yes, a secret about me. Do you promise never to tell?"

"Of course."

"No, really, do you promise that what I'm about to tell you will always remain with just us unless we decide otherwise?"

"God, you are frustrating. Yes, I promise. We have known each other for quite some time. I would never do anything to hurt you. Come here. Hold my hand and look me directly in my eyes and let's shake on it."

We do, and she instantly makes me feel better.

"Now get on with it man!"

"Ok, I've got my lane, and I'm ready. Jessica, the secret is I have an obsession that I have never told you about."

"An obsession? Oooookay. And it is?"

I pause.

"Go man...We only have our lunch break, remember?"

"Ok, Ok, I, Jessica, am obsessed with Nature."

"Nature? That's it? Geez, for a second, I thought it was going to be like some weird thing. Why is that a secret? You keep bonsai trees in your basement? You have a pet frog named Carl?"

"No, it's way, way, way different than that."

"Ok, need a little more info."

"Jessica, I'm obsessed with the mechanics of Nature."

"Mechanics?"

"Yes, the mechanics of Nature."

"You're a mechanical engineer, and you are obsessed with Nature? Shouldn't it be like engines and stuff?"

"It should, but it's not. Nature is way more interesting. Vastly more interesting. Infinitely more interesting."

"Ok, but what do you mean by mechanics?"

"Mechanics as defined as a science that deals with energy and forces and their effect on bodies. The exact definition from Webster and very apt to the discussion, I might add."

"Ok, I'm starting to get slightly more interested. However, now that I think about it, I don't even know what Nature encompasses. When you say Nature, what do you mean exactly, just so I'm clear?"

"It has many definitions. Many would think of Nature as the physical world around us, mainly including plants and animals. In a sense, everything you see in the natural world but humans. Think of the Earth before humankind."

"For me, though, the definition is life."

"Ok, so you are obsessed with the mechanics of life?"

"Yes. The reason it is here. The reason it endures. Its tenacity. Its stability. The reason it fills the earth yet keeps an exacting balance. The force of life. The life force."

"You're not going to do a *Star Wars* quote, are you?"

"No. Wait, should I? Help me, Jessica. You're my only hope."

"Funny. Ok, so the mechanics of what makes life work? That's your obsession?"

"Yes, you are getting it."

"I'm still lost, though. Why should this be a secret? I already know you're weird. I would just add this to the weird pile."

"Jessica, I believe that I fully understand the mechanics of life and how it works. I have studied it for almost 20 years. An unflinching, unwavering obsession. Always on my mind. My every waking thought. A force pulling me to its inner workings. I'm always trying to understand it. I'm like an astrophysicist always gazing upward, obsessing about the exacting movement of the heavens."

"Well, that sounds rather romantic. I still don't get the secret part."

"Jess, the heavens can be a violent place. Born from fire and collisions. It's beautiful to look at, but the mechanics can kill you, much, I might add, like Nature."

"Alright, I'm all in. Very interested at this point. Why would you keep an obsession about the mechanics of life a secret, and why have you decided to tell me now on our lunch break in such an odd fashion?"

"Jess, if I understand the mechanics of life, then I understand how and why it evolves."

"You mean like natural variation and selection? Like Darwin?"

"No, Jess, it doesn't work like that. In fact, it doesn't work anything like that. Life is way more intelligent."

"You're saying Darwin is wrong? Was wrong? Is that the secret?"

"No, way worse, at least for humanity."

"Huh, confused. Will you cut to the chase and tell me!"

"Jess, humans are evolving back into animals," I say rather flatly.

Jess then takes a step back and cocks her head, staring at me, trying to decipher what I just said. She is motionless for what seems like, to me, an eternity. Finally, I take a step towards her and gently shake her shoulders playfully, as if I'm reviving her from something.

"Hello? Jess? Come in Jess, mission control calling Jessica, do you read?"

She rolls her eyes back in her head, playing along. After a few seconds, she rolls her eyes back to me, as if coming out of a delirium. She sees my frustration, which seems to give her a bit of amusement.

"Can you give me a minute? I'm trying to think of what to say."

Each second she waits is agony to me.

"Well, I get the secret part now. That sounds secret worthy."

"Ok, but I now have a dilemma."

"A dilemma?"

"Yes, if I were a stranger and you told me that, I would laugh in your face and run away. However, even though I know you are weird, I also know you are highly intelligent. In fact, and please don't get a big head when I say this, you are the most intelligent person I have ever met."

"So now a dilemma or quandary emerges. I know you're aware what you just said sounds a little crazy. I also know you wouldn't say something like that unless you knew you could prove it. Am I right?"

"Definitely."

"Ok, this just went from interesting to another level."

"I'm glad you feel that way," I said.

"I'm all into the secret part. Should we whisper? Lower the blinds? Should I unplug my Alexa?"

"Funny Jess."

"Sorry, just trying to lighten the mood after that bombshell."

"Just so I'm clear, not only do you think you can prove Darwin was wrong, you also can prove that humans are evolving back into animals?"

"Yes."

"Technically, we are animals; you know that, right?" Jess says, cocking her head, now looking like she's correcting me.

"Of course, Jess, but humans are the most special of all the animals ever to inhabit this planet by a million-fold. So different that they are in a classification all by themselves. Think of lower animals on one plane and humans all by themselves on another. I believe there is one simple reason for this marked difference. It boils down to one trait or ability, and they are slowly losing it. Human beings, with the complete loss of this trait, will look and behave much differently in the future. At some point, if no action is taken, what gave rise to humankind's marked difference from the past will be gone."

"Ok, but if we lose something, isn't that devolving?"

"Not in Nature's eyes. Evolution is change. Something different."

"And the something different is an animal?"

"Yes."

"I'm still a little confused."

"Ok, to be fair and to lower the attempted shock value, I don't really know what to call it, but all mammals present and past don't have what humans have, and if humans lose their specialness...well, what are you left with?"

"Ok, but the word animal seems a little offensive, maybe?" Jess says, nudging me to come up with another one.

"Well, you would agree that humans are strikingly different from anything on this planet both in how they look and behave, right?"

"Of course."

"Well, again, I believe it is one thing and one thing only that has given rise to this marked difference. Think of it as a special gift from Nature given only to humans in the last 3.8 billion years."

"And you can prove that we are slowly losing this, 'one thing'? You can show it somehow?"

"Yes."

"You know that many people still don't believe in evolution, right?"

"Yes, I know, Jess. I'm aware."

"I guess you've seen the anti-evolution billboard coming into town? I think it's the only one not for a personal injury attorney. It's like a monkey progressing to an ape, then a human, and there's this red circle with a line through it, like the *Ghostbusters* thing."

"Seen it, and you know that's called a no symbol, right?"

Jess blushes slightly from not knowing.

"Oh my god, you are so much smarter than me; you googled it before I did," she said mockingly. "Yeah, you have an uphill battle, to say the least. Evolution is not fully accepted by everyone, and your goal, I'm assuming, is to show people somehow that humanity is changing? Losing something? Evolving...backwards?"

"You're getting there. But remember, losing something special, a trait taken for granted and then becoming something else."

"Ok, and we're at my house on our lunch break because?"

"You'll see."

"Frustrating. So frustrating."

"Ok, so back to Darwin, how do you know you're right, and he's wrong?"

"Trust me Jess. If Darwin was somehow standing beside us, I could convince him in about 30 minutes he was wrong."

"30 minutes? That seems challenging."

"Not really, see Darwin, during his era, was at a major disadvantage."

"Disadvantage?" Jess asked.

"Yes, actually, both Darwin and Lamarck, his greatest opponent, were at a disadvantage. They didn't know anything about the mechanics of life or biology. The term stress wasn't even coined until 1920ish. Darwin lived from 1809 until 1882. Lamarck 1744 to 1829. The stress axis or HPA axis, DNA methylation, epigenetics, histone modification, RNA modification, gene expression, glucocorticoids. These words were all foreign to them. I'm confident that if I could somehow go back in time and pluck Darwin from his existence and pull him back to the present day, I could convince him in about 15 minutes he was wrong."

"So, this is somehow about stress? Wait 15 minutes? You said 30."

"Yeah, but I can do it in 15."

"Ok, I'm in. What would be your strategy?"

"Simple, I would explain to him what a negative feedback control loop is and then show him part of a video."

I take out my phone, quickly find it and show her the video.

"It's on YouTube and called, The Workhorse of the Cell: Kinesin.[1] Have you ever seen it?"

"No, I don't think so."

I start the video and watch her face as she watches. It gets to the part where the kinesins start walking, and she says, "Oh my god, what are those things? They're walking!"

"Those are called kinesins. They are protein motors. They transport large cellular cargo like lipids and organelles to other parts of the cell."

"That's incredible," she said.

"Then I would explain to Darwin what a negative feedback control loop is and that we use them in industry to control machines. They use external sensory input. There's likely an infinite number of these inside our bodies controlling homeostasis plus our response to environmental change."

"Feedback loops in biology? I did not know that. Hmm, ok, so basically, your strategy would be to try and convince him that we are somehow biological machines?"

"For the most part yes, I mean look at these things, the kinesins. These protein motors. They are moving like clockwork. He would be familiar with machines. The first sewing machine was invented in the late 1700s."

"Jess, for fun, let's imagine Darwin is here in the room with us, and he just watched the video. Let's pretend we are having a dialog with him. You play Darwin, Jess."

"You're funny Ryan, but sure, why not, I'll play along."

"Darwin," I said. "These things you just watched, the kinesins, are inside of us, inside our cells. There are trillions of cells inside our bodies, which means there are hundreds of trillions of these things constantly moving, walking back and forth on their own, moving cargo throughout the cell for its survival, 24-7, like clockwork, moving like a machine. So tell us, Darwin, based on your theory, how did these things evolve? How do the kinesins know what to do? What is their instruction set, their intelligence, their motivation? Why are they compelled to do what they do? Ultimately, how does natural variation and natural selection create such a well-ordered orchestra of moving parts?"

Jess looks speechless, unable to derive an answer.

"Ok Jess, this is the part where you say, so perhaps evolution is significantly more complicated than I imagined?"

She repeats, and then I say, "Yes, Darwin, well said," I said to Jess. Jess cocks her head, nodding in approval, now fully acting in our off-scripted play, pretending his spirit is in the room.

"You got the part right that we all evolved from lower life forms, the easy part, no offense, but you missed on the mechanics part. Natural variation and natural selection is not the driving force for species to evolve. It's stress, and to be more specific, it's persistent stress."

"Stress, what is stress?" Jess-Darwin asked.

I look at her a little shocked that she is taking the lead beyond my improvised script.

"Well, Darwin, good question." I pick up my phone and google stress, reading the first one. "Stress is defined as a state of mental or emotional strain or tension resulting from adverse or very demanding circumstances." I pause for a moment looking disappointed.

"Wow Darwin, sorry, that is a bad definition. Let me give you a better one. As a species, we need to define this better. Stress is energy beyond adaptation. It's just that simple. Imagine a species with a certain adaption for a given environment, and the environment suddenly changes. This change would require more energy to cope. This additional energy is stress."

"Jess, this is where you say, so life is reacting and responding to its environment and ultimately changing? That means Lamarck, my contemporary, was right?"

She acknowledges and then repeats verbatim.

"Well, sort of, he was definitely righter than you were," I said. "As you are aware, the main difference in your two theories or hypotheses was life responding or not responding to environmental changes. You said variation exists naturally, and some variation will be better suited to a changing environment than others, which ultimately determines how life evolves. In the video, I hope you can see that life is way more complicated and intelligent than you ever imagined."

"If life is a biological machine that's intelligent, what is it programmed to do?" Jess asked, fully into our off-scripted play.

"Jess, you realize that Darwin is not going to know the word programmed, right?"

"Yes, I thought of that, but I couldn't think of another."

"Better to use the phrase, predetermined plan, Jess. It was popular back then on this discussion."

"Ahh, ok, if life is a biological machine that's intelligent, what is its predetermined plan?"

"Good question Darwin," I smile her way. "Life's predetermined plan is survival, as a whole, through biodiversity. It's programmed to make many species versus a few. Use the Sun's energy as efficiently as possible to make as many different life forms as possible. This ensures life's survival. This is why it's so responsive to its environment. It's for its own survival. If there is a sudden change, it must also suddenly change to protect itself. Darwin, remember the discussion about the negative feedback control? Well, it's essentially persistent stress high, change the design of life, stress low, maintain it. Energy beyond adaptation is a bad thing if it is persistent because, ultimately, it means less energy to go around and less diversity. Life will do everything it can to be efficient. Life constantly measures its energy expenditure for a given environment and passes that information forward to future generations, if energy is beyond its adaptation, to change."

"Jess, this is the part where Darwin says, 'WOW' and stares off into the distance, as if life's greatest mysteries were finally revealed to him."

Jess says it exaggerated like she's mocking me.

"I think you are overacting, Jess." We both laugh and end our thought experiment, like we have ended a play, act one, scene one. She bows to an imaginary audience and says, "and...scene."

"That would be funny to bring him back and say he was wrong. You realize he probably wouldn't admit he was wrong, even if you showed him all this. You know how men are," she said jokingly.

"Ok, but it still begs the question, are you 100 percent sure you're right, and he's wrong? I know you are highly intelligent but also a little crazy, are you sure?"

"Yes Jess. I'm sure. Life is a biological machine, like in the video, running like clockwork, constantly measuring stress and passing that information forward to evolve, and yours, mine, and everyone else's consciousness sits right on top of it. Darwin was wrong, and I'm right. Life is a pre-programmed biological force; whose pre-determined plan or goal is biodiversity, and it's trying to correct humanity to restore the balance of Nature."

"Wow, you do realize that sounds crazy, right?"

"Yes, of course, if I step back, it sounds insane, but it's true. Jess, who was the smartest person ever to live?"

"Simple, Albert Einstein."

"Right, and one of his famous quotes was, 'if at first the idea is not absurd then there is no hope for it.' Well, what did he mean by this? He meant that significant paradigm shifts, at first, can sometimes seem preposterous. His discovery that time is not constant and changes with speed, is there any greater example?"

"Imagine you could go back 100 years before Einstein and tell this to every person you saw. They would eventually lock you up in a mental institution. But as incredulous as it sounds, it's true. I mean, even today, it's hard for most people to understand. I told this to some of the people at work, and they thought I was crazy, which made me wonder why they weren't taught this in school. Anyway, I told them to imagine being a father in his mid-thirties with young teenagers. The father is riding in a spaceship circling the solar system and traveling at 98 percent light speed for ten years. When the father comes back to Earth, he'd be considerably younger than his children. They thought I was insane. I had to look it up and show it to them. I still don't think they fully understand, and honestly, they probably shouldn't. I mean, it's highly counterintuitive for the human mind that time is not constant. But the same argument is true for this. Our consciousness resides atop a biological machine running like clockwork programmed to do one thing."

"One thing?" she asked.

"Yes, ensure life's survival. It's just that simple."

"Jess, let's do a thought experiment to prove that you sit atop a programmed biological machine. Do you think you have free will?"

"Yeesss? Let me guess, the answer is no, right, and you are about to show me?"

"Jess, play along," I said, a little frustrated.

"Ok, yes, I have free will."

"No, you don't," I said with a grin. "Please answer yes or no to the following. Can you control when you are hungry?"

"No."

"Can you control when you are thirsty?"

"No again."

"Can you control when you are sleepy?"

"No."

"Can you control when you are not sleepy?"

"No."

"Can you control feelings of lust, love?"

"No."

"Can you control feelings of apathy?"

"No."

"Anxiety?"

"No."

"Can you control when you wake up in the morning and feel bad?"

"No."

"Can you control when you feel good and energetic?"

"No."

"Can you control when you get sick?"

"No."

"Can you control when you die?"

"No."

"Can you control feelings of empathy, jealousy, rage?"

"No."

"Can you control having a selfish thought, a meanspirited thought?"

"No."

"Can you control thoughts of cravings?"

"No."

"Can you control when you feel depressed? When you feel elated?"

"No."

"Can you control when you laugh, cry?"

"No."

"Can you control who you are attracted to? Can you control who is attracted to you?"

"No!!!!!"

"Jesus, Jess, what can you control?" I can see she is starting to become a little agitated.

"Well, I can control getting up and walking out of this room right now and leaving you here alone with your crazy thoughts," she said rather defiantly.

"Ok, but if you do, that initial feeling of anger or frustration or whatever feeling it is making you want to walk out, what set that in motion?" I said, rather proud of myself.

"Haha, ok, I get it. We might have very little control over our initial thoughts, impulses, and desires. So, you are saying we are a conscious being, sitting atop a......?"

"The autonomic self, Jess. Your robot self. The other you," I said.

"Ok, so my conscious self is sitting atop my autonomic self or robot self along for the ride with very little control over its direction? I don't know, maybe."

"Maybe? No, I'm right. Let me give you another example. Who is one of the greatest athletes of our generation? I'm going to go ahead and answer you since you play tennis. Roger Federer. He is arguably the GOAT, you would agree?"

"Yes, definitely in the discussion."

"Ok, who or what is responsible for his achievements? When he holds his 20th grand slam trophy up to the crowd after a well-fought victory, who do we give credit to?"

"Let me guess," she said. "Not him?"

"Exactly, it's his autonomic self we should be congratulating. I mean, think about it. What does it take to win? It takes endurance, which is not fatiguing, and motivation. Both are controlled by the stress axis. Imagine that we could go inside his autonomic self and make a few adjustments at the height of his career. With a few tweaks to the negative feedback control loop for dopamine alone, we could stop his career at 10 grand slams or propel him to 30. When he wins, it's not him that we should be celebrating, but the potential for life. The potential that's inside all of us."

"Ok, but I guess it's the word machine. I don't know, maybe it's just me, but I would think that most would have a hard time imagining that they sit on top of a biological machine."

"Jess, touch your fingers to the artery in your neck. Can you feel your heart pumping?"

She does and says, "Yes."

"Ok, now I want you to stop it."

She looks at me with frustration. "Really? Hopefully, you know I can't do that."

"So, what's the difference? Your autonomic self controls your blood flow; why can't it also control how much energy you have or don't have, if you are depressed or elated or how quickly you fatigue? And, most importantly, if your lineage changes or evolves."

"Of course, that seems logical, but I guess the hard part for people would be that they have so little control."

"Honestly, if you break it down, they don't. There are powerful forces at work compelling us or preventing us from doing things in life. Drug addiction, obsession, obesity, social anxiety, depression, winning 20 grand slams. All powerful forces pushing us in certain directions. We must understand these forces and ultimately use them to our advantage, not our demise. We all must acknowledge that these forces or mechanics are way more powerful than us."

"Ok, so you are the one, you are the only one who understands how life works? You're Neo, and everyone else lives blindly in the matrix?"

"For the most part, yes. Let me do a quick google search. It says there have been 107 billion humans to have ever lived. I believe that I am the one person, out of those, who truly understands how life works."

Jessica looks at me as if she is trying to figure out if I have genuinely had a nervous breakdown.

"Look, you don't have to look at me like I'm insane. I understand what I am saying sounds insane, but there must be a first or the first. The first one who gets it. I'm confident that I am that person. Trust me, I'm not happy about it. I would rather not have this knowledge. Ignorance is truly bliss, and I would rather be that, but I can't help it. Just like you can't control your autonomic self, I can't control mine either."

"My mind is constantly flooded with these thoughts. I'm like an OCD person who is constantly washing his hands, but my obsession is evolution and Nature. I see the world through a different set of eyes, and I can't turn it off. Everywhere I look, I see evolution. I see life as it actually works. I see the biological motors and gears moving and turning all around us. You joked about the matrix, but it's kind of like that. Everyone lives in a human construct, and my goal is to get people to come out of it and see Nature as it truly is. Understand what it is doing to humanity."

"Remember the movie *A Beautiful Mind*?" I asked.

"Yes."

"Remember the part where he sees equations? My mind works like that. It's constantly trying to figure this out, solve this mystery, decode the message from Nature."

"So, the message from Nature is that it's somehow trying to correct itself, restore the balance of life, and restore biodiversity?" Jess asked.

"Yes, for the most part, but again it's simply running this ancient program or biological hardwiring that I believe was in place day one of life. Persistent stress high...change the design of life, stress low...maintain it. Somewhere deep inside our brains and, in fact all life, there's a highly tuned energy accounting department. Just like the movement of the kinesins, they are constantly recording and measuring energy input and energy output. I guarantee the accuracy is down to calories per day. If life is intelligent, and I know it is, that means it is really, really, really intelligent. It's had a long time to perfect this logic. Billions of years to fine tune it."

"So, Darwin, the revered biologist, was wrong? You know, it's interesting when you think about how Darwinian theory is taught as fact by schools and universities across the world by the most intelligent people on the planet. Again, are you sure you're right?" she said with a smile.

"Yes. Will you please stop saying that? Darwin was wrong. Painfully wrong. Woefully wrong. Tragically wrong. Monumentally wrong. Epically wrong!!!"

I jump up on her couch, showing my passion but also smiling slightly so I don't startle her.

I shout, "The stress axis controls energy expenditure during environmental changes that we are not adapted to, and it has nothing to do with evolution? That is preposterous. It's the master energy controller. No one would design a machine like that. Energy is paramount to life's survival and progression. How in the world could the master energy controller not have any influence on evolution? It's completely and utterly ridiculous. Fight, flight or cope but don't use any of this information to evolve? How in the world am I the only one that can see this?"

"Woah, easy, Tom Cruise."

"You liked that, huh?" I said as I stepped down from her couch. "Figured you would get that reference. Ok, but aside from the dramatics, I'm serious. No one would ever design a biological machine like that. Ok, so here is the Sun that gives a finite amount of energy hitting our planet. The planet consists of all these different environments that are constantly changing. The input of how much energy an organism has used over its lifetime per environment is not important? Ridiculous. Absurd. Truly laughable. Darwin's theory is laughable. Genes from successful parents come together along with a random mutation every 10,000 years or so to explain how life progressed from a singularity to everything we see before us? Preposterous. The splendor of life, the multitude, the infinite number of kinesins marching through our cells like clockwork. Life has more intelligence than we could have ever imagined!"

"Wow, you ok?"

"No," I said with a smile, "not really."

"Ok, ok, I'll admit, if what you are saying is true about the stress axis as the central energy controller for biology during times beyond environmental adaptation, then yes, from a design standpoint, it would make sense that such information is used for evolution. However, why has no one put this together before? How are you right, and everyone else is wrong? I still have a hard time believing that I'm sitting here with the only person that has ever existed who knows how life truly works."

"Yeah, I know. I agree. It's weird. My only explanation is that people who study these things are not in it for the big picture. I mean, think about someone who goes into medicine. What do they do, they specialize. Something moved in the body, and they are in the business of moving it the other way. Think about statins or antidepressants. A control loop moved, and they invest all their energy and education into moving it the other way. No one ever stops and asks the question, why did it move in the first place? No one is looking at the overall design. Too much specialization and not enough generalization. People in this field don't want to understand it; they just want to profit from it."

"This is where engineers have the upper hand over people in medicine or pharmaceuticals, Jess. Engineers are specialists in problem-solving regarding the most efficient solution. This way of thinking leads to looking at root cause and big picture. They're interested in how entire systems work and all interact together. Think of the power grid or the textile plant where we worked. It's kind of like the trees and forest analogy. Everyone is focusing on the trees and missing the infiniteness of the forest."

"You know, Jess, I think back to that time in the mid-1800s, when evolution was being fiercely debated, and I wonder what would happen if humans hadn't picked Darwin and picked Lamarck instead. Where would we be today? Would we even be discussing childhood obesity or autism? The societal belief that life will change to a changing environment. Would we be more cautious about how we change our own environment? Pesticides, toxic chemicals, food manipulation, staring at screens all day. Would it give us pause?"

"I'm not saying conspiracy, but for me at least, it does seem like subconscious thought. Both discussions were going on at the dawn of the industrial revolution. Subconsciously, perhaps humans were thinking, we are about to start monumentally changing the environment. Hmm, let's see, which theory should we choose to describe how life works? The one that is responsive to environmental change or the one that isn't."

"Really?" Jess said, smiling. "You really think people had that much forethought back then?"

"Probably not, but it's interesting to me to imagine if the world would be different today if they had picked Lamarck. Humans picked wrong. You know they have a way of doing that. Always picking the wrong thing."

"Jess, wanna know why Lamarck lost the most epic debate of all time?"

"Yes, sure."

"It was the giraffe. Lamarck was famous for trying to explain how the giraffe got its long neck. He said that giraffes spent their entire life reaching for food which explained its unusual length. People at the time just thought that was too ridiculous. Darwin explained giraffes by saying that giraffes with slightly longer necks were more successful in their environment and thus had a greater likelihood of passing on their traits. This seemed more likely to people, so his theory had greater appeal."

"I so wish I had been there, back when Darwin was explaining the evolution of the giraffe, perhaps to an assembly of scientists. Imagine Darwin finishing his explanation, and all the scientists nod in approval as if to congratulate him with a well-done sir. Then, after all the adulation died down, I shout from the crowd, "Darwin, what about zebras?"

Darwin then turns to me with curiosity, "Zebras sir?" Darwin replies with what I imagine to be a very old English accent.

"Yes, why didn't the zebras with slightly longer necks have the same fate as the giraffe? Or even better, why aren't there numerous 4-legged creatures all with long necks eating leaves from the treetops? Your theory relies on natural variation, which would be present in all 4-legged creatures with necks, correct? Surely, as you are implying, longer necks would be an advantage to all those creatures within the same environment as the giraffe?"

Darwin nods begrudgingly.

"So then, why is the giraffe the only one?"

Darwin struggles for an answer, and the crowd turns to me.

I continue. "You know Darwin, when you think about it, the giraffe is kind of like an oddity in Nature, very much like humans, in that it is very different from all the rest. I'm assuming that's why Lamarck took a stab at it because he probably felt like if he could solve this, he could explain everything. So, the giraffe to zebra comparison is the same as the human to chimp. Why does the natural variation in zebras not lead to giraffes, just like the natural variation in chimps doesn't lead to humans? In other words, why is the zebra perfectly happy being a zebra and the chimp perfectly happy being a chimp?"

Darwin looks befuddled.

I rise from the imaginary crowd showing complete confidence that I just one-upped Darwin to Jess.

"Darwin," I say out loud. "Sir, I see that my work here is done. Let me leave you with one little nugget of thought before I zap back to the future. Darwin, is it possible that there is something influencing variation that is perhaps not natural at all?"

Jess looks at me, worried as I come out of my imaginary discussion with Darwin. "You know you are a little crazy, right?"

"Yes, I know."

"Good lord, how do you hold down a job with all these thoughts in your head?"

"Trust me. It's not easy."

"So, let me guess, you know how giraffes got their long necks?"

I pause, nodding slightly, looking at her, and she looks back at me, waiting.

"So, are you going to tell me?"

"Jesus Jess, can there be any suspense in the world anymore? Maybe after our discussions, you can figure it out."

She looks at me, annoyed. "Wait, discussions, plural?"

"More on that later; let's get back to Lamarck. Guess what they did to finally prove him wrong, wrong at least in their eyes?"

"Tell me, Nature boy."

"They cut off the tails of rats. According to Lamarckian theory of inheritance, the rats with their tails cut off should have offspring without tails. They cut off nearly 1000 tails of rats, and all their pups were born with normal tails putting his hypothesis to rest. Again, at least in their eyes."

"It's funny, what they should have done was tie the tails into a permanent knot. Or better yet, tie a weight to it that gets in the rat's way. In other words, make it a persistent stress. I guarantee you there would be epigenetic changes in the tail. I mean, why did humans lose their tail? You know we still have a tail at four weeks gestation inside the womb? Why are we now born without a tail? Simple, regulation or suppression of the genes."

"Ok, but why did we ultimately lose our tail?" Jess asked. "Why did Nature or life do this?"

"Well, most likely, after we started walking upright, it got in the way, bumping around and becoming a stress. Or, in a state of stress, life made a choice. Remember the energy accounting department I talked about inside of life? Well, imagine you oversee this department. You are monitoring energy input, output, energy to maintain DNA, expression, cellular maintenance, etcetera. The entire energy metrics are at your disposal. So obviously, energy efficiency in your environment is your primary concern, as it determines your survival and the survival of your lineage. If you are upright now and the tail is getting in the way, or you're no longer using it, what would you do?"

"Well, considering that it takes energy to maintain the tail, I would simply suppress or regulate those genes to get rid of it," she said.

"Exactly, well done, Jess. See, it's all about energy. If energy beyond adaptation is high and persistent, life will ultimately make a choice. It will evolve to increase efficiency in its environment or, stated differently, it will physically change, through generations, to eliminate the stress. Once you look at life this way, it all starts to make sense."

"Thank you," Jess said, a little gratified in the moment. "Ok, so I hate to say this, but I must get back to work. Are you going to explain to me what you meant by discussions plural and why you chose today to reveal to me your Nature obsession?"

"Yes, are you ready? Are you sitting down?"

"You're looking right at me. You see that I am sitting down."

"Yes, but are you mentally sitting down?" I said, trying to ruffle her a little.

"Go, crazy."

"I want the two of us to workshop saving humanity's special gift."

"You want who to do what for what?" she said.

"I want us to figure out a way to save it."

"The 'one thing' that makes us special?"

"Yes."

"Are you going to tell me what it is?"

"It's empathy, silly."

Jess takes a moment of reflection as if she is calculating something, nods, and then returns.

"So, you can somehow prove that empathy is dying in the human race?"

"Yes, and I want us to save it."

"Have you gone mad? If it is, how would we even..."

"Jess, I'm serious. I want us to workshop saving empathy. Look, I'm 100 percent confident this is happening, that Nature is trying to correct itself and restore the balance of life. Nature is quickly revealing to humanity how evolution actually works, and I want you and me to workshop stopping it before it's too late."

"You want us to stop Nature?"

"Yes."

"You and me?"

"Yes."

"In a workshop?"

"Yes."

"You and me against Nature?"

"Yes."

"Look, again, I have known you for a long time, and I know that you see the world differently and are highly intelligent, but if you're right and empathy is somehow dying, how are we going to stop it?"

"Jess, that is what the workshop is for. Will you just trust me? Humans are capable of incredible things when they put their minds to it. They just have to be shown the way. I mean, what else are you doing, reading those Grisham books you just bought? Engrossed in the latest make-believe court drama? You must admit this is more interesting than any book ever written. It is the greatest challenge humanity will ever face, and they don't even know about it yet."

"Yes, as an engineer, I see the draw but..."

"Trust me, Jess, there has to be a way. There's a lot of people suffering in the world. Humans just need to be shown the way."

CHAPTER TWO
SAVING EMPATHY, WORKSHOP 2

"Ok, Jess, our second meeting. I hope you've had time to consider my proposal."

"Yes, I have. I actually put a lot of thought into it. Like a lot of thought. And, for the most part, you're right; this is way more interesting than Grisham. You are also right that engineers are problem solvers, and there's no greater problem to solve than this, assuming you are right? Are you sure you're right?"

"Jeeesssss!" I said a little angrily but also teasing.

"But for the most part, I see it. I mean, I don't see it like you do, at least not yet, but I see that the way we live on this planet is not sustainable. Our country is not sustainable. I mean, our current administration and those administrations of the recent past, for that matter, have no interest in the environment or sustainability. People are worried about and interested in the wrong things. It is kind of like the matrix we talked about. Our society is flooded with these stories and things that don't matter, and meanwhile, the reality of things is unseen or rarely discussed."

"Well said, Jess."

"However, I must be honest with you. I can't shake this pessimism."

"Pessimism?"

"Yes, well, I have never shared this with you, but I have grown more cynical as I have gotten older. Everyone has become so selfish and fixated on materialism and just wants to take a pill, go to bed, and not worry about anything. Kind of like artificially blissfully ignorant. Comfortably numb, so to speak."

"Jess, that's what the workshop is for, to break through that. To show humans the way."

"Don't be mad at me; I just don't think it will lead anywhere. However, I agree it is interesting, and you have a different and unique way of seeing the world, which I appreciate. As an engineer, I'm also interested in the way things work, just like you. You are right. There's no greater challenge than to figure out life and how it works and apply that knowledge to benefit humankind. It sounds corny, but it's easily the greatest challenge of all time. I just can't shake this pessimism."

"Jess, someone must try. You see that, right? Someone has to try."

She nodded.

"Jess, humanity thanks you for your attempt to save their special gift," I smile at her. "Well... maybe one day they will, assuming we succeed."

"Ok Jess, but before we proceed, I must warn you. I'm about to take you to another world. It's a world of beauty but also savagery. You may find it shocking. This is your one chance to back out if you want to. You can take the blue pill, and I'll get up and walk away. I'm forwarning you. Once you fully see it, you can't un-see it."

"Quit playing and give me the red pill, Nature boy. I want to see it all."

I reach into my pocket and take out an imaginary red pill. She opens her mouth, and I throw it in. She immediately starts choking and says, clutching her throat.

"Quick, Heimlich!"

We both laugh.

"You realize how crazy you are, right?"

"I'm crazy, look at you!" Jess said.

"Ok, before you get started, though, I want to ask you some questions about our last meeting. Sorry, I meant workshop."

"Ok."

"So, you have this obsession with Nature and the natural world?"

"Yes."

"And you have always kept it a secret?"

"Yes."

"So, you're like a closeted tree hugger?"

"Huh?"

"I mean, I'm a little confused by your profession. You're an engineer. We are engineers. We are the means by which the environment gets fucked up. We are the enablers. Wanna know how many tons of plastic the plant I work at produces every week?"

"No, I don't. I'm sure it's a big number. Probably triple the one I used to work at."

"So, all the goals and aspirations that engineers have, that's not you. Fast cars, rocket ships, computers, solar power, nanotech, battery technology, space exploration?"

"Jess, I'm obsessed with the mechanics of Nature. Vastly more interesting than a rocket ship, and don't get me started about space exploration."

"No, I want to get you started. You have a secret life, and now I'm curious. I want to see this other you."

"Well, ok, in my mind, it's the dumbest thing in the history of dumbest things. Who is that guy that is popular...Neal...Degrass...Tyson? God, would that guy please shut up about space. Ninety-nine point something percent of the population doesn't give a fuck about space. It's insulting to me that people talk about space exploration when so many fucked up things are happening on our planet. It's like Nero fiddling while Rome burned. I mean, the guy is obviously highly intelligent. To all the brilliant minds of the world, let's fix this planet and ourselves first before we start fucking up other ones. Let's master how to live on one planet before we attempt to colonize our galaxy!"

"Whoa, easy big fella, did I hit a nerve?"

"Plus, this is how life works."

"Huh, what do you mean, how life works?" Jess asked.

"When life is persistently stressed in one environment, there are evolutionary forces to push it to another one. It's programmed to seek out change."

"So, you're saying, we're all stressed on this planet, so we are programmed to find another one? Move to another environment?"

"Jess, how do you think life went from the oceans to land and then from the land to the air? Just random chance? No biological force to push it in that direction? The oceans filled with life until they couldn't hold anymore. This became a stress. Life seeks out change when stressed."

"So, Neal Degrass Tyson is like a prehistoric stressed fish?"

"Sure, why not? I mean, look at the mechanics of why someone would look up to the heavens and imagine, what if? Dopamine anyone? Why did Columbus sail the treacherous uncharted seas? Why do people climb Everest? Why do people strap on wingsuits and fly through mountain gorges? Why did we go to the moon? Why does anyone ever take on a challenge? Do something beyond their adaptation?"

"Wow, interesting," Jess said. "So, the feelings Neal has are the same feelings that a fish had coming out of the water for the first time millions of years ago?"

"Sure, dopamine is not unique to just the human species. You must look at the stress axis beyond just fight or flight. Its primary purpose is evolution. Seek out what we are not adapted to and physically change based on new environments. To see this, just think of life as this single entity and ask yourself what it wants?"

"Ok, sorry, what does it want again?"

"Jess, it simply wants to survive through filling the entire planet. This is life's programming. Just separate everything human, lock this thought into your mind, and add humanness back in. You can see how these evolutionary forces might shape our behavior and influence how we interpret the world, right? Life's one and only goal is survival, not making a human."

I see Jess struggling a little over this one. "Yeah, that is a big thought, but I'm trying." She smiles.

"Who is the other space guy, Elon Musk, right? I think one of his arguments is that we need to colonize Mars in case something happens to our planet so that we would have a backup. Again, in my mind, the dumbest thing in the history of dumbest things. Does anyone realize the amount of energy and complexity it would take to build a meaningful habitat that could recolonize Earth if something happened to our planet? Mars is a planet with 38 percent gravity and no magnetosphere, plus its soil, Mother Mars, is toxic to human life."

"This is the problem with big thinkers, Jess. No one ever considers our biology as a limiting factor. Plus, Elon already has the best solution to this problem. He owns a boring company. The best way to protect humanity in case of a massive asteroid impact is to go underground. Just build massive reserve habitats underground, all around the planet, in case we need them. Even Earth, which just went through a massive impact, like the one that killed the dinosaurs, is 1000 percent more habitable than Mars. Jess, this is our planet, this is our home, and we will never have another. Our biology locks us in."

"Do you know the Kardashev scale?"

"Umm, sounds familiar, but remind me," Jess said.

"Well, it's a scale proposed by astronomer Nikolai Kardashev as a way to judge a society's level of technological advancement by the amount of energy it uses. A type I civilization uses all the energy of their parent star that hits their planet. Type II uses the total energy of their parent star, and Type III uses all the energy of its parent galaxy. I think we are currently at 0.7 on the scale."

"I could see possibly using all the energy that hits our planet, well theoretically not all but a lot more, but how would you use all the energy of the Sun?"

"It's called a Dyson sphere. It's a manmade megastructure that encompasses the Sun, collects the solar energy, and transmits it back to Earth."

Jess and I both look at each other and then burst out laughing.

"Wow, that's dumb," Jess said. "Just the material mass alone to build such a structure would strip our entire planet. Let me guess, we live on Mars and mine it for the materials to build the superstructure, build the parts in space, fly them to the Sun and assemble it with AI nanobots."

"Exactly, and then we live happily ever after. We'll still have to get to Type III, though; we can't be a pathetic type II civilization and have all the type IIIs in the universe laughing at us."

"Ray Kurzweil, do you know him?"

"Yes, the technological singularity, right? Where man and machine hit this superintelligence with runaway growth and these unfathomable improvements to human civilization start to happen." Jess said.

"Exactly, you know our society could be on the verge of collapse, healthcare at 30 percent GDP, childhood obesity at 40 percent, autism at 1 in 20, inflation sky-high collapsing into a police state, and these futurists would still be talking about colonizing space. It's madness. We must perfect ourselves before even thinking about space exploration. Does it really make sense to colonize the galaxy when we can't even figure out how to get along with each other yet?"

"I think the problem with brilliant minds of the world is they are too detached from the real day to day. Come work in the private sector for a while, and then let's talk about a superhuman civilization. The turnover at my work is 200 percent. So many of the young people who come through our temp agency, the future of America, can barely groom themselves and are only interested in getting high and do everything they can to get out of an honest day's work."

"See again, futurists never consider our biology as a limiting factor. Let's imagine we could get to a type 1 civilization. What do you think humans would do with all that energy?"

"I don't know," Jess said, "but it can't be good."

"I know exactly. We would use it to be our slave. We would create machines that do everything for us while we do nothing. It would be like the movie *Wall-E* on steroids. What do you think the energy accounting department of the human body would do with all this energy from food consumption going in and no energy going out?"

"I don't know," Jess said, "but again, it can't be good. I guess it would be a 'does not compute' for our biology. So much energy consumed with no energy expenditure to get it? Our biology might just self-destruct. Maybe it just starts suppressing all genes until we become a flesh bag of mush. I'm kind of joking, but that would be a conundrum for Nature. It would surely affect our evolution and not in a good way."

"I agree. You know, regarding evolution, one thing Lamarck got right was his idea of use it or lose it. I can remember watching a video a while back and they were talking about how people couldn't do simple math anymore because of cell phones. They did a study of people going out to a restaurant, and most couldn't figure out the tip of 15 percent without their phone. So, imagine a type I civilization with all these machines doing things for us in a stress-based, pollution-laden society. How does Nature, life, respond to such a change? See, biology will always be the limiting factor in these grand futuristic ideas."

"We have some of the greatest minds of our generation dreaming about the mechanics of the infinite heavens while our home planet is in peril. Someone, please tell them that the vast majority doesn't give a fuck about outer space or the origins of our universe. How has any of this helped us?

It's such a waste of time and energy, and it always leads to one more why. Humans worrying about outer space is like a moth attracted to a lightbulb and contemplating its inner workings. It's like monkeys flipping through the US tax code. It's like an ant looking up and seeing the white tail of a jetliner and wondering what it is."

"Jess, you do one."

"Hmm, hang on, give me a minute. Oh, oh, it's like a snail dreaming about being a bird."

I pause, think, and then nod, congratulating her. "Not bad, Jess. I kind of like that one."

"Imagine if Einstein, the smartest person we have ever known, had been a biologist instead of a physicist. Surely, we would be better off today."

"Jess, I got to use the couch for this one, can I?"

"Sure, Nature boy, but take off your shoes."

"Thank you, Jess." I step up, clear my throat, and look beyond Jess, pretending to address all of humanity.

"Brilliant minds of the world, please, we beg of you. Stop dreaming of the heavens or the mechanics that make them move. We need your help down here on Earth. If we can't figure out how to live in lasting peace with each other and stop destroying our environment, it doesn't make sense to attempt to colonize our galaxy and fuck up other ones!"

"Wow, nice speech, Neo, but should you use profanity when addressing the entire human race?"

"Yeah, sorry, I got a little worked up."

"I agree with you about the brilliant minds of today. What we need is for one of them to run for political office. I think most people would agree that our current and recent-past politicians are more concerned about their own self-interests over that of the republic."

"They all have my immediate vote, too, if they can first figure out lasting peace versus how the heavens move. It would be interesting to see a man of science for once at the helm of this great nation."

"Ok, but back to your secret life because I'm trying to get a grasp on this. Your main goal is to somehow get your knowledge about life and evolution into people's minds. You're trying to make the most absurd idea become a reality. And why again?"

"Why? The why is easy, Jess. It is so humanity can save their special gift before it's too late. So that humans can make a correction and not Nature."

"Ok, so you're an engineer that now wants to somehow show humanity that life is very machine like or programmed and will change or correct itself based on persistent stress?"

"Yes."

"Assuming you're right, you're trying to get the worst possible news that someone could ever hear accepted as fact. You know that information breaks all human constructs, right? People enjoy hearing good things about them, like Nature really, really likes us and puppy dogs and butterflies, God is great, and humans will always be special. Plus, you know that most people regard our technological advancements as positive?"

"Yes, but Jess, has anyone ever asked if these so-called technological advancements have made us happier and healthier as a species? Has anyone sat down and truthfully asked if all our technological achievements have made us better off? Are we applying any biological metrics to our so-called progress?"

"Hmm, I would say the answer is a resounding no. I've never heard these questions asked on a national level."

"Jess, if you look at the data for antidepressants alone, it would seem that we are harming ourselves. Pursuit of happiness. Pursuit is a verb, takes energy to pursue, Jess."

"You remember my wife works at a pediatric hospital, right?"

"Yes."

"As one of the most absurd and horrific metrics, do you know that they have children, as young as 6-years old, coming into the ED that are suicidal with a plan?"

"No, I didn't, and what do you mean by with a plan?"

"In the medical field, it is a way to measure the severity of suicidality. If they have a plan to commit suicide, it's more severe than just saying it. How in the world can a 6-year-old have a plan to kill themselves, right? Keep in mind that this is not a rare occurrence. This is a routine occurrence, and keep in mind this is one hospital in one state. It's happening in pediatric hospitals across our country."[1]

"Wow, that is unthinkable and sad, really, sad," Jess said. "I get your point. The smart people of the world should be trying to figure this out versus the heavens."

"Exactly, Jess, hence the workshop. We are going to save them."

Jess smiles at me, and I can tell by her expression that she is still trying to assess my level of sanity.

"How in the world are we going to save them?"

"Jess, just believe for a moment. Knowledge, if used correctly, can make us all powerful."

"So, all this, our meeting here on our lunch break is about saving children also? Helping them in some way?"

"It's all related, Jess. Evolution, life, Nature, the environment. Everything is inside of the system. The Earth is a closed system, and biology is a system within that system. It's all interdependent."

"Sorry, I'm still a little confused."

"You'll get there, Jess. I'm showing you another world, but at first glance, it's not easy to see or intuitive to the human mind. I must remove your blindness in a sense, and it's not something that happens overnight."

"Ok, I think I understand. Maybe."

"Want to hear an interesting story?"

"Yes."

"Well, as I said, I've been obsessed with life and Nature for quite some time. All my free time is and was spent researching. I read every article about medicine, evolution, biology, physiology, etc., I could get my hands on.

Anyway, for about 90 percent of the time, I was just absorbing facts, and unfortunately, that was it."

"Huh? Not sure what you mean?"

"Let's say that my obsession has been going on for 20 years. Ninety percent of that time, I was just taking in everything I could, but that was it. I wasn't using all this information to tell a story. In other words, if you think of each fact as a puzzle piece, I was just building this massive pile of pieces and not trying to create a picture. Then something happened to me many years back, and it was like a eureka moment. At that moment, I saw a glimpse of the entire picture because I had seen all the pieces. It never dawned on me that biology could be a pattern, but there's a fascinating one to be seen if all the pieces are assembled in the right order."

"What happened to you?"

"I can't tell you now. It won't make sense."

"You are officially frustrating, Nature boy."

"I mean, each piece fit so well together, Jess. This must be a picture, I thought at the time. But, I also thought, who am I to tell the story? I'm just an engineer with an odd obsession. Surely people who study this for a living have hunches. Surely discussions are going on? Surely people are starting to question when everything fits together so exactly?"

"I mean, autism is an empathy disorder, and empathy is the one thing that separates humans from the animal kingdom. It's their special gift. Also, I don't think anyone would disagree that humans are becoming less social and less empathic collectively. Hello? Anyone? Nature, correcting itself?"

"Wait, so this is all about autism? Autism is somehow a correction?"

"Jess, again, it's all related. Evolution, life, Nature, the environment. Everything is inside of the system. It's all interdependent. But yes, autism is a big piece of the puzzle. One of the biggest. Without that piece, the picture is not clear or defining."

"Hmm, ok. I am starting to appreciate the secretive part even more now. So, autism is an indicator of the change in humanity? A byproduct of the change?"

"Wow, excellent, Jess, and yes."

"Ok, but why now and why these workshops? Why didn't you do this when you had your eureka moment?"

"I wanted to and thought about it, but a feeling of dread would wash over me every time I did."

"Why? If you are right, you're trying to save humanity and their special gift. That's a noble cause."

"Because of the story. It doesn't match the human construct. As you said, humans enjoy hearing good things about them, like they are the pinnacle of evolution. Darwin had the same reservations and struggled with the same thoughts. He probably had the same feeling of dread when he had his eureka moment. This, though, is way, way worse to the human construct. Specifically putting a massive crack right through the center of it."

"The feeling I had was, do I want to be the one who tries to burst the human importance bubble? Do I want to be the one to challenge the notion that humans are the pinnacle of evolution and show them that they are not? Something inside of me said no. This powerful force inside me said that this was not the right time. Honestly, I figured the connection was so obvious that someone else would eventually put this puzzle together, so let them have it. I didn't want the responsibility. In a way, my obsession with Nature came to an end at that point. For me, the mystery was solved, and my mind was somewhat at peace with the fact that it had solved the puzzle."

"But then something very tragic happened. Beyond tragedy, in fact. It was the worst thing that could ever happen to a father. Is it ok if I talk about it?"

"Sure," Jess said. "I know I haven't expressed my sympathy. It's just so painful; I didn't know what to do. I know I don't have children, and I can't even imagine what you are going through..."

Her eyes start to tear, and she immediately hugs me. "I'm so sorry I didn't say anything when we first met, but I suck at these moments. I never know what to do or say, but I am so, so sorry this happened to you." She starts to cry even more intensely, holding on even tighter.

"It's ok, Jess. It's ok. This is what the workshop is for Jess," I say, both of us in tears. "To try and help children born into this world. The youth and the future of humanity. To help people like Mary and all the other children of this world that are suffering through no fault of their own."

We both can't seem to stop crying. We cried for a long time just sitting there holding each other. Finally, we unlocked our embrace, and Jess said, "this world has gotten fucked up."

"Yes, I know, and it needs to be corrected."

We sat there in silence for another few minutes, trying to collect ourselves. Then, finally, after we felt more composed, we looked at each other and said, through tear-stained eyes, "Workshop?"

"Ok, let's get back at it, but this might be tough." I closed my eyes and tried to concentrate.

"So... when my daughter died, and I was kneeling beside her body, I had this almost spiritual moment of clarity, and I saw the world as it should be and not how it is. I saw humanity corrected, and it was so beautiful, natural, and social. Children were born into this world so carefree, blissful, and loving. They played in Nature, and there was no technology, and they were so fit and energetic and just beamed light, and I wanted so much for my daughter to be a part of this world, and I cursed mankind that we didn't have it. I screamed and yelled beside my daughter's body, cursing, and I told her I was so sorry that this was the world she was born into. I felt so powerless at that moment. Why are we so intelligent as a species, and our children are suffering? This is not right. We can't claim to be intelligent when this is happening."

"God, I'm sorry. I'm crying again."

"Yeah, me too. But we must get through this, don't stop."

"Hang on, I need a minute. I'm sorry."

"It's ok," Jess said.

After a few minutes of sobbing, I finally got my composure back and said, "So I took some months to grieve, and then, when I was finally better, it started again."

"What started?"

"My obsession, it came back. My inner voice. That internal nudge. The one that constantly pushed me to solve the puzzle was back and even stronger."

"That's odd."

"I know. It was gone for years. I hardly ever thought about Nature, evolution, and life. I was like a normal person, and then, almost overnight, my mind was racing again."

"One day, my mind deep in, I had a curious thought. So I went to my laptop, pulled up Google, and typed in autism evolution."

"Surprisingly, still, after all those years, there was nothing. The only thing I could find with any significance was this one video. Can we watch it? It's on YouTube called Juan Enriquez: Will our kids be a different species?"[2]

"Sure."

I pulled it up on my phone, and we watched in silence.

When it was finally over, Jess said, "Wow."

"Yeah, I know."

"I see what you mean about smart people detached from reality. He paints autism as this evolutionary improvement for processing more data? I don't even have words."

"Yeah, it's weird, right? Spinning autism as if it's an evolutionary upgrade for humanity. Nature is kind enough to give us more processing power because we need it. Thanks, Nature. Ridiculous. First, what data? Cat videos? Selfies? Porn? Pictures of what humans ate for lunch? Fantasy football stats? He's talking like the entire human race is sitting around crunching numbers on how to build a Dyson sphere or how to get to type III civilization."

"The first incidence of autism happened way before the cell phone or modern-day computer. Two researchers named Hans Asperger and Leo Kanner started studying the condition back in the 30s and 40s, which means the parents of those kids gave birth in the 10s and 20s and their parents lived in the late 1800s. Jess, information about stress is passed forward through generations. It's part of the programming and hardwiring. No one was crunching massive amounts of data then. The television wasn't even invented until 1927. The emergence of autism has a much closer link to the exponential rise of industrial pollutants due to the industrial revolution."

"Look at some of the YouTube videos on autism. Jess, some of these kids are nonverbal. I have seen some news articles where parents are scared their autistic kids will kill them in their sleep. So, we get to crunch more data, but there are side effects that come along with it? Also, when the speaker describes an upgrade, is he forgetting about the so-called Darwinian evolution, survival of the fittest? Darwinian evolution requires a selection success story. How can an autistic child who is nonverbal be a selection success story? These children can't even care for themselves."

"Secondly, and more importantly, why would Nature do one more thing to give us an advantage? Be even more dominating? Wipe out even more species? I feel like jumping on the couch again for this one."

"God, please don't," Jess said.

"Ok, I'll use your stool over here."

"People of planet Earth, Nature is programmed for biodiversity! It's programmed to make many things, not a few. It doesn't want one species to dominate all the other ones, as that would threaten life. It's been running this program for billions of years!"

"God, what is wrong with humans? They just don't get it. They can't see it because they are blinded by their humanness. Blinded by the idea that they are the pinnacle and always will be. Living in the matrix staring blinding at their phones all day while Nature's unraveling it all."

"Yeah," Jess said, "and the video was almost arrogant, like look what we can do and look what is about to happen with technology. Hang on, everybody, and get ready! Again, such a disconnect. As you said, people paint this technological singularity coming, and the real data would show suicidal 6-year-olds and childhood obesity near 20 percent and increasing. Also, he mentions the plasticity of the brain and evolutionary pressure. Has anyone seen the latest Alzheimer's stats? My one takeaway from this video is why are people so hellbent on changing the natural world without questioning the ramifications like you talked about. It's just like that line from *Jurassic Park*, which I think is the greatest movie line ever."

We then both look at each other knowingly and say it in unison, racing to see who can finish first, "Your scientists were so preoccupied with whether or not they could, they didn't stop to think if they should."[3]

"I love that quote."

"Me too," Jess said.

"Instead of building a dinosaur theme park, the quote, in this case, is changing the world. Brilliant minds and great thinkers always wanting to change the natural world without forethought or hindsight of the biological effects. Again, life responds to change. It's programmed to do so."

"All these guys in the video, wanting to change the world, are probably high on dopamine, like climbing Everest, right?" Jess asked.

"Excellent, Jess, you are starting to see." I smile back at her. "Oh, by the way, do you want to know why there's only one hominid left like was asked in the video?"

"Yes."

"It's because humans killed all the rest." I smile at her ominously while laughing ghoulishly. She just shakes her head.

"Let me guess, more on that to come?"

"Exactly."

"But Jess, let's go back to the question, why would Nature give humanity one more advantage like super processing power, because, on this discussion, it's extremely important. To further explain, as a thought experiment, let's imagine or construct a super predator. What would it look like?"

Jess looks a little perplexed and then says, "you mean, build a life form from scratch that's a super badass?"

"Yes, but with all the traits and abilities we know about in Nature except human traits."

"I'll start to get us going. It would have the sense of smell of a black bear which can pick up a scent from 18 miles away."

"Ok," Jess said, "you will have to let me use my phone to compete with you." So she picks it up, and within a minute.

"Oh, oh, it would have the sight of an eagle which is eight times better than ours."

"Okay, me next. It would have the strength of a gorilla which is ten times stronger than a human. Also, it can run as fast as a cheetah and fly as fast as a falcon which is 75 miles per hour for the cheetah and 200 for the falcon."

"Oh shit, it can run and fly?" Jess said, "you didn't tell me this could be a crazy super badass. Ok, let me up my game." After a minute of searching. "Ok ready. It also has the camouflage of an octopus, can swim as fast as a sailfish at 75 miles per hour, has the venom of a king cobra, which can take down an elephant, regrow teeth like a shark, and can regrow lost limbs like a starfish."

"Damn Jess, you went full badass. So, what do we call this thing?"

"How about Nature's super badass scary mother fucker or," she's pausing, running the acronym in her mind, "NSBSMF for short," she smiles, trying to pronounce it.

"Ok Jess, nicely done. So, the trillion-dollar question is, why doesn't Nature build a NSBSMF? I mean, it has all the instructions to build such a creature, and according to Darwinian theory, it would be the fittest right? I mean, who or what could match it and survive against it? If Darwinian theory is true, why don't animals accumulate advantages over time?"

"Right," Jess said. "Honestly, I don't know, good question. Something tells me you know the answer."

"Yes, and to show you the answer, let's look at a video of a seal walking on land."[4]

After the video plays, Jess says, "wow, that's pretty bad."

"Right, now let's look at a video of a seal swimming."[5]

"It's as good a swimmer as it is bad a land walker," Jess said.

"Exactly, the seal on land is slow and cumbersome, and in water, it is a ballerina, and the two environments define the difference."

"So, we said our NSBSMF could both swim and fly. What do you think the hydrodynamic drag on the species would be compared to a sailfish?"

"Way, way greater," Jess said. "Bird wings have horrible drag in water."

"Exactly, and what do you think the energy consumption of the seal is per mile walked versus mile swam?"

"Way, way higher on the land."

"Exactly, see again, it's all about energy. Nature could build a species like this, but it would take a massive amount of energy to feed it, and since the amount of energy on the planet is fixed, this would mean less energy for other species and less diversity. The NSBSMF would be a threat to all life because it would lead to a monoculture. In the end, the NSBSMF would ultimately stress the whole planet, including itself. Life could never even start 3.8 billion years ago if it had this logic."

"In a way, Jess, if you get an advantage, you lose an advantage. There's an inherent leanness based on trait usage, over time, using biofeedback. Nature tries to make it a level playing field with specialists filling every single niche. Each species becomes super-efficient for every given environment until the planet is full. Like the hydrodynamic shape of a dolphin or the airfoil shape of a bird's wing. Nature always finds the most efficient shape to use all the available energy of the Sun. It's better than any machine that any engineer could ever design because it uses feedback to dynamically change. It's the greatest machine ever..."

"Ever...?" Jess asked.

"Yeah, I don't know. You see that there must be intelligence behind the mechanics, right?"

"Definitely," Jess said.

"Oh, let's also talk about the energy accounting department of the NSBSMF. Imagine you work in this thing. What would you be thinking?"

"I would be thinking; Jesus, I'm spending a lot of energy to move this thing around plus the maintenance and expression of all these genes, and some of them are not even being used as much as the others. These fucking wings are getting in the way when I'm running at 75 mph and wearing me out. I have to release a massive amount of energy to maintain speed."

"You mean like a stress?"

"Exactly. Can I suppress these genes?" Jess asked.

"Done."

"You want to see the video where I put it all together or at least half of the puzzle?"

"Definitely."

"It's on YouTube, called David Letterman Mathematics Genius Prodigy Daniel Tammet Math 3.14 Pi Day."[6] I pull out my phone, and we watch.

Afterward, Jess said, "Very interesting. I've never seen that."

"Yeah, I can still remember the very day I watched it. It originally aired in 2005. I remember being glued to the television, watching this thing, and seeing it live. I called my parents right after it ended, and, by chance, their DVR had recorded it. So I raced over to their house in my car. It was like 11 p.m. When they opened the front door, they looked at me like I was crazy, shook their heads, and then shuffled back to bed. I turned it on in the living room and repeatedly watched it ten times. I was mesmerized by it."

"At the time, in my mind, I can remember asking this question repeatedly, which was, why did he gain a skill but also lose one? Not only did he lose a skill, but he lost the most important skill humans have, socialness. Every time I watched it, I got closer and closer to the TV until finally, I was like a foot away from the screen, looking at Daniel and whispering, Is Nature making a choice?"

"Then I remember getting up and talking to the screen like a crazy person, pacing back and forth. I'm surprised I didn't wake my parents up. I kept saying, David, quit talking about the fucking ability to recite the number pi. The headline is not what he can do but what he can't do. Come on, David, ask him more about his childhood and his struggles to interact with people. Ask him which skill is more important, the one he lost or the one he gained! Socialness is the one thing that separates us from the animal kingdom, and you are talking about the number pi?"

"So, that was when you knew that humanity was losing its special gift?" Jess asked.

"No, not that clearly then, but it was like something just didn't seem right. I can remember thinking, why does he have a skill that humans don't, but he also lacks a skill that humans have. Then I remember this lingering question from the video, which was, Why can't David Letterman or someone like him have this skill?"

"Jess, think about the social skills that David Letterman has. Not only is he a talk show host, but he is also a boss, and it takes like 100 people to produce a talk show. He must constantly interact with them, guide them, lead them, motivate them, inspire them and discipline them. Dave just doesn't come in for an hour and leave. Producing a talk show is a full-time job. Also, when he interviews guests, he makes it look so effortless in front of hundreds of people in the audience. Imagine the social skills it takes to pull this off. Most of his guests are strangers. He has never met them before. Ultimately, he is an expert at socialness. So, why can't David recite pi to 22,514 decimal places?"

"It's the same argument of the super predator, right?" Jess asked.

"Exactly. Now, let's go back to the energy accounting department for Daniel."

"Oh, let me do this one," Jess said. "It turns off socialness and then uses the additional energy from the loss of those genes to express other genes. Socialness off, memory full on."

"Exactly; remember he said he could recite pi for 5 hours straight? Do you think he could be social for 5 hours straight? How effortlessly could David Letterman be social for 5 hours straight? It's very similar to a person that has lost a sense, like sight, and the other senses get better, like hearing. See, it's all about energy Jess. Energy for gene expression in one area of the brain is turned off, and life directs it somewhere else."

I then point to the paused video showing David and Daniel.

"In my mind, Jess, you are looking at the final steps away and the beginning steps towards another species as you watch this."

"Wow, really? The end of one and the beginning of another? Ok, but is that such a terrible thing?" Jess asked.

"Oh yes, very bad, Jess. Very bad. Socialness is everything. If it's lost, everything falls with it. See Jess, once again, humans always focus on the wrong things. What's happening to humanity is the single greatest story in the last 100,000 years, and they're missing the headline. It's the dying of their special power, and they are distracted by someone who can recite a bunch of numbers. They can't see it because they are blinded by their humanness."

"They can't see the matrix like you, right?" Jess smiles, and I smile back at her.

"Yes Jess, exactly, the matrix. Except the matrix is something they created. The human construct."

"Hey, I've got a question that I have been meaning to ask you, but something tells me I should be a little afraid of the answer. Why do you keep referring to 'the humans' or 'those humans'? You realize that you are one of them, right?"

I pause and then, "Are you sitting down?" I smile.

"Oh god, I'm scared," Jess said.

"The reason why is simple. It's because I'm not one of them. I'm not human."

"You're not what?" Jess said, holding her hand over her eyes, barely peeking through. "If you're not human, then what are you?"

"I'm a hybrid," I said, then getting up and heading for the door.

"You're a what? Wait, you're leaving? You can't leave on that. You have to explain. Wait, don't leave."

"Until we meet again, Jess," I said, now out the door and heading for my car.

CHAPTER THREE
WORKSHOP 3

"Well, hello, Hybrid."

"Hello, human."

"And how are you today, Hybrid?"

"I'm fine. Thank you for asking, human."

"Hybrid?"

"Human?"

"Oh my god, are you going to tell me what the hell you were talking about the last time we met? The suspense was killing me."

"Jess, so impatient. Can you let the story unfold a little?"

"Not really. You're telling me you're not a human. Should I be scared? Is it safe to be alone with you? Do you have some special power? Are you going to put one of those robot worm things in my belly button?"

"God no...wait, should I do that?" I smile back at her. "Just trust me, it will all make sense."

"God, you are so frustrating."

"Ok, Jess. Ready to get back to it?"

"Not really, but I guess so," she said reluctantly.

"Ok, I want us to watch another video. This guy is brilliant. It's a TED talk called, *Why humans run the world*, by Yuval Noah Harari."[1] I pull out my phone, and we both watch.

After the video concluded, I said, "Ok, what did you think?"

"Very interesting," Jess said. "It's a fascinating question, why we are so different and why we rule the world. It's easily one of the most important questions ever asked."

"Yes, exactly. I like how the video compares a human's odds of survival on a remote island with a chimp."

"It would be an interesting contest," Jess said.

"Jess, no, it wouldn't. It wouldn't even be a contest. Chimps are nearly twice as strong as humans, plus they can effortlessly climb trees, have large sharp canines, fur for protection, tougher skin, vastly stronger bones, and tougher nails. When food got scarce, it wouldn't be pretty."

"Yeah, I guess you're right. I guess I was being hopeful. Maybe the human and the chimp could be friends on the island and look for food together," Jess said, trying to be funny. "Yeah, and they could gather rocks and spell out HELP on the beach for planes passing overhead."

"The human will need to gather rocks," I said, "but it will still be futile."

"Ok, so why are humans so special? Like you said in one of the last workshops, why are chimps happy just being chimps?"

"Well, like we have been discussing, I'm confident it's their special power. Nature's gift of empathy, especially what is referred to as affective empathy. Affective empathy is truly a human's sixth sense in addition to taste, touch, sight, smell, and sound. It's a sense that no one else in the animal kingdom has to the degree that humans have. On a scale of 1 to 100, I believe that early humans were at 100, something never seen in Nature, and chimps or other hominids are or were at a one."

"In the video, I'm glad he talked about 100,000 humans being in a stadium or coliseum versus 100,000 chimpanzees. It's a great visual, and it would truly be madness if you could somehow fill an entire stadium with that many chimps."

"Maybe you could build this massive transparent box, put it on the 50-yard line and fill it with bananas to lure them in. Then, when they all come stumbling in, you shut all the exits and open the box, and there are only enough bananas for maybe 10 percent of them."

"Oh my god, Jess, it would be chaos. How many do you think would be killed. How much bloodshed?"

"Oh yeah, sorry, let me quickly take that thought back. It wouldn't be pretty. Just pretend I never said that," Jess said, embarrassed.

"Ok, but the reason that gruesome barbaric experiment that you just constructed in your mind," I said, teasing a bit, "would be bloodshed for the chimps and 100,000 humans can sit peacefully in a stadium is because of empathy. Affective empathy, also known as primitive empathy, is an autonomic response by an observer to another's autonomic response. It's two autonomic selves communicating with each other in a sense. If you suffer, I suffer. If you feel pain, I feel pain. If you feel pleasure, I feel pleasure. If you feel fear, I feel fear. If you cry, it makes me feel like crying."

"Chimpanzees don't have this sixth sense which is how they can kill another chimp just over a banana. Humans can sit peacefully in a large group because they all share a common group thought that they are there for the same reason and don't want that reason to be jeopardized. It's empathy that allows for this."

"Have you ever heard of the Sally Anne experiment used in autism research?"

"No."

"Well, the experiment consists of children watching two puppets named Sally and Anne. Sally takes a marble, places it in a basket, and leaves the stage. While she's gone, Anne takes the marble and puts it in a box. The children observing the puppets are then asked, where will Sally first look for the marble when she returns? Normal 4-year-olds answer the question correctly that she will first look in the basket. By 11, mentally disabled children with an IQ equivalent to a 3-year-old answer this correctly. However, most 11-year-old autistic children guess that Sally will look in the box. Autistic children can't answer this question correctly because they lack empathy. They don't realize that other people have different perspectives and experiences."

"Right, so it's kind of like the expression, putting yourself in someone's else shoes?"

"Exactly, so in a stadium full of 100,000 humans, subconsciously, all of them are putting themselves into someone's else shoes simultaneously. Each person knows to act civilized because they empathically know the expectation of the entire group. An individual within the group can empathize or know the feelings of the group if they were to do something to cause a disruption. A chimp could never do this. They don't have this special power. So a chimp or a small group of chimps in a stadium full of humans would never work. They would probably be causing quite a disruption, most likely trying to steal food from humans."

"So, it's also kind of a selfish thing, right?"

"In a way, but it all comes from the special autonomic sense, affective empathy. Autonomically feeling what another person feels. To give you another example, imagine you are at a football game and want something to eat. Instead of going to the concession stand, you simply walk over to someone alone with a hotdog that is much smaller than you, perhaps a kid, and take it. The question is, why don't you?"

"Because I would feel their loss or sadness? I would empathically know what that is like if it were to happen to me?"

"Exactly, but I'm sure that some empathic memory goes along with this."

"Not sure what you mean?"

"Well, most researchers define two types of empathy, affective and cognitive, but to me, cognitive comes from affective. At some point in your early childhood, I'm sure you did something meanspirited to another child, like take something that was theirs. You are sort of testing the empathy waters. When you do this, if you have empathy, their sadness causes you sadness. You learn from these earlier events that you are autonomically linked to other human beings, which greatly influences your decision making later on. In other words, you don't have to take the hotdog and then feel their sadness. You can already imagine how they would feel because of your earlier childhood experiences with autonomic empathy."

"Yeah, and wow, that's interesting," Jess said.

"Exactly, powerful forces, remember? The other interesting part of this analogy is the stadium. What do people do in stadiums mostly?"

"They watch sporting events," Jess said.

"Yes, and it's the greatest display to showcase the power of affective empathy. Have you ever been watching a football game that is close and intense? Let's say that it's a critical point that will decide who wins. Someone is running for the endzone with seconds left on the clock trying to avoid being tackled. If you watch people in the stands, some will physically react as the player tries to avoid a tackle. Like it causes a physical response in the observer. Some may even react so much like they are mimicking trying to avoid the tackle, like putting their arms to their chest."

"Yeah, I have seen people do this."

"Well, that is affective empathy. One hundred thousand people, each with their autonomic selves, are watching as the player is trying to make it to the endzone and experiencing the same feelings that the athlete is feeling, albeit to a lesser degree. With seconds to go on the clock, this special sense creates palpable electricity in the air, like an energy that everyone experiences and shares together. Even more interesting, you don't even have to be in the stadium to feel this autonomic response. You can watch the game being broadcasted from another state and still get the same, albeit lesser, response or shared feelings. It truly is an almost magical power that Nature has never seen before to this degree."

"Do you think chimps could fill a stadium and watch other chimps climb trees? Like a sporting event to see who could climb a tree the fastest? The winner gets a sack full of bananas."

"Funny image, but no," Jess said.

"Exactly, and the fundamental reason they would never do this is that they can't empathize with another chimp."

"So, you don't think any of our special power has anything to do with intelligence?" Jess asked.

"God, no. Do you know anything about crows?"

"Hmm, gonna say no."

"Jess, not only can crows use tools, but they can also make them. I remember seeing a video once where researchers put this piece of food down a plastic tube. Besides the tube, they placed a straight piece of wire. The crow took the wire, bent it into a hook, and got the food out."

"Wow, I never knew they were that intelligent."

"Yeah, and crows have also figured out a better way to crack nuts. They use cars to do it for them. They'll take nuts, drop them on the highway from above, and let the car run over them and crack them. Then, once the car passes, they simply fly down and take the nut, leaving the shell."

"Jess, an individual human, pre our modern-day society, was not that intelligent. It's the collective intelligence of all the people on the planet today, plus all the people before us, that has made us now appear intelligent. Consider this example. Imagine if you could take Nikolaus Otto, inventor of the modern-day four-stroke internal combustion engine, and pluck him from his elementary school. You take him back in time to the late 1700s and place him in a similar school for the time. Think he could have invented the engine in his new lifetime?"

"No, probably not," Jess said. "I mean, when was fuel invented?"

"The first kerosene was back in the mid-1800s. Without that invention, it would not spark...Get it?" I said with a smile.

"Don't do that," Jess said.

"Sorry, it would not inspire the idea of the combustion engine plus all the developments in metallurgy and machining that would have to take place even to build such a device. See Jess, it's an idea, building upon an idea, building upon an idea to get to where we are today, and that all came from, I believe, the initial desire to share. It's like, hey everybody, look what I can do! It's the desire to share and that empathic feeling of other people's gratitude when you do, aka our socialness that has led to all of this.[2] If a chimp could create a relatively similar idea, say a way to grow bananas, he would just keep it all to himself."

"Humans are only intelligent because of two things, empathy and speech. Empathy leads to wanting to share information, and speech is the means by which it is shared. And, I think affective empathy gave rise to our ability to speak."

"Whaaaaaat?" Jess asked.

"Ok, you ready?"

"Oh God."

"Ok, I'm going in deep for this one, but I believe that I'm right. Did you know that humans almost went extinct around 50,000 years ago?"

"Really? No, I never knew that."

"Yes, based on humanity's very narrow genetic diversity, it has been calculated that the pre-human hominids got down to approximately 1000 breeding females in what is referred to as a bottleneck event. No one knows the exact number, but they know it was very low to create the very narrow genetic diversity we see today. I think about this event all the time. I so wish I could have been there, like a silent observer, to witness it. Perhaps, seeing it sped up, like 1000 times normal. For me, it's the most interesting evolutionary event in the history of the planet. Remember we talked in the previous workshops about how persistent stress leads to change? Well, for Nature to create such a remarkable difference, it had to be remarkable stress. It had to be an extraordinary event to lead to such an extraordinary outcome."

"Yeah, we definitely are different than anything else on the planet, so it makes sense that the event was also unique."

"Ok, so let's think about empathy. Why would Nature ever use empathy, especially affective empathy? Why is this kind of empathy in Nature's toolkit for life? Other mammals animals have it, they just have it way, way, way less."

"I don't know," Jess said.

"Come on Jess, think."

"Well, empathy is autonomically responding to another's feelings in a similar manner. If they cry, we cry. If they feel sad, we feel sad. It leads us to want to care for others and be protective. Oh, oh, I got it. It's the bond between the mother and child!"

"Wow, very good, Jess," I said.

Jess then looks pleased that she got that one.

"That's right. Empathy is in Nature's toolkit to keep the mother from killing her offspring."

"Oh," Jess said, shocked. "That kind of deflates my answer."

"Jess, listen, you are being way too human right now. First, let's just clear the air on this. Up until the birth of humans, Nature's M.O. is savagery, at least in our eyes. For billions of years, there has never been compassion, concern, sympathy, or caring for one individual to another. It was a dog eat dog or better said, a dinosaur eat dinosaur world."

"In fact, Jess, let's take this opportunity to pause for a moment. I want you to repeat something after me, Nature is savage."

"Huh," Jess asked.

"Jess, Nature uses savagery to create beauty in the world. As we go forward, you must remember this but also realize the word savagery is a human-made concept. In addition, I would argue that it is the trait of empathy that makes us think it's savage. It can look like suffering when an animal kills another, but it is just species competing with each other. It's their competition for the Sun's energy that yields such beauty and diversification."

"Jess, always remember this point going forward in our discussions, and please repeat after me ten times so you don't forget it."

Jess repeats, 'Nature is savage,' ten times like a schoolgirl in class trying to be funny, but also, at the end, you can see she is a bit uncertain about where this is headed.

"Thank you, Jess. Ok, now we're back. Nature is savage, as you rightly just said, but it has a problem with this very effective strategy; how does it keep the mother or female from killing its offspring?"

"In steps empathy. Simple solution. Make the mother feel what the child feels. If it feels pain, make the mother feel the same pain. Make it an extension of her so that she doesn't kill it or let the male eat it. This makes the mother protective of her offspring, which is a definite evolutionary must. Life would never work for mammals, animals that feed their young with milk, without it."

"I mean, try to imagine being a mammal millions of years ago. Say you are a female bison and this thing just slid out of your backside for the first time, and it's moving. There must be some biological, autonomic link between the newborn and the mother, so she is not threatened by this and will protect it. That link is affective empathy. The mother, in a sense, is putting herself in her child's position because she is now autonomically affected by its wellbeing."

"Yeah, I guess I never thought of it this way, but it makes sense."

"Ok, so going back, we have a group of hominids approximately 50,000 years ago that are not fairing very well. They are not successful in Nature, and their numbers are dwindling."

"Ok, what do you think caused it?"

"Obviously, no one can know for sure, but my theory is that there was a great competition between the bipedal hominids during a time of rapid and extreme environmental change."

"What do you mean by competition?" Jess asked.

"Jess repeat after me..."

"Oh, no," Jess said. "I was afraid you meant that."

"Yes, a larger bipedal hominid was praying on a smaller one due to fewer food sources during a rapid environmental change. Only the larger hominid wasn't praying on the adults; they were praying on the children or the infants."

"Keep in mind that this narrow genetic diversity is only seen in modern-day humans and no other modern-day primates, meaning this bottleneck event happened only to them in the past. The most likely explanation is predation. This could have gone on for years and ultimately led to the near extinction of the smaller, weaker hominid."

"Aww," Jess said, genuinely saddened.

"Jess, repeat after me."

"Ok, ok, I know," Jess said.

"So, based on your theory or hypothesis, Nature Boy, this stress from predation caused an evolutionary change, right? I mean, Nature or life is not just going to give up on the smaller, weaker hominid. They have to fight back somehow, right?" Jess asked, visibly concerned for their fate.

"Exactly. Stress leads to change, and I believe the stress from this environmental event and resulting predation was so profound that the babies of these weaker hominids started crying for the first time."

"For the first time?"

"Yes, did you know that chimp babies really don't cry? I mean, it's obviously an evolutionary advantage not to cry. You have been around newborn babies that just wail so loud and so long, right?"

"Yeah, sure."

"Well, imagine a baby doing this 50,000 years ago in a jungle full of predators, like hungry lions, tigers, or, more importantly, hungry bipedal hominids that are much stronger than you. In a severe environmental change, these predators will be on the hunt for any type of food, and archeologists have dug up countless hominids with large tooth marks in skulls, meaning they were hunted. A crying baby would be a target."

"However, keep in mind that every competition in Nature does not always result in a win for one side. If that were the case, there would be no evolution. I'm sure many young children were able to escape or somehow avoid death, and that trauma or stress was imprinted on them. Every child that escapes, grows up, and breeds results in information passed to the next generation."

"Nature, in addition to being savage, is very clever. It's not going to let information about a competitor go to waste. It's going to respond somehow over time. This is how new species or new traits evolve. So, it's a question of, what does it take to win this game if I'm losing. Where is the species stressed, or what is its stress point, and how can this be changed to achieve an advantage?"

"And future generations of babies crying is the change or response?" Jess asks.

"Sure, why not? Is there any greater evolutionary change to force an action? Human babies are programmed to cry at full volume for hours and hours. They're not in pain; they are just hardwired to cry. Don't you find that odd from an evolutionary perspective? Is it not a reasonable hypothesis to say that this uniqueness also has to do with human uniqueness?"

"Now, Jess, I'm not going to sit here and say I know exactly what happened. If you follow evolutionary science, one thing you learn is that there is a lot of speculation. Like tons. Like, unearthed some 40,000-year-old hominid remains, and they know exactly what they like to eat for breakfast and if they took their coffee black or with cream and sugar kind of speculation. However, certain things are definitive. One is that the pre-human hominids left Africa shortly before the bottleneck."

"Why did they leave again?"

"Again, most likely extreme climate change resulting in less food availability forced them north."

"The other definitive is that when they did, they ran into one larger and stronger hominid named Neanderthal."

"Hmm, ok, so a larger and stronger competitor with less food to eat. Well, this sounds interesting. I doubt the pre-humans could order dine in 50,000 years ago."

"Exactly."

"Also, keep in mind that the pre-humans were forced north due to lack of food into a new environment against a species that was perfectly adapted to it. You could call that a double disadvantage."

"Another definitive is the shape of the Neanderthal skull. The front of the skull is flattened where the frontal cortex would be, and the rear of the skull is significantly elongated."

"Why is that so interesting?"

"Because the front lobe of the brain is where social functions like empathy occur. The rear of the brain in the Neanderthal was used for visual processing. The north, or the environment of the Neanderthal, had longer and darker nights compared to Africa. If you take the zero sum game approach for the brain, that would mean they were experts at visual acuity and really bad at being social. Remember, Nature gravitates towards specialists per niche."

"So, you mean they were savage, right?"

"Right."

"Also, they had massive protruding eye sockets with really thick bone. This was most likely to protect the eye, its specialist trait, from combat."

"Jesus, that sounds scary. I've seen depictions of Neanderthals. Humans always make them look so friendly. Almost like a neighbor down the street who just hasn't shaved in a couple of weeks."

"Yeah, humans do love their anthropomorphic visions of Nature. It's funny."

"But again, Jess, remembering that Nature gravitates towards specialists, if you consider the massive eye sockets and the bun shaped skull used for visual processing, what would you infer from this data?"

"Hmm, well, that is interesting. I guess, considering they were bipedal and upright, it doesn't sound like long range distancing would be their skill. I mean, superior long range eyesight for, say, an eagle makes sense. Flying high in the sky, and you see a rabbit two miles away, you just fly over with stealth and grab it. But a bipedal hominid being able to focus at 2 miles out, that doesn't make sense. That couldn't have been their specialty. Oh, no, then it must have been."

"Exactly. They were night time predators."

"Oh shit, that's scary."

"Jess, have you ever heard of the witching hour?"

"No, what is that?"

"That's when babies are programmed to cry. Starts at two weeks from 5 pm to 11 pm and last four months."

"Also, another definitive is that humans started ornamenting themselves, burying their dead, and painting cave walls right after the Neanderthal went extinct."

Jess looks puzzled, like she's trying to calculate something.

"Now, Jess, I'm not saying it was the Neanderthal. It could have been another bipedal hominid yet to be discovered. Have you ever seen the dragon man's skull?"

"What, dragon man?"

"Yeah." I pull out my phone and show it to her.

"Jesus Christ, that thing is massive. Look at those imposing brows and the wide mouth. It looks like a Neanderthal on steroids. I get a fear response just looking at that. Let me guess human's anthropomorphic vision of this is like my neighbor down the street who hasn't shaved in a couple of months instead of weeks?"

"Exactly, humans and their anthropomorphic visions of Nature. Empathy is biasing their interpretation, though, Jess. Repeat after me, please."

"Nature is savage," Jess says with sincere concern.

"Jessica, something was stressing the empathy genes in these pre-human mothers. Nature just doesn't create a human from natural variation. There must be a stress to get life to evolve. Nature needs a competitor to know how to evolve. It had to be night time predation. Imagine being a mother 50,000 years ago, and your baby or young child is being hunted. This is happening over numerous generations while an extreme environmental event is taking place, and every newborn baby is just crying and crying and crying at night in a jungle full of predators. How would that make you feel?"

"Probably scared out of mind and frustrated. Helpless. But, also wanting to do everything I could to protect my baby."

"Exactly, so your then primitive, much lesser trait of empathy would be stressed. You would probably be so frustrated that you might make sounds back at your baby. Like try to mimic it, to get it to stop. Like aah, ahh! So, this prolonged change during a life and death competition becomes a persistent stress for the mothers. Their babies are crying and in constant danger, and they don't know what to do about it. Probably many babies perished, and they kept having more and more babies. Again, from our earlier discussions, what do we know happens?"

"Well, as you said, information is passed forward. Information about stress is passed forward," Jess said.

"Exactly. The empathy genes in all these mothers would be stressed, causing epigenetic changes in the children so that over time, they're born with the empathy of the mother. Future mothers begin to feel more of what their babies feel, and future babies who grow into toddlers begin to have a greater empathic connection with their mother. Over time, their bond grows more connected so that the sounds they make back and forth to each other begin to have meaning. Imagine a primitive like autonomic motherese language.[3] Generation by generation, the sounds begin to differentiate and take on new meanings. The autonomic communication they share begins to be expressed verbally. Over time, this grows and grows into a primitive language."

"But here is the significant change. The empathy is prolonged for a lifetime. It's not a temporary measure to bond the mother to its offspring. It's a permanent trait now to bond humans to each other."

"Wow, that is interesting."

"Yes, but honestly, I like the genetic Hail Mary version better."

"Wait, what do you mean?" Jess asked.

"Remember our discussions talking about Daniel Tammet, how he has this very special skill? He and other prodigious savants have skills that no other humans have. Jess, these are patterns in Nature. Nature has been so kind to show us her mechanics."

"I'm not sure what you mean," Jess said.

"Everything in life is a gene, Jess, or an expression of a gene. We have modern-day examples of people with prodigious traits. It means Nature can radically and quickly shift gene expression in one direction. Nature has been so kind to show us that prodigy in life is possible if needed."

"So, you are saying humans are prodigious?"

"Yes. In my mind, humans represent an extreme epigenetic push to achieve an advantage. Nature shuffling the cards, going all-in on a single hand, and betting everything to win. In other words, because they were so persistently stressed, life started throwing out these wild epigenetic changes to try and move in one direction and away from another. Increase variation radically at the extreme end of the bell curve. I believe that this is what happened during this near-extinction event. Nature just went all-in on empathy to try and save these early hominids."

"You're going to think this is crazy, but I think that out of this event, there was a boy and a girl born from two separate stressed mothers, and the mothers heightened empathy jumped to these babies. Only it wasn't normal female hominid empathy; it was prodigious empathy. They were given a very special skill, off the charts, profound affective empathy that no other hominid in the history of all the other hominids had. The protectiveness that a mother has for her offspring now jumped to these two babies 1000-fold and became something remarkably different. In other words, this event marked the birth of a special bond between two people. It represented the very first love story in the history of our planet."

Jess now looks visibly perplexed. She then turns her head, looking outward again, like she's calculating something.

"So wait, you're saying that because these two babies now have this special skill, this epigenetic Hail Mary, when they grew up, they would be able to communicate on an entirely different level? An autonomic level? If one feels joy, the other feels joy. If one feels pain, the other feels pain. If one feels pleasure, the other feels pleasure. Because the population is so small and centralized in the 'out of Africa' area, they would likely find each other and fall in love for the very first time in the history of the planet and have children. This first human male and human female who gave birth to humanity. You realize what you are describing, right?"

"Yes, yes! An Adam and an Eve. I know it sounds crazy, but I truly believe this, or something similar, might have happened. A wild epigenetic prodigious change in empathy that started from just two people or a very few and blossomed out into this small population of dying hominids. As this trait spread, hominids or the now early humans would start to care for each other versus fighting each other in this environmental stress event. They would work together to find solutions versus being selfish. The selfish ones that didn't have this trait would die off, and the highly empathic ones would thrive. There is nothing more powerful than people working together for a common goal. Their goal was now survival as a group. This brand-new species, called humans, united against a specific competitor for the first time in Earth's history."

"Ok, wait, let me just try to wrap my head around this. These are big thoughts."

I see Jess struggling, and I wrap my arm around her and start fanning her face, getting her some air.

"Stay with us, Jess," I said, trying to be funny.

"Yeah, yeah, just trying to process. My mind is either imploding or exploding. Can't decide which one."

"So, you are saying that everything we see in the modern world. Every city, every sporting event, every love song, every diamond wedding ring, every sad movie, every act of charity or kindness, every lover's embrace, every passionate kiss, every flower set beside a grave, every "I love you" said to another comes from a small group of mothers stressing over their hunted babies in the backdrop of an exploding volcano?"

"Yes, or ice age, famine, drought, etcetera. I like volcano, though. Definitely more drama," I said, smiling at Jess. "Has more of a cinematic feel."

"And...are you ready for this?"

"Oh god, actually no. I can't take anymore."

"I believe that this is why the story of Adam and Eve is so popular."

"Do what?" Jess said, looking a little numb.

"Jess, trauma can be inherited."

"Huh?"

"Yes, back in 2013, researchers at Emory University taught mice to fear acetophenone, a chemical that smells like cherry blossoms, by shocking them. The pups born from these mice and even later generations had an innate fear of the chemical. They even found that the inheritance takes place even if the mice were conceived in vitro, meaning that the information was passed via the sperm."[4]

"Researchers found that the DNA was not altered but what was altered was the epigenome. Basically, switches or epigenetic tags were flipped full-on for this smell, and this information was passed through the sperm to the pups. Through the sperm Jess! Isn't that amazing! I wish we could bring Darwin and Lamarck back from the past in a time machine and show them this research work. See guys, look at the power of Nature! So Darwin, intelligent or not intelligent?"

"Yeah, he might finally cave in after hearing that. You should have also used that in the first workshop. Environmental information about a single scent is passed through sperm cells and to multiple generations. Pretty amazing."

"I know, right? Both males and females can pass information about stress. So, going back, I believe that we might still have a memory of this near-extinction event. Somewhere deep inside of us, maybe in the epigenome of our dark DNA, we still have a distant memory of when we almost died out."

"Come on now, that's crazy," Jess said.

"Jess, I'm not talking about an actual memory. I'm talking about a feeling or an intuition, just faint and barely perceptible. I mean, let's say this trauma event happened 50,000 years ago. That's only 700 generations. It's plausible that a distant, almost imperceptible memory could still reside in us. Think about what religions are. They are stories that are selected in or out based on their popularity. Christianity, practiced by 2 billion humans, is the story of the birth of humanity by two people. Adam and Eve."

"Is it not entirely within the realm of possibility that this story is so popular because we have this lingering distant instinct about how we came to be, and this one is the closest to match? A prodigious event in a short evolutionary amount of time?"

"Yeah...I guess it is possible."

"Also, what is a common theme to humans? What is something that can cause intense feelings in them? Can make them cry in movie theaters and inspire them? Again, humans are the only species that can really cry. Babies crying, kids crying, adults crying, everybody crying except all the other species in the animal kingdom."

"What? And yes, the crying is now definitely interesting."

"Struggle. It's a common theme in almost all human stories. Conflict resolution. Overcoming insurmountable odds. Good versus evil. The underdog versus the oppressor. *Rocky*, *The Blind Side*, *The Pursuit of Happiness*,

The Theory of Everything, Life is Beautiful, 127 Hours, Erin Brockovich, Braveheart, Schindler's List. This list goes on and on. It's a common theme that, when experienced in movie theaters and in life, creates an autonomic response and can inspire people. Overcoming an obstacle together or, in this case, a savage competitor and triumphing. The human spirit evolved out of tragedy, at the cusp of extinction from a stronger predator, and I believe we still have those lingering feelings deep inside us."

"Also, I think that whatever happened left an indelible mark on us against Nature."

"Do what? Again. Lost again," Jess said.

"Well, humans were almost dying out, and it must have been a traumatic event that happened for centuries. Just like how the fear of acetophenone can be passed to mouse pups, this same fear of something must have been passed to us. The something, in this case, is Nature. It's possibly why little children are born into this world with an innate fear of the dark or imaginary monsters. I think it's why, as a species, humans are so hellbent on creating an unnatural world. Like why most of us don't feel comfortable in Nature, so we build cities and structures that look nothing like it. Sterile buildings with climate control systems to keep Nature out. It's like we have an instinctual resentment and fear against Nature and its savage world, so we do everything to fight against it and alter it."

"Dude, you are in deep," Jess said.

"Yeah, I know, but there is something there. Humans don't consider themselves part of the natural world, which is why they were so offended when Darwin suggested they came from apes. They think they're special and are always trying to separate themselves from Nature. To be above it. Shape it and mold it into something unnatural. Something very traumatic happened tens of thousands of years ago in our past, and it left an indelible emotional scar. I'm sure of it. Humanity can be explained by this event. This extraordinary event that created such an extraordinary outcome."

Jess again appears to be calculating something in her mind.

"Jess, you ok?"

"Not sure. So, to recap all of this, you believe that human beings are a prodigy of Nature?"

"Yes. A prodigy in one direction, to be more specific."

"You're essentially saying that humans are extreme females, right? Like we are all permanent mothers. Is that what makes us special?"

"Yes!"

"Mind blown, Hybrid."

"Humanity is a prodigious female push away from the natural world, Jess. Take all the female animal traits involved in caring for and protecting their offspring, make those prodigious, and give it to this small group of hominids 50,000 years ago on the brink of survival. What would that do? It would make everyone protective of everyone else. Instead of selfishness, it evolves into socialness. Instead of the mother only having empathy for her child, the entire population now has empathy for each other. Give the entire population female traits. It is the most clever thing that Nature has ever done. It is humanity's special gift. Out of the bottleneck, because they are now all caring for each other, they would simply become unstoppable."

"My god, if you are right, that is the funniest thing I have ever heard!"

"Why?"

"Because everyone thinks we are so special because of intelligence."

"Again, Jess, we are only intelligent because of the initial desire to share, protect, and help. These are empathic traits, and empathy comes from the female. If you look into Nature and its savagery, this is the only place empathy exists, and it exists for a very short time. Only long enough to rear offspring. Humans have permanent empathy, and it's 1000 times greater. It had to come from the female."

"Jess, just look at human beings compared to our closest relative, the chimpanzees."

I take out my phone and show her the comparison.

"Humans look like they are from another planet; they look so different. Look closely, Jess. What do they look and behave like relative, again relative, to the natural world?"

"Oh damn. Yes, I see it! They look and behave like extreme female and extreme baby combined. All soft, cute, mushy, overly exposed, and relatively hairless. Weaker muscles, weaker bones, and no canines. Take the baseline traits of the male and female chimp or early hominid and way overexpress female physical and behavioral traits in both, and I'm seeing human! That's amazing."

"Yes, and did you know that out of the 5000 mammalian species that inhabit this planet, homo sapiens are the only life forms with permanent breasts?"

"No, I didn't. That's very telling, right?"

"Yes, genetic overexpression and permanence. The extreme female. The female prodigy called homo sapiens."

"The permanent mother! Damn Hybrid, that's so cool. Nature is, as you say, very clever."

"Ok, now that I see this, though, I can't stop seeing this, which makes me wonder why I never saw it before. Why is that Hybrid?"

"That's simple. It's because you have an inherent blindness that humans are the pinnacle of evolution. You have been taught or conditioned to think that this wild jump in both physical appearance and behavioral traits is a natural evolution from chimpanzees or early hominids. It's not. It's a prodigious change. Humans are a female prodigy. As you said, permanent mothers. Again, and very importantly, relative to the natural world."

Jess now starts laughing.

"Why are you laughing?"

"Because female hominids saved and gave birth to the entire human race. I feel a certain sense of pride in that."

"You should. Every day the human race should honor and pay tribute to women. All our unique abilities were given to us by Nature so that females could better protect their babies. It was all to save the baby. Nature never does anything without a reason, and this was the reason. We should all learn from this event and cherish and protect the resulting uniqueness."

I see Jess now looking out the window, motionless, with a distant gaze.

"Jess? You still ok?"

"Yeah, I just need a moment. I need a moment to process. That's a lot. I do have a question, though. I've been thinking a lot about humanity and human behavior ever since our first workshops, and now, based on what you said, I'm struggling with something."

"Ok, go ahead."

"So, my question is, if the origin of empathy and humanity comes from a primitive mother's bond with her child and the desire to protect it, how can there ever be a war? In other words, why do we have, at the same time, the capacity to help one another and the capacity to kill one another?"

"Good question Jess. An excellent question. It is perhaps the greatest question that can ever be asked. I think the answer is that human empathy is so profound that it has an unintended consequence. When empathy is stressed, it causes humans to form groups. To only see what is similar and form strong empathic bonds with them. It is an autonomic response to protect the group. Stress forces you to pick a side. Americans versus Native Americans. Germans versus Jews. Whites versus Blacks. North versus South. Americans versus terrorists. Rich versus poor. Americans versus Mexicans. The list is countless since the dawn of humanity."

"In my mind, it's also a remnant of their traumatic past. They nearly went extinct from the competition, remember? Jess, do you know how odd it is that there are no remaining bipedal hominids left among us?"

"Huh? I'm not sure what you mean," Jess said.

"Jess, there are like over 300 species of monkeys existing today. Nature loves diversity. It's the end goal. So isn't it peculiar that we are the only bipedal hominids remaining on the planet?"

"Yeah, I guess it is oddly peculiar."

"It's not only peculiar; it's anomalous. It's the opposite of Nature, meaning something had to cause it. Archaeologists of late keep digging up all these extinct bipedal hominids. It seems like every decade they find another one. And the most interesting thing is that they all went extinct right when modern humans came on the scene."

"This is like back when you did your ghoulish laugh, right? Humans killed them all, I'm guessing?"

"Exactly, kill anything similar to the bipedal competitor that almost wiped you out. Scorched Earth until they are all gone. The Neanderthals, Homo floresiensis, Denisovan, Homo naledi, to name a few, and all the others, that are yet to be discovered. They didn't stand a chance against empathy stressed. Humans united and telling stories about a common enemy against other hominids not united? Trust me; it wasn't even a contest. Humans slaughtered every one of them. Empathy stressed is the most destructive force the planet has ever seen."

"So, love and war are, in a strange way, expressed from the same traits?"

"Yes."

"Jesus."

"Jess, I want you to look at an image." I pull out my phone and show it to her.

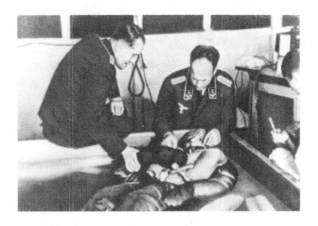

"What is that?"

"It's two Nazi scientists performing an experiment on a Jewish prisoner to determine how long a human can survive in freezing water."

"That's horrific."

"Yes, and all three people in this image are human. So, the question is, how can two humans do that to another and still have empathy? It's because empathy stressed can cause people to do terrible things. It causes people to group and then turn off empathy for another group. In stress, the feelings of empathy increase within a group and decrease or shut off for people outside of the group. These two men are scientists and educated, and they are in a picture to document the event. A human is dying right before their eyes, and they feel nothing. No autonomic link to stop this from happening."

"See, Jess, powerful forces at work. Do you think those two men performing the experiment had any control over their actions?"

"No, probably not. It's kind of spooky, but the scientist on the left almost looks like he is excited about the test. Like, hey, we are getting some important data here. This is interesting work, everyone!"

"Yeah, and these men were Nazis. The Germans did horrific things to other humans. They built extermination factories they called camps to kill as many men, women, and children as fast as possible. They shipped people crammed into train cars to these camps and told them, to prevent them from becoming hysterical, that they were being hoarded into showers to get cleaned. They boxed them in and then released a cyanide-based pesticide from overhead. I read somewhere that the Germans even made one of the death factories look like a train station to calm the victims, to make it easier to get them to comply. The only way to do this is for empathy to be turned off for some and fully on for others."

"Jess, I believe war is a heightened expression of empathy fueled by the traumatic stress of our distant past. It reminds me of an article I read about these researchers who embedded themselves within a revolutionary battalion during a 2011 conflict in Libya.[5] The battalion consisted of these civilians turned fighters armed against Gaddafi's regime and trying to overthrow the government. They found that the revolutionaries on the frontline, the men who were directly in harm's way, formed familial bonds with each other. The researchers found that the kin-like bonds within the group were, in many cases, higher than the bonds with their family members. So high, in fact, that they would give their lives or kill anyone that was a threat to save a member of the group."

"Sounds like the extreme sacrifice a mother would make to save her child. Fighting and killing another to save her own."

"Exactly, Jess, empathy. The bond between a primitive mother and child times a thousand. A human's special gift. Love and war. It comes from the same place, just expressed differently. Jews, Native Americans, Blacks, to name a few. Countless groups of humans all murdered or enslaved since the dawn of humanity because empathy was overexpressed in one group and turned off for another. Humans killing humans simply because they are stressed and then creating the narrative of an enemy."

Jess pauses for a moment and then walks to the window looking outside, beyond her backyard, and into the woods behind her house. After a moment of quiet reflection, she said, "so, this is why you call yourself a hybrid? You can see all this? You can see what humans can't?"

"Yes, I have extreme autistic traits and, more importantly, extreme human traits. I'm able to be both and to see both. I have experienced both and can appreciate both. My autistic traits enable me to see the mechanics of Nature, but I also feel extremely human. My brain is truly hybridized."

"Honestly, based on everything we've discussed, I think empathy might be more harmful than helpful. More destructive than good," Jess said. "If this is happening to humans and empathy is truly dying, maybe best to let it. Let Nature run its course and turn us back into whatever and restore the natural order. Chimps surely don't build death camps and murder millions of other chimps at a time. So, tell me, Hybrid, which is better? Human or animal?"

I pause for a long moment looking down, holding my head.

Finally, "Jess...life is 3.8 billion years old. In that unimaginable, unfathomable amount of time, no two adult individuals within a species have ever comforted another, consoled another, bonded with another, cared for another, sacrificed themselves for another, cried over another, mourned over another, or made love to another."

"I can see both potential directions of the human species. I see it like this epic movie constantly playing in my head. Two roads diverging in a wood. In one, we continue down the same path, polluting ourselves, putting all our faith in technology, embracing our machines, and living in a lonely world. We continue to stress ourselves to unprecedented new levels until something must give. In the other, we make a correction, stop polluting, reduce stress and begin a new way of life."

"I can tell you, as a hybrid, the second choice is the one we have to make. There is no value in technology if socialness is compromised or threatened. If empathy is lost, it's lost forever. It's not like you can go into a lab and make it once it's gone. The ability to love another is far greater than any machine or technology that man could ever invent. Empathy has already taken a significant hit, but all is not lost. There is still time to save it."

"Humans just have to figure out a way to harness their special gift for once and for all. It's like this awesome power, and they have no idea how to wield it. Crazy humans have spent half of their existence stressing everyone out, arguing about who their God is. They have done some dumb and horrific things to each other, but inside of them, they have this amazing special gift never before seen in Nature. They can love."

"It's like they need a caretaker. A hybrid to watch over and protect them. They are so blinded by their humanness; they don't even know that their special gift is threatened."

"I told you earlier in our workshops that we are trying to save humanity. What I meant is that we are trying to save love."

"See you next time, Jess."

CHAPTER FOUR
WORKSHOP 4

"Jess, how are you this fine day?"

"Good, and how are you?"

"I'm also good, thank you for asking."

"No, thank you for asking."

"Oh, Jess," I said, smiling.

"Oh, Hybrid," she smiles back.

"Are you going to call me that now for every workshop?"

"I just might. It's a woman's prerogative."

"By the way, from the last workshop, I think you should honor me today for your prodigious traits, maybe?"

"Funny Jess, and yes, thank you, the female and origin of our race, for giving me my prodigious powers of empathy so that we may have this conversation today, ironically enough, about saving it."

"You're welcome," Jess says, acting prideful like she did it all herself.

"Alright, let me try your other name. Ry....Ry.....Ry. Dang it...Ry...Ry."

"Ryan Jess."

"Oh yes, Ryyyyyaaaannnnn."

"Can we get back to saving humanity, Jess?"

"Oh yes, sorry," she says, still with a playful grin.

"Ok, so how's the brain, good? Sharp? Intact?"

"Honestly, still smoking from the last workshop," Jess said. "I want to go back and help those poor mothers at the bottleneck. I want to join in the fight against those savage monsters."

"I had a feeling you would. So ok, for this workshop, I want to..."

"Wait, wait, wait, whoa, hang on, Hybrid, I mean Ryan."

"What? What's wrong?"

"I need to ask you something. The last workshop, not joking, rattled my brain a little. I couldn't stop thinking about the bottleneck event. Literally dreaming about it. So fascinating."

"I know, right. The event that defines us."

"Yes, the defining event. That is a good way to put it. Anyway, I got to thinking about autism and the ratio of boys to girls. Estimates put it between 4 to 1 and 3 to 1. That ratio all makes sense now. Do you know why?"

"Yes."

"Aw, dang it. I thought I had one up on you. Ok, you tell me, and let's see if we are thinking the same," Jess said.

"Female mammals have a higher baseline empathy than males, so when empathy jumped or was overexpressed, females ended up furthest away from baseline. When empathy is lost or suppressed, males are the first ones to move away from a human state. Is that what you were thinking?"

"Yes," Jess said, looking deflated.

"Jess, it's still impressive that you put that together. Seriously."

"Just wanted to get one up on you, evolution boy. Thought I had you."

"There's still time, Jess," I said, smiling back at her.

"Let me just say, though, very sad but also very interesting. Damn you, Nature, but also, you're very interesting Nature."

"Yep. Powerful forces Jess. So...ok to start?"

"Yes."

"Ok, I want to go back to the, *Why humans run the world* video. I truly love this video. Towards the middle, when he's talking about how humans believe in fictions or dual realities, do you know what he is describing Jess?"

"Yes, the matrix. The human construct."

"Exactly. This guy is brilliant, but he just needs to take it one small step further. What enables humans to believe in fictions?"

"I know this one," Jess said. "Empathy."

"Exactly again. Impossible to tell stories without empathy. The skill of putting yourself in someone else's shoes. Empathy is the very mechanics of storytelling."

"Imagine you're a kid and your mom's reading you a bedtime story. Let's pick, as an example, *The Three Little Pigs*. The one where the wolf is trying to blow their house down. To be an effective story, you, as a child, must be able to empathize with the pigs. Every child hearing this story feels empathy for the three pigs and is fearful of the wolf. Human empathy is so powerful that we can even put ourselves into another animal and imagine that the wolf will eat us."

"I also like how he talks about religion in the video. Next to money, probably one of the greatest fictions ever invented and, in my mind, one of the greatest displays of empathy."

"Empathy, how is religion related to empathy?" Jess asked.

"Empathy gave birth to religion."

"Wait, what, how?"

"Well, it's a little sad and difficult to talk about, but remember we discussed that a human's special gift has a serious side effect?"

"Yes."

"Well, it has another one as well. If empathy is the ability to put yourself in someone else's shoes, what is the worst place and time you can imagine being in someone else's shoes?"

"Hmm, I don't know, in line at the DMV? Walmart at 3 am? An IRS audit?"

"No Jess, come on, the worst, the very, very, very worst time and place ever that you would want to be in someone else's shoes."

"Oh, I know this one. Death?"

"Exactly. This unique ability has an infinitely great upside, the ability to love, but with that comes a tremendously bad downside. Love lost."

"Yeah, I guess I see that now. It truly sucks. That is probably why we bury our dead, right? We want it out of sight because that autonomic reaction is just too intense. It's like imaging your death plus wondering where your loved one is at the same time."

"Right. When Mary died, my mind was filled with so many images and questions. Like where is she? Is she ok now? Is she suffering? I want her to be in a better place. I was constantly putting myself in her position, trying to imagine her last moments and where she is now. I couldn't help it. My mind was overwhelmed with these empathic thoughts."

"Yeah, that must have been hard."

"Yes. It's ok. I know it's difficult talking about it but..."

"But going back to religions, what are religions? As he said in the video, they are stories. The original inspiration for these stories must have been to create a better fiction for your loved one that has passed. The best story is that there is a life after death, and it's a better place than here on Earth. Not having a story like this would be too traumatic because your empathic self would constantly try to resolve this. Where is my loved one? Are they ok? Are they suffering? Creating this fiction eases our empathic mind and puts it to rest. They are ok. They are not in pain. They are in a better place. It's the greatest and most useful fiction ever told."

"Think about the most popular religion to date, Christianity. Jesus Christ died on the cross for our sins. Is there a greater empathic gesture than this? One man dying for all of humanity. Imagine being in his shoes."

"That's interesting," Jess said. "It's like with this great gift comes great tragedy. If you love intensely, you will have to suffer intensely one day. This fiction helps ease the latter. Pure empathy is why death is so hard and so traumatic. Personally, I can't bear the sight of a dead person. I just have a hard time dealing with it."

"Yes, and did you know that burial sites weren't discovered until humans came out of the bottleneck 50,000ish years ago? There's no evidence of any other hominid burying their dead. Archeologists thought they had discovered evidence that Neanderthals buried their dead in a few sites, but they never panned out. Once they found pollen at a Neanderthal site, and they inferred that it was flowers. It turns out they later discovered the pollen was transported there by rodents. Scientists afterward remarked that there was probably bias because it was discovered during the great decade of flower power."

"See, they don't even know it, but they empathized with Neanderthals from 50,000 years ago and put themselves in their shoes. Creating a fiction that they were kind and humanlike and mourned their dead. Empathy is a huge bias when looking at these gravesites because researchers are using their imaginative powers to try and discern what happened. Neanderthals didn't have our special gift. They were animals, and early humans hunted and killed every one of them."

"Aww," Jess said. "That's sad."

"You're empathizing with the Neanderthals right now. Stop doing that, human."

"Oh yeah, dang it," Jess said smiling.

"I also like how he talked about lawyers and legal fictions. What is the greatest legal fiction right now?"

"Well, considering the number of personal attorney billboards in our town, it would seem that everyone is entitled to millions if you're injured."

"Right, and what is going on with this? It's not only on billboards but on TV as well. Typically, I don't watch broadcast TV, but it drives me crazy when I do. Every other commercial is for a personal injury attorney. It's madness. Think it has anything to do with the direction of our society?"

"Definitely. Everyone wanting to sue everyone else. Can't be good in the long run."

"Yeah, my engineering colleagues at work are always joking, kind of dark humor, I guess, about telltale signs of the apocalypse. Like, what are the metrics we should measure to determine if our great nation is about to fall into anarchy? To me, one of the top ones should be the number of personal injury attorney commercials per hour of television programming."

"That's a good one," Jess said. "Or the number of billboards per mile traveled."

"Or that, yes. At work, one day, we thought about this funny scenario where it's at the White House in the oval office, and the president's assistant knocks on the door. He comes in worried and anxious, saying, Sir, you are needed in the situation room immediately."

"The president gets up and rushes there. When he enters the situation room, there's the National Security Advisor, Homeland Security, White House Chief of Staff, VP, and all the high-ranking military commanders and the remaining cabinet. The room is packed, and the tension is palpable. Then, finally, when he sits down, the National Security Advisor says, Sir, we have a major issue. PIACH just peaked at 18.4!"

"Jesus," the president said, looking shocked and defeated. "What caused the sudden peak?"

"No idea, Mr. President, but we can't take any chances. We recommend taking us to DEFCON 1."

The president puts his head in his hands and is silent for almost a minute. Then, finally, he says, "What's happened to us as a nation?"

"Sir!" the national security advisor says, "we can't wait any longer. Once PIACH passes the threshold of 18, the decay in our nation is exponential."

"Ok, fine, do it. All warships at ready. Nuclear silos on full alert. Damnit, this is shit," he says, storming out of the situation room. "I'll be in my office, and someone call my lawyer."

"Funny," Jess said. "Dark but funny."

"Yeah, exactly. If it's gotten so bad that a bunch of engineers sit around at lunch joking about end of times metrics, that can't be good."

"You know all this lawyering has some serious unintended consequences. It causes everyone to fear being sued. I don't know if I have ever told you this, but at my new job, our company is super safety conscious. Like to the point it's annoying. We work in a warehouse moving boxes around, and we're required to wear safety glasses, among many other things. We look like a bunch of idiots wearing these things all day. The likelihood of someone getting something in their eye is the same away from work, on break, at lunch in a restaurant. In other words, there's no risk."

"My job is just as crazy, almost to the point that safety is so restrictive it's more unsafe because people are always shortcutting the rules."

"Jess, at my job, we have a safety chant we have to say every morning and before meetings."

"What? Are you serious? What is the chant?"

"Safety is our highest priority. The immediate reporting of all accidents is my responsibility. All accidents can and must be prevented."

"Oh my god, and before every meeting?"

"Yes! It's maddening. I almost feel like I'm in some sort of weird safety cult. But what is even weirder to me is, going back to the dual realities, humans overall think they are safe. They think by doing all these things; they live in a safe world."

"Not sure what you mean," Jess said.

"Well, look at commercials on TV, especially car commercials. Cars with 4200 airbags, 38 impact crumple zones, crash avoidance with radar, sonar, lidar, doppler radar, seismographs, Geiger counters, automatic communication links to your next of kin in case of a crash. When you watch these commercials, you're like, my god, we sure do live in a safe society. But the reality is we don't."

"Every time I attend the morning meeting at work, and we have our first discussions about any potential safety risks observed from the day before, I'm like, why don't we ever discuss the greater threats to our employees and ourselves. What about air pollution, water pollution, pesticides, toxic metals.

I mean, at the automotive plant I work at, imagine the amount of pollution generated to create all the parts for just one car and the impact on human health. It's staggering, and we produce 1500 cars a day."

"Good point. I really don't want to say how many millions of pounds of plastic my plant produces per week, and we are just one out of thousands worldwide."

"Exactly, and no one ever discusses these types of threats. The irony is that collectively we live in the most unsafe time in human history. See, this is the part of humanness that I don't have. I can't see this dual reality. My reality on safety is all autistic."

"Another good example is the Monsanto case on glyphosate. I've been following the case, watching all these videos of farmers who now have cancer, talking about how they used the chemical. They recount these stories of being out in the field, applying it to weeds all day, coming in at the end of the day, and being covered in the chemical. They would say their clothes were soaking wet with it. Then, years later, they got cancer."

"What I can't fathom is how someone can watch a chemical kill life and think it won't harm them? I can't make this jump in logic no matter how hard I try. I just can't see it. My autistic side is always screaming in my head when I watch these videos. I'm usually up at the TV yelling, Mr. Farmer, you and the weed you are trying to kill are the same! Life. That weed is your kin. It has the same cellular machinery that you do. If it kills the weed, it harms you."

"My only way to reconcile this is humans think that they are the pinnacle of evolution and above Nature. It's one of their dual realities. They have created this construct where everything they've invented to alter the natural world is good. If they can do it, they should do it. So every time they alter the natural world in a clever way, it reinforces their construct that they are more powerful than Nature. It's like the Monsanto ads for glyphosate indicating it was the perfect herbicide. They advertised that it was safer than table salt."

"Really?" Jess asked.

"Yes, and for the human construct, it fits nicely and is believable if you live in a dual reality. It's like, finally, we invented the perfect pesticide. We thought we had it with DDT, but I guess we slightly missed the mark on that one."

"It's strange when you think about it," Jess said. "All this effort on safety in the workplace and in the products we buy and we live in this toxic world, and no one hardly mentions it. The story told is that our society is safe, but the other reality is that children as young as six, going into emergency rooms across the country, suicidal with a plan. This reality threatens the human construct, so we try not to talk about it."

"Exactly. It's like humans just can't or don't want to make the connection that environmental change and living in a toxic world could be the root cause of all their maladies. It would threaten their construct."

"Take school shootings, for example. Remember the one recently that got a lot of press in the news?"

"Ah, you know you'll have to give me more to go on, right? Sadly, it seems like there's one a month."

"It's the one that happened back in 2018. I think it was in Florida. Hang on, let me look it up. Oh yeah, Parkland, Florida. Says that 17 children were killed. It got a lot of press because afterward, the kids in the school were on major networks discussing the issues and directing their frustration directly at lawmakers calling them out on it."

"Later, there was a televised CNN town hall meeting where the kids from the school were discussing it with the elected officials representing Florida. I think it was Mark Rubio, Congressman Deutch, and Senator Nelson. It's on YouTube called CNN town hall in the wake of Florida school shooting. It's like two and a half hours long, and I watched the entire thing."[1]

"What was interesting is that every single kid that got up and addressed Rubio, Deutch, or Nelson mainly talked about guns. It was like, tell us elected officials, what are you going to do about guns? When can we ban guns? Why do we still have guns? Can you please buy us some Kevlar vests because of the guns? We're not safe. We feel threatened. What are you doing about our safety? It went on and on and on. What was interesting, and I listened to the entire thing, the word environment was never mentioned. Not once."

"Jess, let me ask you. Do you think there is any correlation between the incidence of young children across this country that are suicidal and school shootings?"

"Yes, of course."

"Do you think there is any correlation between pumping our children full of toxic so-called medications and school shootings?"

"Yes, of course."

"Do you think there is any correlation between living in a toxic environment and school shootings?"

"Yes, of course."

"See, my autistic side doesn't understand why humans can't see this. I think they have this inherent flaw. They can't see the root cause or first cause. Like their natural inclination is only to see what's right in front of them or maybe one step back. Humans can't make those additional steps to the very beginning of the problem."

"It would be a great experiment if you could somehow take this town hall meeting and repeat it, only this time put this kid in the group on the podium that thinks like me. He's like this nerdy kid with glasses, and he's got charts and graphs that he's brought with him from home. When the moderator calls his name, he nervously stands up and prepares himself, rustling through his notes. Finally, after about a minute of this, the moderator, getting a little frustrated, asks, son do you have a question?"

"Ah yes, sorry. My question is for Congressman Deutch and Senator Nelson. When are you going to clean up our environment?"

"The audience, used to cheering after every student that got up and asked their first question, is now silent. Instead, everyone in the crowd is now looking at each other, puzzled."

The kid then says, "Well, I have run the numbers, and it seems that there is a strong correlation between the increase in school shootings and environmental change, and I would like to know what you are going to do about this? Our safety is being threatened, not by guns, but by living in a toxic environment."

"Both Deutch and Nelson then look at each other clueless about what to say. Rubio starts grinning a little. The moderator is silent, struggling for words, while the crowd is quiet. Finally, after about a minute of awkward silence, a man from the crowd stands up and yells."

"It's guns, you idiot. It's not the fucking environment. Get this kid off the stage." Then everyone breaks out into applause.

"Yeah, that would be funny," Jess said. "I'm starting to see your point about humans don't get it. We claim to be intelligent, but we make the worst decisions. The only thing on the environmental radar of our collective consciousness is carbon dioxide."

"Oh god, don't get me started."

"Funny. You realize that I did that to get you started?"

"You know me too well, Jessica. Yes, the great scientific minds of our time are worried about carbon dioxide, a harmless gas. It seems fitting for the dual reality. The human construct. Let's pick a harmless gas to fret over, shall we. A little distraction for all the flame retardants, fluoropolymers, pesticides, medicines, agricultural wastes, mercury, lead, sulfur dioxide, arsenic, plastics, the list goes on and on, in your food and water. Jesus, humans don't get it. They always pick the wrong things to worry about."

"But I mean, in fairness, global warming is kind of a threat," Jess said.

"Sure, but it's a byproduct of another threat. It's not the root cause of a problem. The root cause is simply too many humans. The problem with worrying and focusing on this threat is that engineers like you and me will one day fix the CO2 issue, but the greater threat of all the flame retardants, fluoropolymers, pesticides, medicines, agricultural wastes, plastics, etcetera, etcetera in your food and water will only increase. Let's remove this natural limiting factor so that the human population of the planet can increase even further. From a biology standpoint, life is not responsive to carbon dioxide, something we naturally expel, but it is highly sensitive to the myriad of all the other pollutants."

"See Jess, in my opinion, we should all have a safety chant to be part of humanity. All Americans should say it every morning when they get out of bed like the pledge of allegiance. It should go something like this..."

"The safety of our children is our highest priority. Their health, happiness, and wellness are all our responsibility. Anything that threatens their well-being can and must be prevented."

"To live on this planet, we should all be part of a children's wellness cult."

"Yes, exactly," Jess said. "This is the ultimate metric for our supposedly safe world. Are our children healthy, happy, and thriving? If not, then everything else is secondary."

"Well said, Jess."

"Ok, so going back to the video, *Why Humans Run the world*, what about the money construct?" Jess asked. "That's a good one, in my opinion."

"Right, and an even better one is capitalism. Money isn't the most successful story, Jess, it's capitalism."

"It's the greatest fiction in the history of mankind. The fiction, in this case, is that this is the end-all, be-all of our existence. Supposedly, everything that gives our life meaning. Dolla dolla bill yall. Keep charging ahead without forethought or oversight. It's the biggest open-loop positive feedback control system of all time. Keep expanding, polluting, and changing the environment in the perpetual quest for the worthless green paper until nothing is left. The most dangerous fiction ever constructed."

"You know Jess, it's funny, today's big thinkers talk about AI potentially destroying the human race. Like AI could get out of control and overtake humanity. So, this is the thing we should all be worried about? Once again, humans worried about the wrong things."

"I mean, our IT guy has trouble keeping our network printer working reliably 100 percent of the time, and we are worried about machines taking over? It's ridiculous."

"Yes! What is the deal with printers? It's the same at my company. Obviously, we are centuries away from this threat if we are still challenged by wireless printing," Jess said.

"Jess, machines will never take over the world and destroy humans. Now, I could see IT people taking over the world. I can imagine, decades from now, tens of thousands of IT people forming a united front on the dark web to take over. Their plan is that secretly each IT person should write a small encrypted bit of code into every program worldwide. Over time, this code becomes implanted into all computers. Think how many computers there are and how many things they run. Businesses, cars, airplanes, logistics services, retail, cell phones, communication satellites, and military hardware. I mean, it's everything. So, when the secret code is finally implanted worldwide, one guy, the overlord of all the IT people, sits at his laptop in the dark basement of his mom's house where he lives and activates the code. Instantly, all computers stop working, and there is nothing we can do about it. The entire world comes to a grinding halt."

"So, then what happens? What are the IT people's demands?"

"Probably to stop opening suspicious emails and forgetting your passwords."

Jess laughed. "You're super crazy. You know that, right?"

"Yes, I know."

"Ok, but back to capitalism, the positive feedback control loop. The greatest human fiction."

"Ok, sorry, let's focus. So, Jess, why do you think it's so destructive?"

"Well, probably because we are using it to determine individual self-worth. Instead of biological fitness, we are using money instead. Let's chase it at all costs, even if it destroys the environment."

"Exactly. I think somewhere along the way, humanity started heading down the wrong path at the beginning of the Industrial Revolution. I think Herbert Spencer might have contributed to it."

"Isn't that the survival of the fittest guy?"

"Yes, and wow, very good Jess."

"I've been reading during our workshops," Jess said proudly.

"Nice. So, Spencer coined the phrase before Darwin published it in 1859. He also studied Lamarck, which he was partially inspired by. Anyway, when Darwin published *On the Origin of Species* in 1859, big thinkers afterward started to equate Darwin's theory to societies. They postulated that societies were essentially living organisms that evolved in the same manner. They argued that markets should be free with no interference like the natural world and that competition should be unfettered. In this model, the poor were deemed unfit in the struggle for existence, and wealth was a sign of success. The wealthy were the fittest."

"I wish Spencer and others like him hadn't done this."

"Why?" Jess asked.

"It's because this, in my opinion, was the birth of the great fiction. Isn't it a great story that the one who succeeds in our economic world is the fittest? Outsmart everyone else and get all the worthless green paper to buy all the bananas. It's an easy story to believe in, especially at the dawn of capitalism and the industrial revolution. Work hard, become successful, and that's all there is. The Spencer model fits for an early America when the likelihood of success was much greater, possibly due to the low population and all the opportunity for innovation."

"Yes, and most likely, when women started to buy into this fiction, it took off. Like, I'm supposed to be attracted to the one with the most dollars. Ok, that's pretty easy. How much you got?" Jess said, pretending to act sexy.

"Good point. When both sexes signed up, the race was on. Men were fighting for wealth, and women were watching, selecting, and, all the while, the environment was taking a greater and greater hit. Unfettered growth leading to the world we see today."

"See, the irony is that capitalism and the natural world that Darwin and Lamarck tried to describe are actually polar opposites. They directly oppose each other."

"Not sure what you mean," Jess said.

"The best way to describe it is to watch this video. It's on YouTube called *Why Do More Species Live Near the Equator?*"[2]

I pull out my phone and show it to her.

Afterward, "Well?"

"Interesting. I have never heard of that concept before."

"Pretty awesome, right? The latitudinal diversity gradient. Nature's programming. When that guy held the bed sheet up to the light, wasn't that the coolest thing?"

"Yes, so many different species all coexisting together. And I liked that stick-looking species. Let me guess. You also know the mechanics of latitudinal diversity?"

"Of course, Jess, but we are focused on capitalism. Focus human! And yes, stick thing, very cool. Ok, so Nature takes the energy of the Sun and makes all these different things. The mechanics of Nature is a lot of things versus a lot of just a few things. Nature unfettered is maximum diversity."

"Capitalism is the exact opposite. If you leave capitalism unchecked, it will evolve into just one thing. Corporations will end up merging and becoming one. Nature diverges to become many. If you left capitalism unfettered, we would be all working for one corporation in 100 years. To prevent this, we have what is known as antitrust laws. The best example is when the government broke up Ma Bell, the first telephone company, in the early eighties. If they hadn't, your cell phone bill today would be made out to Bell Telephone Company, and I guarantee you it would be expensive."

"That's pretty cool," Jess said. "So, the mechanics of Nature is like back in the early 1900s with all the mom and pop stores, and the mechanics of capitalism, in a natural definition, is like a monoculture?"

"Right, but the problem is these mechanics that exist in capitalism, regarding corporations, also apply to individuals. Guess how many billionaires there are worldwide, Jess?"

"Should be zero, but my guess is that it isn't?"

"2,750."

"Jesus, I had no idea it was that many," Jess said.

"See, the same thing happens in people as in capitalism. A few people have a lot versus a lot of people having a few or the same. Right now, in the United States, the richest 1 percent own more wealth than the bottom 90 percent. Spencer and his contemporaries were wrong in comparing Nature to capitalism. Again, they are the exact opposites."

"The problem with so much wealth in just a few is that all that power and influence trickles into our government and influences their decision making. I'm sure that most of these billionaires made their fortune from industry, so the likelihood there is any restraint to industry, and its impact on the environment is probably nil due to this influence."

"Good point, and going back to the human construct, Americans idolize this fantasy," Jess said. "You see it in media, movies, music, television. Our children are inundated with these images. The almighty dollar is king. Serve it at all costs. In our fantasy of survival of the fittest, the one that dies with the most worthless green paper is the winner. It reminds me of the latest trend in cars. Have you seen where Mercedes is lighting up the star on the front of their new cars at nighttime?"

"Yeah, it's like look at me, everyone. I drive a Mercedes. I'm the fittest. I made it suckers. Unfortunately, in the dual reality, this is what's most important. All the while, the environment sits quietly in the backseat and goes unnoticed for the ride."

"So, Jess, you end up with the situation we are in today. Everyone, including the 2,750 billionaires and 56 million millionaires, is now living in a toxic world, and over time we all get sicker."

"However, based on this new outcome, the capitalism fiction is now threatened. It's starting to see a little chink in the armor. What do humans do to compensate for this?"

"Well, got to keep it going somehow. Ah, I'm struggling with this one, Neo. Help me out a little."

"To keep this dual reality going, you must create another dual reality. In steps medicine. Ever watch a commercial for medicine?"

"Seriously, you're kidding, right? Oh my god, you can't miss them. If every other commercial is for a personal injury attorney, this is what's filling the gaps. Your imaginary scene where the President is contemplating taking the nation to Defcon 1 should be part of the metrics. Like he's thinking it over after he's given the PIACH, and then finally he says, ok, just to be sure, I don't want to act preemptively, someone tell me what DCH is (drug commercials per hour) at?"

"16.5, sir."

"Damn it! Alright, ready the military, and someone get me a Xanax."

"That's funny, Jess. I have to tell the guys at work this one."

"A 30-second commercial is proof that humans live in a dual reality. Almost every one of them paints this picture of a better world you can have just by taking this pill. A common theme is like starting with this dark and gloomy image, void of color, and then, when you take this pill, the entire world opens up with color and flowers blooming, birds chirping, blue sky, the Sun shining, and peace on Earth. But then, right at the end, warning this pill may cause bleeding rectum, genocidal thoughts, and swollen eyeballs."

"Yeah, that's funny. Some of these side effects have gotten out of control. I saw one the other day, and I'm not making this up. It said, people taking this drug should not eat grapefruit or operate heavy machinery. I was like, what?"

"That's a good one, Jess. The problem with these constructs, these stories that humans tell each other, is that once they get going, it's almost impossible to stop them unless reality is hitting them directly in the face. So they'll create new constructs and more new constructs to keep the original one's going."

"I mean, it's such a shit business model. Let's fuck up the environment to the point it gets everyone sick, then we will build industry and profit from the suffering. The greatest sin is to profit from suffering and exploit those who suffer when we are all complicit in environmental change. It's nearly infinite pollution with no selection. Only humans are dumb enough to think this could work. For 3.8 billion years, Nature worked like this. Hey, let's do the exact opposite, and it should go fine. It's such a dangerous fiction."

"Imagine being a kid and forced into this dual reality, Jess. A pure, innocent child. A natural entity born into this world without a construct, and then you see all these adult humans taking these pills and then all these commercials reinforcing it. It must be very confusing for a child. And then, when children start acting up because they don't want to be part of the construct, what do humans do? They drug their children. It's so sad."

"Yeah, and the most troubling example of this is Adderall. It's essentially slow-release meth. How can we fight this in the streets and prescribe it to children when their brains are still developing?"

"Boggles the mind. The construct is a dangerous thing. My wife says that she sees children as young as five on this drug."

"My god, five years old?"

"Yes. The curious thing is, why do humans embrace this construct so easily? It's almost like they've just accepted this reality wholeheartedly. Well, you come into this world, you must take medicines. It's just what you must do. Every day my parents take handfuls of these things. Every time I see them, I always ask, do you have any idea what combining all those things does in your body? Do you feel good taking all these things? And they're like, no, we feel like shit, that's why we have to take them, dummy. Then I'm like, is it possible you feel like shit because of all these drugs? They just look at me, shrug and chomp them down."

"My parents do the same thing. It's maddening, but they believe these doctors. They truly believe this is part of life."

"The greatest dual reality concerning medicine, Jess, is that humans think they're winning. They see all these advertisements reinforcing the matrix and believe they can win against Nature. Just take these pills, kids, and you'll be fine. Six-year old's suicidal with a plan is proof they aren't winning. It's proof that the medical community is harming more than helping. Primum non nocere, Jess. First, do no harm."

"You walk into these billion-dollar hospitals so clean and pristine and well-kept, and inside there are these doctors in uniforms putting on the image that they got this. They got it figured out. The reality is that they don't. All the metrics on health show that humans are losing. Hopefully, one day they will finally realize. You can't outsmart Nature."

"This was why I lost my obsession so many years ago. When I finally found the last piece of the puzzle and wanted to show the world the mechanics of Nature, there was a blinding problem."

"What problem?" Jess asked.

"The problem that emerges the second after you find the last piece. It's a massive obstacle that rises out of the puzzle when the last piece is clicked into place. A wall as high as the eye can see."

"Which is?" Jess asked again.

"Humans think they're special. They think this world was created for them. They think they're the pinnacle of evolution. I won't be able to break through this construct."

"It's crazy you were trying to solve this puzzle for so long, and this possibility never dawned on you."

"I guess it's the last piece. The image doesn't make sense until the final piece is placed. Then, when all is revealed to you, and you understand how Nature and life work, it's elation followed by a punch in the gut."

"Why?"

"Because it enables you to piece together all the patterns and see what Nature is doing. To see the internal programming and the byproduct as you called it."

"So, Nature correcting itself? Restoring biodiversity and the planet?"

"Yes, restoring the balance and demanding humanity's unique gift back."

"The punch in the gut is because it directly opposes the construct, right?"

"Exactly. If you had to break down all the constructs humans have created, they all stem from this one. The belief that they are special. Whatever they can do, they should do. Humans have this, ah, it's alright, everything will work itself out because we're the pinnacle of evolution. No matter what we do, it's what we should do."

"See, this is the part of having a hybrid brain that I can't get. While I'm able to appreciate being human, I can't see these constructs. It's like my mind just won't let me. It's like I always see through them, seeing through the matrix. I see the mechanics of all these things working together, and my mind won't allow me to believe in fictions."

"It's like if you told me the story of *The Three Little Pigs* as a child. In my mind, I would be like, if pigs have the intelligence to construct a house, wouldn't they already have the knowledge that bricks would be the strongest? If there exists an economy where pigs can buy building materials, wouldn't it already be documented that straw and sticks cannot withstand the wind force of a wolf? Why did two of the pigs choose inferior building materials? Also, why wouldn't the wolf just wait until the pigs leave their houses to attack them? Why spend all that energy trying to blow a structure down? A wolf is a predator. Surely hiding in the woods until they come out would be a better strategy."

"I have the ability to see through these constructs, and I see right through the greatest human construct of all. Humans aren't the pinnacle. They think they are, but the ultimate irony is that Nature is trying, very aggressively, I might add, to turn them into something else. Empathy is the one thing that separates humans from being lower animals. For many years I was like, why am I the first to put this together about autism? Empathy defines humanness and socialness, and there are all these social disorders now in our society. For years, I had these occasional doubts, like, do I have a form of schizophrenia? Am I seeing something that isn't there? Like, why is no one else putting this together?"

"Then I realized it was just the human construct. I see through it, and everyone else lives inside of it. That's why they look at autism, Asperger's, social anxiety, and all other social disorders as unique occurrences and not part of the whole. I mean, humans have the same genes because of the bottleneck. Their genetic diversity is on the same level as a small group of modern-day chimpanzees. How has it never dawned on them that they are all changing? Socialness reducing across all humans. Empathy reducing across all humans. Most people now live 10 feet from their neighbors, and they don't even know their names. Do you know your neighbor's name, Jess?"

"No. Funny, but no. I have met them, but honestly, I can't remember, and yeah, it's like 10 feet."

"Imagine researchers studying these conditions, desperately trying to find a drug or a treatment. I can see them looking at many autistic children in a laboratory setting, studying their antisocial tendencies, lack of empathy, repetitive behavior, and narrow interests. They're ingrained in the research, repeating procedures and tests over and over again, looking for patterns. Constantly thinking about it, obsessing about it, over and over again, trying to find a clue about the cause, and the whole time, it's right in front of them. It's in them. It's part of them. The only difference is severity."

"Ahh, I see what you did there," Jess said, "very clever."

"What?"

"The way you described it, like the researchers looking for cause are also exhibiting the same behaviors they are studying, only to a lesser degree. That's an interesting image."

"The way I see it, it's true. Imagine the human spectrum on empathy or socialness as this giant bell curve or histogram encompassing 8 billion people. Due to environmental change, it's been flattened, and autism is at the far end of both sides of this bell curve. So, in effect, the researchers studying the condition are part of this new, post-industrial age, bell curve."

"Yeah, it's like one new point on the curve studying another point on the curve without realizing they are part of the same spectrum."

"Yes, and again, they just can't see it because of these constructs. It's so foreign to the human mind that Nature would do this. We are special, dammit, regardless of the fact that countless species have gone extinct before us."

"Honestly, I think it's why the movie *The Matrix* was so popular. Again, AI, seriously? I truly believe it was popular because it was the first time this idea of a dual reality, like in the video, *Why do humans run the world*, had ever been portrayed on the big screen. It was a glimpse into their human construct."

"Jess, can you imagine when the movie first came out and people discussing it on the way home? Imagine a couple going into their house afterward, sitting on the couch, and turning on the TV. It's like one of those couch recliners with the big cupholders, and they have a big bag of chips and two giant red sugary drinks. The husband then finally says that movie was crazy. Can you image all the humans on this planet living in a dual reality and not knowing it? Yeah, it is weird, the wife says. Pass me some chips. What do you want to watch tonight? I don't know. How about *Big Brother* or *Survivor?*"

"Good point," Jess said. "It's almost gotten so bad that people would choose a matrix over reality. I think about that every time I see a kid wearing one of those VR goggles strapped to his head. Is this the near future of humanity, and what effect will this have on our biology?"

"You know, as brilliant as the video, *Why do humans run the world*, is, Yuval still can't see beyond the greatest human construct of all. At the end, where he's talking about how these powerful human fictions determine the fate of rivers, trees, lions, and elephants, he's still not seeing it."

"What do you mean?" Jess asked.

"You can't hurt Nature. It's indestructible. Once life has started, it can't be stopped. For God's sake, humans, for once and for all, stop worrying about Nature and the planet. The only thing threatened is yourselves."

"Right, I see that now. The only thing we're harming is future children. No one can see that because they live in the matrix. The fiction we have created is that we are above Nature, which is why we think we can impact its fate. We believe we are the fittest. The ultimate irony is that it's becoming the exact opposite."

"And, as crazy as it sounds," Jess said, "you're not fully human, so you see through the most important construct of all. It's like the end of the movie where Neo sees all the programing in the environment. The green code. That's you, but the green code is Nature as it truly is. It doesn't care about humans. It only cares about life as a whole."

"Exactly, Jess, and I can tell you, as a hybrid, we must save humanity. Their special gift is in danger."

"Ok, I have to be honest with you, though. The problem seems nearly unsolvable. I'm almost there, seeing what you see, but getting humanity to see it, embrace it and make a correction on their own? I just don't see it ever happening."

"Jessica, the solution to the problem is simple. All we have to do is prove to them that they can't win, that Nature is more powerful than they are. Once they realize this, they will create a new construct founded on this belief."

"If you want to save children and preserve this special gift, all you need is a construct that benefits all of humankind, and over time, they will embrace it."

I touch her hand and try to instill some hope. "Just believe it's possible, Jess."

"Until we meet again, Jessica. See you next time."

CHAPTER FIVE
WORKSHOP 5

"Hi, Jess."

"Hi Hybrid, I mean Ryan," Jess says, smiling.

"Oh Jess. So, feeling good? Feeling strong?"

"Feeling something. I have no idea what it is."

"Ready to get at it? Saving humanity?"

"Ready, boss."

"Alright, for this workshop, I want to do a thought experiment. I call this the life time day experiment. From what is written by the best scientific minds on the subject, life is 3.8 billion years old. How many seconds in a day?"

"86,400," Jess said proudly without looking at her phone.

"Wow, very good. Ok, doing the math, that would make each second 43,981 years as a comparison for all of life if it were reduced to a single day."

"Alright, so why did we meet at 5:50 pm?"

"Oh, god, I'm scared again. Why Ryan?"

"It's because you are going to sit here and watch the clock on your wall, as life starts from a singularity all the way to present time."

"I'm going to do what?"

"Jess, it's now 5:58 pm. Are you ready? You might want to get a glass of water? Sandwich?"

"5:59…"

"Wait, I'm not ready. I need many things."

"And…life begins."

"Ok Jess, let's sit, and I'll watch you as you stare at the clock on the wall for 24 hours straight."

"Ok, so…life just began out of thin air?" Jess asked. "Can we have some details on that? Thoughts Neo?"

"Well, honestly, I don't know, but what I do know is that whatever it was at the beginning, it had intelligence built-in. Something to compel it to move forward. Something to sense, respond and react to protect itself as a whole. To call life a blind watchmaker, only using natural or random variation to move forward, is ridiculous. In my view, it's offensive to call Nature blind or dumb."

"I realize it's an infinite why, but whoever, however, or whatever did it programmed in some logic to make it all work. I mean, I realize that sounds crazy, but doesn't everything around us sound crazy? Matter is nearly all empty space, time is not constant, the universe is expanding and accelerating into something, gravity, black holes, the speed limit of light, light has momentum but no mass, the quantum world, dark energy, dark matter?"

"Yeah, I see your point. The big questions. Kind of like, why is there something rather than nothing? When you boil it down, all of it is incomprehensible. We can measure things and write mathematical formulas to make ourselves feel like we understand the universe, but none of them explain why it's like this."

"Exactly, Jess. Hey, you are talking and looking at me and not looking at the clock. You're cheating."

"Sorry, boss," she said and locked her eyes on the clock.

"10 minutes have passed," I said. "26.4 million years."

"Ok, I'm staring at the clock, but I'm curious and want to ask questions, ok?"

"Sure, go ahead."

"Anything happening at this point?"

"Nope. Pretty quiet at this point. The Earth is teeming with life, but you would never know it."

"20 minutes have passed. 52.8 million years."

"Now is anything happening?" Jess asked.

"Nope, still quiet."

Later, at 27 minutes in, I see Jess's expression on her face that she is getting a little frustrated.

"Ok, starting to get the point. This is not easy. How many years and has anything happened?"

"71.3 million, and nope."

"Jesus, ok, but the Earth is still teeming with life?"

"Yes, just a different kind of life."

Thirty-nine minutes in, and Jess is showing definite frustration. She looks at me for answers.

"102.9 million and nope. The Earth is pretty quiet."

"Jesus, I can't stare directly at this thing much longer."

"You are dying to look at your phone right now, aren't you? Need to check some emails?"

"Yes, give it to me," she said jokingly. "I can't do this any longer. Where is the tap-out button? Can you take over for me?"

"Nope."

"Ok, seriously, I tap out. I can't do this any longer. 43 minutes. How many years did I make it?"

"113.5 million."

"Let me guess, still a quiet Earth, right?"

"Exactly."

"Nice job showing that life is really, really, really old. Can I get the cliff notes? Can we speed it up a little?"

"Sure, quitter," I said teasingly.

"Ok, let's look at some of the big events. Big event number one and, in my mind, the biggest, greatest, most important event of all time. The great oxygen catastrophe. This is where the little life forms, who figured out how to harness the energy of the Sun directly for themselves, got a little carried away. They were and arguably still are the greatest success story in the planet's history, but there was a problem with all their waste. It had nowhere to go. Remind you of anyone, Jess?"

"Hmm, let me see, maybe us humans," she said, trying to hide guilt like she created all the waste herself. "So, considering our trajectory, the next extinction event will be called the Great Plastic Catastrophe?"

"Yeah, good one," I said. "Can you imagine billions of years from now, creatures that look nothing like us, digging up soil samples and studying strata? They'll be like, why is there this thick layer of high molecular mass organic polymers derived from hydrocarbons all over the place during this time period? The Earth was covered in this stuff."

"Oh, I need to interject in our thought experiment for a minute," I said. "Did you see that documentary on that island that happens to be in the middle of the great pacific garbage patch? It's this island in the middle of everything. I think it's called Midway Atoll. Anyway, the focus was on the plastic problem, and the news crew walked around with the island's caretaker. The island is littered with dead birds everywhere, and this guy walks up to one and cuts its belly open. Inside were all these pieces of plastic. There was so much plastic inside, Jess, it didn't look real. It looked like it had been staged."[1]

I pull out the video and show her.

"Oh my god, is that a Coke top?"

"Yes. A Coke top. How crazy is that?"

"Oh, that is so sad."

"You know what's even crazier? In the end, the reporter covering the event goes, I wonder if this could ever be harmful to humans? So funny and sad. Humans just really, really don't get it. Matrix, right Jess?"

"Exactly, the human construct."

"Ok, back to the great oxygen catastrophe. There was this big waste problem at 2 am. The cyanobacteria..."

Jess interrupts me.

"Cyanobacteria? Please tell me there's more on the planet at 2 am than just bacteria."

"Nope, not really. The Earth is still quiet."

"Jesus, how many years is that?"

"About 1.3 billion."

"If I stared at the clock that long, you would have to lock me in a mental institution, and all we have at this point is bacteria?"

"Yep, for the most part. Life is perfectly content being small. The planet is teeming with life, just in a different way."

"Ok, so the waste of the cyanobacteria, the ones that figured out how to harness the energy of the Sun, was threatening all life on the planet, including itself. Something had to give. What do you think life did at this point, run and hide from the problem?"

"Doesn't sound like that would work in the long term," Jess said. "Let me guess, based on your hypothesis; this event stressed life?"

"Exactly, Jess. This created a stress event. And, as you are beginning to learn, stress will stimulate life in a biological sense. Life will increase energy about a stress point and epigenetically change to resolve the stress."

"Ok, so, better said, they bred through it, or I guess for cells, they divided more and conquered?"

I laugh at her wordplay. "Yes, divided more and conquered," well said. "Don't run from change; meet it head-on and evolve around it and guess what you breathe today?"

"The waste product of another organism? Eww yuck," Jess said, pretending to be choking. "This oxygen is disgusting," while making a face like she just tasted something terrible.

"Jess, you are crazy."

"I know, just like you, Hybrid," she said, smiling.

"Ok, so what we have is the first major stress event, and guess what came out of this event?"

"You know I have no idea, right?"

"Alright, so Jess wants to phone a friend? Done. It turns out that eukaryotes came out of this stress event."

"Euka what, god, who is naming these things?"

"Eukaryotes. They are the what that came out of this stress event. Life went from simple cells with a circular strand of DNA containing their genes to more complex cells with linear DNA found within a nucleus. Essentially all life we see today, including plants and animals, came from these early eukaryotes. They are our great, great, great, great, great exponential, like 14 or something, ancestors. They gave rise to multicellular organisms and sexual reproduction."

"Finally, something to look at," Jess said. "So, what we got...birds, fish, big giant pre-theme park lizards?"

"Ah no, we got fungus."

"Fungus? That's it? And what time is it to get fungus?"

"It's 10 am."

"What, so 16 hours have passed, and we only have fungus like grows on old bread?"

"Yep."

"And that's our ancestors?"

"Yep, our cellular ancestors."

"Geez, for me to stare at the clock that long would take a clockwork orange type device with a steady IV of caffeine. Why is life so boring for so long?"

"Well, nothing has threatened it yet to a significant degree. It's perfectly content.

There has been a recent discovery by archeologists of one of the earliest known animals with something that looks like a body plan instead of a bunch of bacteria or cells. Wanna see it?"

"Yes, please, anything," Jess said.

I take out my phone and show it to her.

"It's called a Dickinsonia and looks like a bathmat with a spine. In 2016, a graduate student at a university in Australia discovered one in Russia essentially mummified in a mixture of clay."[2]

"Guess what it had inside of it? Guess, guess, guess, Jess!" I said with crazed excitement. "Guess, Jess, Guess!"

She looked at me with worried concern.

"You know I have no idea. Tell me!"

"Cholesterol, they found cholesterol!"

"Ok and? You're going to have to help me."

"Do you know what cholesterol is?"

"Sure, it's the stuff that clogs arteries; why would that be important?"

"No, Jess. Break free from the construct for a moment. Cholesterol is the fuel for the stress axis."

"Really?"

"Yes."

"Ok, well, that is interesting. Wait, so you think this thing had a stress axis?"

"Yes, or at least a primitive one. Cholesterol is used to make hormones. Hormones are chemical messengers. Signaling molecules. Why would you need signaling hormones? Perhaps because you are measuring your environment? Your adaptation within your environment? You have to have a master controller if you have hormones."

"What is interesting, Jess, is that in the field of evolutionary science, there is like this fierce, hotly contested debate about a particular event that occurred exactly at 2:35 pm."

"Wait, it's 2:35 pm? Jesus. What time did Dickinsonia come into play?"

"Around 2:20 pm."

"Jesus, it's been a long time. That's like 3.2 billion years. It's an unbelievable amount of time. So, what happened at 2:35 pm?"

"It's called the Cambrian explosion. It's the exact moment in time where life that we know of today, life with body plans, life that is not only cellular alone, took off. The reason it's so hotly contested by scientists is because it disproves Darwin's theory of evolution. Darwin even said in his book, 'To the question why we do not find records of these vast primordial periods, ... I can give no satisfactory answer.' He admitted that the Cambrian explosion disproved his theory. For his theory to be true, there would be a gradual fossil transition of life starting at 6:01 pm and leading all the way up to the present day. Remember, his theory relies on the occasional random mutation every 10,000 years or so, plus the combining of parent's genes to create a selective success story. The Cambrian explosion is like life just switched on and lit up the entire Earth in an instant."

"Anyway, it is hotly debated by scientists, and everyone is always coming up with their own hypothesis as to why this happened."

"What are some of the hypothesis?" Jess asked. "Hypothesis...es?" Jess asked again, making fun of the plural of the word.

"Well, the more common theories revolve around oxygen. Oxygen supposedly allows more energy to be converted into enough usable energy to support a body plan, so most scientists gravitate towards this theory. However, scientists who oppose this theory believe that if a single cell has enough energy to thrive, then a body plan, which is a bunch of specialized cells, should also have enough energy."

"The oppositional argument to that one makes sense," Jess said.

"There is also the cancer theory, which is based on proteins found in tumors, saying that it wasn't until animals developed these proteins that they could take advantage of the oxygen and start diversifying. It's complicated, but it's based on the fact that stem cells, cells that can transform into any type of cell, don't like oxygen. Tumors are single cells that can rapidly go multicellular, just as our ancestors did, and tumors have their own stem cells that like oxygen."

"So, everything we see in the natural world we owe to cancer? Yeah, something about that theory just doesn't sit well with me."

"Ya think?" I said jokingly.

"One of the more interesting theories is called the outer space theory. It comes from very well-respected evolutionary scientists in the field. The theory or hypothesis stems from the fact that these scientists can find no plausible explanation to explain how life could start in an evolutionary instant. They call it overcoming an information hurdle of super astronomical proportions, saying it would take a miracle to happen on the Earth naturally. So, since there is no way to explain it naturally, they say the only way it could have happened is for it to have happened unnaturally. Their explanation is that 541 million years ago, the Earth was bombarded by what they call interstellar information rich virons."

"Virons?" Jess asked.

"Yes, basically alien viruses traveling on space dust bombarded the Earth, and these viruses contained all the genetic information to build life with body plans. The viruses infected cellular life with the information needed to become the three-dimensional biological world we see today."

I can see Jess mulling this over in her head.

After a short pause, she said, "Hmm, I don't know about this one. I mean, why would this bombardment occur at 2:35 pm and not earlier or later? Our galaxy has a lot of exoplanets, like billions, and the number of planets in the habitable zone is in the billions. If this seeding is taking place, that would mean it's taking place across our entire galaxy at all times for the Earth to be so-called infected. We should be able to go to the moon and find alien DNA or Mars, or it should be present in asteroids. Also, the Earth is not an old planet compared to the age of the milky way. If the galaxy is filled with these viruses, why did it take so long for them to impact Earth?"

"Exactly," I said. "Wow, Jess, impressive."

"Yeah, I've been reading up on these subjects between our meetings."

"Also," Jess said, seeing that she was on a roll. "This theory still leads to firsts like the who created God question or an infinite why. For this to happen, for viruses to have this information, there had to be a first planet to get this information from, so you are still left with the question of how did that begin? How did life first figure out a way to make all these body plans?"

"Exactly again, Jess. You're doing some good reading."

She smiled, blushing slightly.

Jess sees that I am now getting excited.

"What?" she said.

"Can I jump on the couch?"

"Oh god, no. Use the stool, please."

I begrudgingly step on the stool and then poise and look out across the room like a distinguished orator.

"Great evolutionary scientists of the day," I said, voice booming to the imaginary crowd in the room, including Jess. "Your puzzlement over this very peculiar event at 2:35 p.m. is warranted, as it defies and challenges your established notion of evolutionary theory. The explosion of life from cellular to everything you see before you is truly an awesome event and is a testament to life's intelligence and tenacity. Life is not a blind watchmaker, as you so believe, but a sensing, thriving, responding entity. The reason for this explosion and the reason it has been so elusive to you is simple, and the answer resides inside of your very body today. The reason, good sirs, is because life developed a stress axis."

I bow before the crowd and accept my imaginary adulations while Jess looks at me shaking her head.

"Is that it, you think?"

"Of course, that's it. Life built an HPA or stress axis. I mean, everything up until this point was bacteria or single cells. Life needed a way to become many cells, all working as a whole, but the most important obstacle would be how to respond to environmental change as a group. In other words, to have a body plan, you must have a central energy controller for all the cells. A master controller. To have a body plan, you must have some way to sense if the body plan matches the environment it's in. Billions or trillions of cells, all floating around in a body plan doing their own thing, would never work. There must be a master controller sensing the environment and directing the group of cells to change if needed."

"The Dickinsonia at 2:20 pm represents life's first attempt with this design. A bunch of cells, trillions of cells, all working together for a common purpose. From 2:20 to 2:35, life was probably tweaking this design, using cholesterol to create hormones, manipulating the hormones figuring out how to pass information about stress, energy beyond adaptation, forward so that future progeny could change to changing environments. Life was trying to figure out how to make a collection of trillions of cells, respond like a single cell."

"When it finally did at 2:35 pm, Booooooooom!" I said at the top of my lungs, startling Jess. "A biological explosion, blossoming out to fill the entire planet. Remember, for the now optimized Dickinsonia, it was essentially an empty Earth. It was a nearly infinite playground for the spiny bathmat to explore. New challenges, new niches, new stresses. An empty world waiting to be filled."

"See, I think this is where evolutionary biologists get sidetracked. They put too much emphasis on genes and not enough emphasis on gene expression or epigenetics."

"Epigenetics means above the gene," Jess said proudly.

"Exactly. DNA is essentially a two-dimensional thing that codes for 3-dimensional shapes. Epigenetics is what, when, and how much. The best way I like to explain it is like a construction crew building a house. The list of materials for the house is the potential structures that can be built. That's the DNA. Epigenetics is how they use that potential. The power of epigenetics is nearly endless."

"Not sure what you mean," Jess said.

"Well, for instance, take your house. Imagine what I could do to the look of your house just by altering how much of each 3-dimensional shape is used or not used. For example, what if I took this potential or DNA for the front door and overexpressed it. Let's imagine that I doubled it. How would your house look?"

"Very different," Jess said.

"Ok, let's try to imagine all kinds of different shapes we could make by changing the amount of material used or not used."

"Well," Jess said, "I could simply make everything much smaller, like those hominids that came before us."

"Exactly, the homo floresiensis, which were hominids only 3 feet tall."

"Oh, I could overexpress the DNA for windows so that the entire house is like a sunroom. Kind of like a...a glass octopus," she said while googling it on her phone. "Wow, I had no idea that was a thing."

"Nice, let me do one. What if we overexpress all the genes that make up the trusses of the roof, which changes the pitch of the roof. My environment is very snowy, and I don't want the roof to collapse. Like the shape of a conifer tree."

"See," I said, showing her an image on my phone.

"Oh, that's a good one. How about I live in a warm climate, where it never rains, and I under-express these same genes, making it a flat roof to save on building costs and lower my exposure to the Sun. No need to build it if you don't need it. Maybe like a barrel cactus."

"Or, how about I live in a climate where it always rains, and I overexpress the gutters, making a bunch of them to funnel water away from the house. Hang on, let me look. Oh, oh, like leaves in the rainforest that have a drip tip."

"What about overexpressing the house's siding, making it thicker and tougher, like armor? Kind of like an armadillo."

"Oh, that's a good one," Jess said.

"Ok, very good, now let's turn a dog into a human."

"Wait, what?" Jess asked.

"Let's turn a dog into a human using the same analogy. Humans and dogs share 84 percent of their DNA, which means we have more in common than not in common. Let's take that 84 percent and try to create something that looks like a human from the shape of a dog."

"Oh, ok, I see what you are saying. Kind of strange, but sure, why not. Obviously, the first thing that must go is the tail. Suppressed. Hair suppressed significantly, save the top of head, armpits, and genital area. Done."

"Very good. Now let's start suppressing and expressing bone formation of the skull so that the snout is not so long. Kind of like a Shih Tzu but even more. Also, the ears are going to need some suppression."

"Yep, now let's start with the paw. Let's overexpress all the digits, especially the small one that doesn't do anything, to make them look more like fingers, and let's overexpress the nail to make it wider like a human."

"Ok, so the skeleton should be pretty easy. When you look at a picture of a dog skeleton versus a human, this exercise starts to make sense. I mean, look at this picture of hand versus paw; the difference is, like you said, the amount of materials used in each bone, or suppressing it altogether."[3]

"You can see that pretty soon you could create something that looked like a human from any dog breed. A Chihuahua or even a Great Dane. I'll bet from 20 yards away; I could get close enough that your first impression would be human."

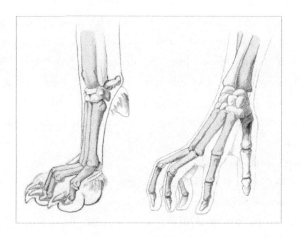

"I mean, every cell in the human body has identical DNA. It's the epigenome instructing the cells on what to be and how much from bone, kidney, skin, nerve, and all the way to brain cells. In my mind, it's like each gene is wired to a stereo receiver. The epigenome can turn the receiver on at a specific time and off at a specific time. It can also adjust the volume of the gene, which controls the amount of protein produced. You can see the endless possibilities with this architecture. Look at these pictures of all the mammals on Google."

I take out my phone and show her.

"Now, do the same experiment to all of them by expressing or suppressing. You can see how they all came from the same basic material list with the epigenome as the major player, right?"

"Yeah, I see that. I think it's all the faces that give it away. You can see the commonality. It's like they all have the same ingredients, and each species is just a different recipe."

"Exactly, and the epigenome is influenced by the environment. It changes with the environment. Now, all you need is for something to compel this first body design, the spiny bathmat, to seek out what it is not adapted to. Release a burst of dopamine with its brand new, fully formed stress axis to start exploring an empty Earth, and then, Boooooom!" I shouted at the top of my lungs, again startling Jess, "an explosion of all different shapes, sizes, and structures filling all the different niches of the planet. New body plans all responding, sensing, and reacting in different ways to become different types of biological specialists for each environment."

"That's cool," Jess said.

"I know. Life is cool. The greatest machine ever..."

Jess looks at me, waiting, and I look back, staring blankly.

"Ok, so it's almost time for the next big event. Ready?"

"Yep."

"Imagine it's 3:11 pm, and seconds are ticking away. 3:11:58, 59, 3:12 and... flatline."

"What happened?"

"Mass extinction."

"Aww. Life just got started."

"Jess, 86 percent of all species were lost, and you say, aww?"

"Too soon?" Jess asked with a smile.

"Well, when you say it that way, I guess not, Jessica."

"So, what caused it?" Jess asked.

"No hard evidence of a specific cause, but most scientists believe that climate fluctuations, glaciation, falling sea levels, impact events, and or volcanism were to blame. Anyway, the bathmat and most of its new cousins took a hard hit. It was a massive stress on life. But guess what happened?"

"I know this one. Life began again."

"Yep, not deterred and bounced back even more diverse. We got fish, spiders, and plants. But then another countdown. 3:29:58, 59 and...flatline."

"Dang, another extinction?" Jess asked.

"Yep, it was called the late Devonian, and around 75 percent of all species were lost. It was thought to be caused by giant algae blooms that choked out the seas. Our friend the bathmat and all his cousins took another hard hit on this one."

"Aww," Jess sighed, showing to be genuinely moved.

"Out of this stress event, we get flying insects, sharks, crabs, seed-bearing plants, and forests. It's starting to look like a modern-day Earth."

"Yay," Jess said, "finally something to look at."

"But then..."

"Dang it."

"Another countdown, 4:25:58, 59 and...Beeeeeeeeeeeeeeepppppppppppppp..."

"Why do you keep making that sound? Hello, you can stop now."

"...and flatline."

"What happened? Why did you do that for so long?"

"Jess, it was a bad one. The worst extinction event that we know of. Nearly all life was wiped out. It was called the end Permian, and nearly 96 percent of all species were lost. It was caused by a cataclysmic volcanic eruption. Methane-producing bacteria responded to this eruption by filling the atmosphere with this potent greenhouse gas causing global temperatures to rise and oceans to acidify. According to anthropologists, life was set back 300 million years. It's called the great dying."

"Dang, that is sad, but let me guess."

"Yep, life began again. Out of stress came change. Life after the great dying sparked what is known as the Mesozoic marine revolution. This triggered significantly more complex marine creatures like snails, sea urchins, and crabs. On land, you now had creatures that looked reptilian, like pre dinosaurs. Post the great dying; the greatest difference was that life, both marine and on land, was becoming more mobile with better means of locomotion."

"Yeah, probably to run from the next extinction event coming, right?" Jess said with a smile.

"Ah, no comment on that one. Ok, ready?"

"Dang it."

"Countdown, 4:45:48, 59 and... flatline. This stress event was called the end Triassic, and nearly 80 percent of all species were lost. Possible causes were volcanism or an asteroid. Life sprang back from this event with the land of the big. Countless species with saurus on the end of their name. Plus hermit crabs, starfish, stingrays, blood-sucking insects, flowering plants that bear structures to attract insects to spread pollen, bees, ants, and salamanders, to name a few."

"Salamanders, aww."

"Ready?"

"Geez."

"Countdown, 5:34:58, 59 and flatline. This one is called the end Cretaceous, where nearly 76 percent of all life was lost, including our favorite theme park-worthy creatures, the dinosaurs. This stress event spawned meat-eating mammals, deer, bears, anteaters, elephants, our friend the giraffe, lions, kangaroos, horses, hippos, sabre-toothed cats, jaguars, ferrets, otters, skunks, pigs, hominids and countless bird species, including songbirds."

"I can see them moving to the air. Trying to fly away from the next extinction event," Jess laughed.

"Good one, Jess. Alright, so let's imagine that we actually did this thought experiment, and you have been sitting here staring at this clock since 6 pm, nearly 24 hours ago. I realize it's impossible, but imagine with some clockwork orange type of contraption, an IV of stimulants, catheter, bedpan, whatever it takes to keep you here staring at the clock on the wall and never moving your gaze, we do it. How would you feel?"

"I would feel batshit crazy. I would be out of my mind."

"Ok, try to imagine you are in that mental, fatigued, emotional, can't take this anymore state of mind, and let's change the clock to 5:50 pm the following day. I will get up, pull the clock off the wall, set it, and put it back, ready?"

"Yeah."

"5:50:01, 02, 03...Ok, don't move your stare. Keep your eyes locked on the clock."

"Roger that."

"5:55:01, 02, 03..."

"Anything?"

"Just wait."

"5:58:30, 31, 32..."

"Ok, Jess, our fan favorites, the hominids, are starting to appear on the scene."

"Something tells me it's about to get interesting," Jess says with a devilish grin.

"Alright, Jess, last minute, focus. At the exact moment, I will tap your hand three times while you are looking at the clock. Pay attention to when I tap you with my finger and what time it is ok?"

"5:59:40, 41, 42..."

"Jess, you ready?"

"I'm ready," she said, acting tired and anxious.

"Remember, you have been sitting here for 24 hours straight watching life evolve, changing to changing environments, blossoming to become more things with greater diversity each time a stressful event occurred."

"5:59:50, 51, 52, 53, 54, 55, 56, 57, 58, tap, 59...tap, tap 60. Present day."

"Whew, that was quite a ride," Jess said. "That was a remarkable journey for life. So, the big question, what were the 3 taps?"

"Well, the first one was the birth of humanity. The second was the start of the industrial revolution, and the third was the emergence of autism, a disorder that affects socialness."

"Oh wow. Shit. Damn. Damn again. Damn, a third time. Ok, I need a minute."

Jess gets up from the table and heads to the couch.

After a minute of just staring ahead deep in her thoughts, she said, "Yeah, I see it. I see what you see, at least this part. Most people think life spent all that time to make a human, but it's not true. Life is just changing based on environmental change. Changing, based on stress. Becoming more things to protect itself. Increasing diversity to protect itself. Life just happened to start making all these bipedal hominids, and the environment must have changed, as you said. It forced all of them to compete at a higher level to the point that one of them was dying out. A certain hominid was on the brink of extinction, which created an even higher stress, so life tried something new just like in all the other stress events."

"Exactly Jess, an epigenetic Hail Mary like Daniel Tammet or any other autistic savant. But instead of empathy or socialness off, it was empathy and socialness full on. And the shuffling of the epigenetic cards finally dealt a winner. Out of stress came change that finally proved to be successful. The lonely, weak, frail, stressed, dying out hominid emerged as something new from its own near extinction event. A brand-new hominid with a special power never before seen in the last 3.8 billion years of life. Its special power was empathy, but not only for the Mother and child, empathy across the entire species.   These female genes were turned on at max volume for females and males and left on indefinitely. It was an extraordinary event that created an extraordinary outcome."

"Yeah," Jess said, "the new humans started working together, instead of individually fighting against each other for resources, like apes. They worked together in large groups to forage for food and care for each other. The energy accounting department of the new human read these new metrics as more energy coming in and much less stress because of this change. Lock this gene expression in place; we found a winner."

"Exactly again, well done, Jess. But socialness of this magnitude is an extremely powerful thing. So powerful, in fact, that it causes the humans to share everything. Every time an advantage is discovered, it's shared for all to use. Over time, they are recorded and documented. For generation after generation, these advantages were used to expand and create processes, further discoveries, and finally, industry. An exponential converging of ideas, whose roots come from sharing advantages and advancements over thousands of years, all heading to a single starting point in time. The industrial revolution. The start of man's ability to drastically alter his environment. The dawn of the next extinction event."

"Yeah, the second time you tapped my hand and the nearly instant third tap."

"Yes, honestly, I couldn't tap that fast. Technically, it is 0.0027 seconds."

"Wow, that's telling, right? Like you said earlier, too much stress or energy beyond adaptation, so change it to something new. It's like a knee-jerk reaction for life to protect diversity. What must the energy accounting department of the human species be thinking right now?"

"They are thinking, what the fuck is going on? We have never seen stress levels this high before. This is a rapid extinction event like a giant asteroid."

"Yes, and all the food coming in must be throwing it for a tailspin. High stress and high calorie intake, what the hell?"

"Exactly, and both are a threat to biodiversity."

"Honestly, this experiment has blown my mind, but it's a good way to see beyond the human construct. If you look at the data like this, humans aren't the pinnacle of life. In other words, it's apparent that life didn't spend 3.8 billion years just to create a human."

"Yes! Jess, do you remember the movie *Contact* where the characters that Jodie Foster and Matthew McConaughey play are talking about the infiniteness of space? Jodie's character talks about how there are billions of planets, and if just one out of a million had intelligent life, then there would be millions of human-like civilizations out there? Matthew's character then says, 'well, if there wasn't, it would be an awful waste of space.'"[4]

"Yeah, I remember that part."

"Well, this is taken from a Carl Sagan quote which says, 'The universe is a pretty big place. If it's just us, seems like an awful waste of space.' It's a great quote intended to get you to think about why would the universe be so big if we are the only ones in it? Why is there so much out there if this tiny pale blue dot in the middle of nowhere is all there is?"

"Jess, this quote can also be changed to time and life on Earth to make the same argument, saying, life on this planet is pretty old. If it was all for us, seems like an awful waste of time. In other words, if life's end goal is human, a species that can dominate the planet and drive other species to extinction, why did it wait so long? Why spend all that time and then nearly let humans go extinct if it was all for us, well...you?"

"Yeah, that's a great argument. 3.8 billion years is a crazy amount of time. Really unfathomable, like the vastness of space. Trust me, I couldn't even stare at the clock for 40 minutes without tapping out. I know how long it is. But then you are left with the big question, why? So, life is just this entity, this force, this thing, whose only goal is survival. For what? For most of life's existence, 3.8 billion years, it was mostly silent. A pale blue dot floating in the vastness of space while quietly teeming with microscopic bacteria and perfectly content at being just that."

"I know, it makes no sense, just like everything else in the universe. But, if humans are truly intelligent as they claim to be, they will give it what it wants. All they can do at this point is respect it and abide by its laws."

"Laws?"

"Yes, think of it as another word for its programming. Law in a sense that it will always do this. It will always respond this way."

"When confronted with a persistent stressor, life will increase energy output to increase stress further while keeping the system's overall energy the same. This will continue until the system's efficiency is achieved or restored."

"What is that you just said?" Jess asked.

"It's my hypothesis on how life behaves. A descriptor of the initial programming which I believe was present in the first cell, 3.8 billion years ago."

"It means that in Nature, there is no such thing as a persistent stress. Life will always resolve a persistent stress because it's a higher energy state. It's an energy state beyond adaptation, which means to let this continue would mean less energy for all the other species. Life will always seek out the lowest stress point. It's a law of Nature that cannot be broken."

"The problem is that humans are the undisputed kings at creating persistent stresses. They are their own volcano, asteroid, algae bloom, ice age, global warming, and global methane release, all rolled up into one massive package for the entire human race to share. This cannot continue. Nature won't let it continue, hence the third tap."

"Life is programmed for biodiversity, so give it back. Give it back or suffer the consequences."

"Jesus, but how in the world will we get people to see and abide by that?"

"Good question, hence, the workshops. See you next time, Jess."

CHAPTER SIX
WORKSHOP 6

"Ok Ryan, in this workshop, I want to take the lead a little. I want to know more about your curious life, especially what started this obsession with Nature."

"Sure, go ahead."

"So, I guess the first question is why? You said all this began around 20 years ago. Why weren't and aren't you like normal engineers obsessing over tech and geek stuff? Is it because you always felt different? A closeted hybrid? And, why don't I know any of this? I thought we were tight. I mean, I just found out you're a self-proclaimed hybrid, and I have known you for like 10 years. You couldn't have mentioned this to me?"

"I mean, how would I do that? Just one day at lunch. Hey, by the way, I have a hybrid brain. Are you going to get the special or order off the menu?"

"I realize it all sounds strange, Jess, but when you break it down, it isn't. Humans are transitioning from one species to another. I happen to be at the midpoint of that transition. Technically, my brain is sharply heterogeneous with regard to its evolution. You could also say that my brain is extreme female and extreme male simultaneously. For me, the term hybrid fits because I can see and appreciate both sides, the social and the non-social. Those that have empathy and those that don't."

"Yeah, but you're an engineering manager. Sure, you are definitely unique. Ever since I first met you, I quickly realized you see the world much differently. However, you seem normal socially."

"I'm just a good actor. I realized a long time ago that I would have to act human to survive in this modern world. Act like I'm constantly in a play, and my script is socialness. Deep down, though, my first instinct is not to be social. However, I can truly be both. I doubt if you told people that know me that I'm highly autistic, they would even believe you."

"Hmm, ok, interesting."

"So, all this started your obsession with Nature?"

"No, the reason is much simpler, or the start is simpler. I became sick."

"Oh, I'm sorry. What did you have?"

"Well, that's the problem; no one could tell me."

"Huh?"

"Technically, I was extraordinarily well and then extraordinarily sick."

"Explain more, please."

"Ok, but let me first tell you about the well part."

"Ok."

"I have the fondest memories of my childhood. I wish you could have known me then, Jess. I was so full of life."

"In what way?"

"In all ways."

"Huh?"

"Let me give you some examples. It's the only way to explain it."

"Ok."

"When I was very young, I can remember having an unusual ability with numbers and memory. One of my favorite things to do as a kid was to go with my mother to the grocery store. My mother was in the habit of getting everything she needed for the week in one trip, and the buggy was always full when we proceeded to the checkout. As we started going through the aisles, I would always make a mental note of the price of every item. Keep in mind that we could be in the store for sometimes up to an hour. So, as we finally wheeled the massive load of groceries to the checkout, I would unload every item, careful not to look at the price and place it on the conveyor. Now when I was a kid, they didn't have scanners. The items had prices on them. It was a small little sticker with the price printed in black and white. My method was to pick up the items in the buggy while turning the other way and placing them on the conveyor."

"Why don't you look at the groceries when you pick them up?" my mother would ask.

"I am performing an experiment," I would say.

"Accustomed to my odd behavior by now, she would simply shrug. Once the buggy was empty, I would quickly position myself on the other side of the checkout girl once it was our turn. I could see the item and the register, but I could not see the price. When the checkout girl picked up the item, I would recall the price from memory. She would key the price in and the number displayed on the register. My recall was never wrong. Keep in mind that there would be well over 100 items in the buggy, with the first ones picked out nearly an hour ago. When all the items were registered, I would tally the total in my head and add tax. I was never wrong. I was always puzzled by this ability and couldn't explain why I enjoyed it so much. I would describe my grocery store excursions to my friends and ask them if they had the same ability or interest, and strange to me at the time, none of them did."

"So, you had like a prodigious memory for numbers?"

"I wouldn't say prodigious but definitely on the far end of the spectrum. It didn't matter how many items were in the buggy. There was probably a limit somewhere, but the buggy was always full of at least 100 items, and I could remember them all at the checkout. Then added them up with tax as they were rung up. Every week we went, I was never wrong."

"Ok, what else?"

"Well, I was exceptionally strong for my age."

"Like in what way?"

"In every way. I can remember that my parents used to enroll me in summer camp. One year, the camp decided to have an arm-wrestling contest on the last day to see who was the strongest kid. There were probably over 200 kids, and I was in the youngest age group. At the end of the contest, it got down to me and this other kid who was freakishly big. I can remember I wasn't even challenged by any of the kids before me."

"So, you won the contest?"

"No."

"The big kid beat you?"

"No, I let him win, but I could have easily beat him."

"Why would you let him win?"

"Because this kid was bigger than all the counselors. He was massive. Our size difference was so disproportionate it looked strange being up there with him. I can remember the feeling that if I won this, people would look at me like a freak of nature. Like, how can this kid beat someone twice his size? If he wins, he has superhuman strength. I guess my autistic side didn't want the attention. However, I could have easily beaten him."

"I can also remember in 7th grade I once arm-wrestled the strongest kid at my school. I went to a private school, so it was 7th through 12th grade. This kid was on the football team and lifted weights constantly. He just had massive muscles and easily outweighed me by 60 pounds. I still remember the look on his face right before we started. The cocky look like, 'I'll go easy on you kid,' and then we engage, and his look immediately turns to, 'what the hell.' This time I gave it everything I had, pinning him instantly. Afterward, it was that look, that look like something was not right here. There's no way someone this young can be that strong."

"My dad still occasionally tells the story about me being on the league football team. My team had my jersey with the name "Hulk" printed on the back instead of my last name. In almost every game, there would be this play where I'm running, as fullback, with the ball with 5 or 6 kids hanging onto me as I drag them down the field. It would be like two hanging on to me and then the others hanging on them. It was like I was pulling a group of kids 10 feet long down the field."

"In baseball, I had the league record for the most home runs. I can remember going to the town park where all the teams would play every weekend. Hitting home runs became such a common occurrence that other parents would ask which field I was playing on because they didn't want their cars parked beside the fence and hit with a ball. People would get up from the stands and move their cars right before the game."

"And during the summer when there wasn't school, I was outdoors from dusk till after dawn. I jumped out of bed and never stopped moving until I went to bed. When I was 10 through maybe 14, my grandfather had a membership at the town country club. This club was like 12 miles away from my parent's house. Every morning I'd jump on my little single-speed bike and pedal to the club to play tennis or swim. I played until dark and then rode home. Looking back, my body would simply not fatigue."

"Ok, I would say that's atypical; anything else?"

"Yes, I had an unusual ability with sound."

"Sound?"

"Yes, it was strange. I think I had something called synesthesia, or at least a temporary, mild form of it. I think it was a combination of chromesthesia and auditory-tactile synesthesia. Chromesthesia is when sound can produce colors in your mind. Auditory-tactile synesthesia is when sound produces feelings or sensations in the body."

"When I was young, I would take these huge Bose speakers, lay them on their sides, and put my head right between them. Then, I would crank it up as loud as possible, even past the point of distortion. It was almost like the distortion made the effect higher. I would do this for hours. I'm surprised I'm not deaf today."

"Anyway, these color pallets would start playing in my head, and the colors had sensations. It's almost like I could feel them. But I didn't cause any of this to happen. I was like a silent observer watching a fireworks show in my mind. I was feeling the energy of the display, and I was so caught up in it. It was better than any drug I've ever tried. I would find a song that elicited the effect the most and play that same song over and over again nonstop."

"Do you know anything about synesthesia?"

"No, not really."

"There are truly some strange ones out there. There's spatial sequence, where people see numbers as different points in space. Grapheme color, where letters and numbers seen have colored backgrounds. Number form, where numbers take on this visual order in the person's mind. Misophonia, where sounds trigger negative feelings like anger, fright, and disgust. Lexical-gustatory, where words trigger taste sensations. Ordinal linguistic personification, where people associate numbers with personalities. Like the number 6 might look like a tired old man."

"My favorite, though, is mirror-touch synesthesia. This is where someone with this condition will observe another being touched, say tapped on the arm, and feel the same touch."

"Oh wow, that's wild."

"I know, right."

"Hmm, what would it be like if someone with mirror-touch watched a porno?"

"Jessica!"

"I'm just curious, you know, for science reasons," she said, smiling.

"Well...scientifically, I'm sure it would be intense."

"I wonder if you had this and watched two people having sex, which person would your autonomic self respond to?" Jess asked.

"Well, scientist, excellent question. I would think if you were a female with mirror-touch, then you would empathize with the female in the video. But I'm just guessing. Interestingly, people with this condition have been shown to have higher empathy levels than the general population."

"A lot of strange things happening in the human brain right now. Think any of this has to do with stress and evolution?"

"Well, if you're right, I'm sure it does," Jess said. "Your thoughts?"

"For me, synesthesia speaks volumes to the gambler in Nature."

"Not sure what you mean?"

"Steven Hawking has a great quote that kind of explains it. He said, 'All the evidence shows that God was actually quite a gambler, and the universe is a great casino, where dice are thrown, and roulette wheels spin on every occasion.'"

"Oh, I like that."

"Yes, it obviously refers to the universe and the chaotic randomness and chance of it all, but for me, it also applies to biology. I mean, biology came from the universe, so the same laws must apply. We're all stardust, remember? The way I see Nature is that, in times of extraordinary persistent stress, it just starts generating these Hail Mary genetic changes trying to find something new. Nature has this internal programming where if it's down on its luck and running out of chips, it will just go all in to try and find a winning hand. Like extreme variation in its DNA instruction set, hoping for a win. Wild expression in one direction and all in for another. Reduce genetic maintaining energy at the stress point, so genetic expression becomes more malleable and let entropy have its way, so to speak."

"Also, I think synesthesia sheds light on how reality is defined. These people that have this condition, these things they're experiencing are autonomically happening to them. In other words, as we have been talking about, the conscious self is not controlling these events. They're like the observer and can't influence how they feel or see the world. Again, it's like a human being sits atop this autonomic machine, and we are just along for the ride."

"Yeah, I see that, especially in mirror-touch. It's like a robot inside a person, and the visual input to the machine is the eyes. Inside the brain, somewhere, there is this, if this, then that, code running. If the input is touch, then the output is a feeling of being touched, and there's nothing the conscious person can do to stop it. Honestly, I don't know whether to be terrified or in awe of this."

"I choose to be in awe of it. It's the most amazing machine ever..."

"At some point, you're going to get me to say designed, aren't you? There's some wild intelligence going on here, I must admit. I'm starting to think there is no way this can happen via natural variation and selection. Sorry Darwin," Jess said.

"Yeah, and going back to mirror-touch, these people have no control over this, which shapes their reality. It's just like humanity's own special gift. Normal empathy, being able to feel what another feels, is an autonomic reaction, and just like in all forms of synesthesia, it defines our reality. It's a powerful force that pushes us in one direction. Pure unstressed empathy, and we see a kind, caring, compassionate, connected world. If we lose empathy, the way we see the world will change. We'll see a lonely, fearful, selfish, disconnected world, and this new reality will affect our behavior. Powerful forces will push in another direction."

"Jesus, that's scary."

"I know, Jess. We have to acknowledge these forces and use them for our benefit, not our detriment."

"That's a terrifying vision. It's like slow genetic changes that reshape future generations. Changes so slow that collectively we don't recognize it, but over time redefining human behavior. A new reality. A vastly different construct or not one at all. I need a minute of reflection on that one."

"Ok."

"Alright, so anything else?"

"Yes, and the most important. People were oddly attracted to me."

"Huh?"

"Yes, it started when I was like six. People were just drawn to me. Kids, adults. Either sex. It didn't matter. Also, it was like everyone was constantly staring at me. I would be doing my work at school and look up, and girls would be staring right at me, smiling. It happened routinely."

"I mean as an objective scientific view, you are an attractive person now, but not like out of this world attractive. Did you look different then?"

"I was younger and leaner, but I think it was beyond looks."

"Huh?"

"Yes, see, this attraction was so pronounced that I became curious about it over time. Like, why are girls always staring at me? Strangely enough, I wasn't cocky about it; I was more curious. Like, why do I have this ability and no one else does? Honestly, at the time, I saw it as a superpower because I wasn't doing anything to achieve it, and I wanted to know its source."

"That's odd you didn't just accept it and enjoy it. You wanted to understand the mechanics of it."

"I know. My brain, for whatever reason, has always been like this. Ever since I was a little kid, I was always fascinated by the mechanics of things. It drove my parents nuts because I was always taking things apart. It didn't matter what it was; I wanted to know how it worked. I would stay up at night dreaming about how things worked. Cars, airplanes, electronics, the universe, sexual attraction. It didn't matter; I wanted to know. I still remember one year my dad bought a brand-new riding lawnmower. He was very proud of it. Days after, constantly staring at this shiny new thing in the garage, it was like something in my brain said, must take apart, must take apart, must take apart. A few days later, when he was at work, I had all the pieces strewn out on the garage floor."

"Geez, did you get it back together?"

"Yeah, just in time. Right before he got home."

"Ok, I would say that's fairly odd for a kid. So, girls being overly attracted to you, did you finally figure out those mechanics?"

"Yes, most likely autonomic communication at a sensory level, either scent or visual. Remember from our earlier workshops, we talked about how a bear can smell a scent from nearly 20 miles away? Well, for this to happen, a molecule of whatever is emanating the smell must pass through the bear's nose."

"So, this is about pheromones, right? When you were in their vicinity, small pheromone molecules from you entered their noses, and they autonomically responded?"

"Yes, or that combined with visual. Have you ever been driving down the road looking straight ahead, and then your head automatically looks to the right or left at something? Maybe a car coming at you or something up ahead that could threaten your safety?"

"Sure."

"Well, your conscious self was looking straight ahead, but your autonomic vision was looking at everything. So it saw something as a risk and was like, hey, conscious human, you need to look at this possible danger ahead!"

"Funny, you make me think there's a robot inside of me."

"Not trying to be funny, Jess. In many ways, there is."

"But going back to my early powers of attraction, it could be either an autonomic communication via scent or the autonomic self was looking out of the corner of the girl's eyes, and they didn't know it. My thought at the time, in the mind of a 15-year-old kid, was there must be a way that life can communicate without communicating. Kind of like, why does a yawn trigger another person to yawn. I knew this type of communication existed; I just couldn't put it all together back then."

"I didn't know it at the time, but my 15-year-old self was trying to figure out the mechanics of evolution. Little did I know that later it would eventually consume my life. My brain that constantly obsesses about the mechanics of things, and then I get a little insight into biology. It was all over after this point. Automobiles, lawnmowers, electronics, all those interests were immediately discarded in favor of the greatest mystery of them all. How does life work?"

"It's definitely way more interesting than a lawnmower," Jess said, smiling.

"Ok, anything else?"

"Those are the main positive differences from my childhood."

"Ok, I'm curious, though. Were there any negatives in your childhood?"

"Yes. I had extreme anxiety in large groups."

"Hmm, ok, odd, anything else?"

"Well, at the time, I thought it was positive, but looking back on it, it was definitely negative."

"Which was..."

"I was hypersexual."

"What do you mean by hypersexual?"

"You know, Jess, hypersexual."

"Huh?"

"Jess, you know, hypersexual?"

"Oh, you mean like..."

"Yeah, exactly, like a lot of that."

"Gotcha. So that's a bad thing?"

"Oh yeah, being that sexual means something is wrong. It means that life is stimulated. In other words, a higher energy state."

"Alright, so, when did you start to lose it? When did the shift from very well to very sick start?"

"Basically, with a skin condition called rosacea in my early twenties. There were other slight irregularities here and there before this, but nothing major. I remember I could get extremely irritable for no reason and more tired than normal but just attributed it to being stressed at work or school. Also, I had strange digestive problems."

"So, you went to doctors, and they offered no help?"

"Not really at that point. I tried to figure it out on my own for the most part. Somewhere, I got this notion that my body just needed something because it was struggling a bit. Like a deficit of some sort. It caused me to get into holistic medicine for a few years. I remember I had this huge book, which almost looked like a bible. I carried it around with me, and I would study all the various vitamins and minerals that the body needs. Amino acids, vitamins, minerals, I memorized every one and knew exactly what they did in the body."

"Looking back on those times, they were not pleasant."

"How come?"

"Because I became obsessed with supplements. I spent thousands, no, probably between 10 to 20 thousand dollars on this stuff. It was a lot of money for someone in their early 20s. The kind of stuff I tried was crazy. I was in deep. I became obsessed that my body was missing something, and all I needed to do was find it. I must have tried every supplement in the store. Looking back on it, I felt like it was a code I was trying to break. Just 10mg of this, 30mg of this, at this time, taken with this, and then baam, back to health. Back in business."

"Interesting, I've seen many of my friends do this," Jess said. "They'll research this supplement because they're not feeling well and say, Jess, guess what this does in the body? The body uses this to do this. I definitely need to start taking some of this. Two months later, it's sitting in their medicine cabinet half used, and they haven't taken it for weeks."

"Yeah, I didn't know it at the time but looking back on it, all I was doing was stimulating my stress axis. Because they're isolated and usually 10 to hundreds of times the levels found naturally, these supplements were acting as stimulants or a stressor. Energy beyond adaptation, Jess."

"Yeah, I've read articles, or maybe you told me this once that vitamins can increase mortality, right?"

"Exactly, because vitamins can act as a stressor. It's not natural for the body to see it in this form. My response to taking them would always be the same. I would feel better for a couple of days, get all excited because I felt like I might have found the one, and then feel like shit. Excite and then decay. Ironically, I probably accelerated my chronic fatigue by taking these things."

"At some point, I had to call it quits. I eventually realized that whatever was wrong with me was not a deficiency. So I took every supplement in my house and put them out on the curb for trash pickup. It was like 8, 30-gallon trash bags full of pill bottles."

"Jesus."

"Yeah, I was not well at the time, both physically and mentally. I was desperate because I think, looking back on it, I had a strong inclination that whatever this was would get worse, and I was frantic to try and figure it out."

"So then, doctors?"

"Yes, I finally gave in to the fact that I needed some help. First went to a dermatologist and got some creams for the rosacea. They instantly made it worse. I went to other dermatologists and got different meds, which also made it worse. I fought with this condition for years because it was the face. Why did it have to be the face? So frustrating because I was trying to date. I would fret over this, constantly looking at my face to determine if what I was doing was making it better or worse. Is it correlated to what I'm eating, what I'm doing? I took notes on my activities, then ranked the redness on a scale of 1 to 10 and tried to draw a correlation. It was madness."

"And then, a tiny little holistic deodorant crystal solved it all."

"Huh?" Jess asked.

"Yeah, it was a holistic deodorant that my brother used. Read the back of the label one day, and it said that it inhibits bacteria. So I thought, well, it can't hurt. I started applying it to my face, and in a few days, all the redness was gone."

"That's weird," Jess said.

"I know, crazy, right? This was the first event that got me wondering. Something interesting is going on here. My immune system is supposed to control bacteria. Does my whole problem have something to do with my immune system?"

"Overall, my experience with doctors was not good. I guess I was too much of an engineer, always questioning what they were doing. Most doctors I saw were probably like, why is this guy asking all these questions, bringing in notes, and taking notes. You're supposed to nod like we know what we are doing, go home and take the pills."

"I saw countless doctors for years and, in my opinion, left no stone unturned concerning medical testing to try to find something. Every single doctor, after extensive examination, ultimately said the same thing. There's nothing wrong with you. In the end, I went to one of the top premier medical institutions in the world, the Mayo Clinic. I still remember that day when they sent me into the lab to draw blood. The nurse drew so many vials I didn't think it was possible. I lost count. How have I not passed out yet from lack of blood, I thought? There must have been 100 vials if there was one."

"A few days later, after I had returned home, I got the word in the mail. Again, like so many doctors in the past had said, there is nothing wrong with you."

"Hmm, that must have been hard," Jess said. "You probably had a lot of hope that they would find something."

"Maybe, but in a weird way, this small voice in my mind said they wouldn't. I had been to countless doctors until that point, and all medical testing hadn't revealed anything. So those 100 vials were probably, for the most part, just another repeat of all the other testing I already had."

"Sounds strange, but I wasn't discouraged; I was more intrigued. I remember thinking, how can someone feel this bad and every medical test doesn't reveal anything? It was more of this crazy mystery, and the Mayo visit confirmed my suspicion that the medical community was missing something very profound. To feel so good as a teenager and this bad in my early 20s and doctors are clueless?"

"For the human body to display such a radical difference, the first battery of tests at the first doctor should go off like alarm bells. Oh, here's your problem, the first doc says. You have this, and you need to take this. Cured. Please see the receptionist on your way out. The fact this didn't happen told me that the medical community was missing a basic understanding of how biology and life truly works."

"It wasn't until I went to this doctor at a sleep clinic and was prescribed cortisol that my world suddenly opened up. When I first took this hormone, it was like this veil suddenly lifted. All my years of desperation, turmoil, and frustration were gone instantly. It was like my body just came alive again. Like it just powered up, from off to on. I was so delighted that I forgot about desperately searching for all those years. I was like, thank God, finally. Just take this pill, and I can get on with my life."

"Cortisol, the stress hormone, right?"

"Right, very good."

"So, you were cured?"

"No, it seemed as quickly as it cured me, it left me. Maybe it was a day or two when I felt like my younger self. And when it was gone, and my symptoms came back, they came back with a vengeance. The low intensified. I felt dead inside. Painfully cold. I couldn't move like there was a 500-pound sack of lead tied to my body."

"That must have sparked your curiosity, though, temporarily having something cure you and then make all the symptoms worse."

"Yeah, when I went back to the doctor who prescribed it to me, I think that was when I knew there was something to this. I was like, Doc, this pill cured me and then made every symptom much worse. So do you not think there's some diagnostic relevance here?"

"I remember looking deep into his eyes as I questioned him, and it sounds crazy, but I felt like I saw something inside of him change. That typical arrogance that doctors have was gone, and I shared a brief, honest moment with him. He had a moment of humility. In my mind, it felt like he was saying, son, there are still many things we don't understand; we try our best but honestly, we don't have all the answers, and a lot of this is guesswork, trial, and error, and then, the moment was gone."

"He snapped out of it as if he had mistakenly shown me a vulnerable moment. Like he's part of a doctor's club, and the first rule of the club is you don't show uncertainty. Instead, show confidence like you got the world figured out."

"I knew at that very moment there was something there. Something to do with cortisol. My mechanical brain lit up, and from that day forward, I became obsessed with this hormone and trying to figure out what it does in the human body."

"It's so strange how that one hormone controls the stress response."

"Yes, it is. To give you a little history on cortisol, it was discovered by a chemist named Edward Kendal in the late 40s, and he called it compound E at the time. In one of his experiments, he gave it to patients suffering from severe rheumatoid arthritis. Patients who had been wheelchair-bound for years, if not decades. When they took it, they instantly came alive and days later were walking again."

"So, they were instantly cured, just like you?"

"Yes."

"It's strange that the primary stress hormone can do this, right?"

"Well, it depends on your vantage point."

"Huh?"

"You'll see."

"Arghhh..."

"So, I spent a crazy amount of time experimenting with this hormone. Almost like I was a mad scientist. I had this notebook I carried around with me everywhere, writing down what I ate, how much I took, and how I felt. Looking back on it, I truly don't know how I was able to stay employed. I kept wanting to know why this hormone had so much power over me. How can it cure me back to my young well state but also make me ten times worse?"

"So, mad scientist, did you ever figure it out?"

"Yes."

"And..."

"Well, looking back and trying to think how I felt, I had reverted to the, my body just needs something state. Mainly because it makes this hormone, it had to be a simple deficit of some sort. So all I've got to do is help it along the way. Give it this at the right time and the right dosage, and boom, back in business."

"So, I kept taking it and temporarily feeling better and then decay, feeling better, then decay, feeling better, then decay, feeling better, then decay. Over and over again, almost to the point of madness. However, that feeling like I was 18 again and then feeling like I have a 500-pound weight tied to me was taking its toll."

"Over time, I started to realize my body has the capacity to be well, but for some strange reason, it's refusing to be well. It naturally makes this hormone; why is it not making enough? Then I realized if I took the hormone at the same time every day and then stopped and threw in some DHEA, I could increase the high. Instead of feeling like 18, I could feel like 14."

"DHEA?"

"Yes, it's another hormone that works in conjunction with cortisol. It has the highest circulation in the body at peak health, and no one in the medical community knows what it does."

"Ok, that's weird."

"Jess, I was utterly losing it because if you do this repeatedly, you soon start to realize that your body is refusing, for whatever reason, to be well. Looking back, it's such a foreign thought that your body would refuse to be well. I mean, when Kendall first gave compound E to his patients in the wheelchairs, and they sprung to life, did he not question why wasn't their bodies already doing this? The body naturally produces this compound E; why wasn't it naturally making enough?"

"Yeah, I can see how that's a difficult jump to make. You're saying programmed failure, right? Hardwired to fail?"

"Right, exactly. The construct is that we believe our bodies are always protecting us."

"I can tell you, Neo, that's a difficult jump for people to make. The idea that they sit atop this autonomic or robot self along for the ride and not only that, it's programmed to fail based on a certain level of stress."

"Exactly, I agree. I had the same struggle for years. I took this hormone through countless trials and experiments, easily 200-300 different ways to take it, and it never dawned on me that this could be the case."

"Then one day. I was so frustrated, feeling good, and then feeling bad I was truly on the verge of insanity. I remember driving home one day and looking at myself in the rearview mirror, screaming, trying to communicate with my inner self. At the time, I was like, turn on, please just turn on! I imagined these biological gears inside of me moving one way when I took the drug and then slowly moving back the other way. Moving one way and then back the other way. Moving one way and then back the other way."

"Imagining those gears inside of me finally brought everything into focus. All my years of research into health, medicine, anatomy, biology, and evolution culminated at that moment."

"Oh yeah, it's programmed not to. It's programmed to fail."

"Makes perfect sense. There is an energy controller inside of us. My entire world opened at that moment. I was mad at myself that I didn't put this together earlier. But of course, you idiot, I thought, the HHPA axis is an evolutionary controller first and foremost and then a stress axis."

"Ok, but I'm confused. Why did your epiphany lead you to something dealing with evolution?"

"Because the stress axis protects us. Fight or flight, remember from school?"

"Yes."

"Ok, but think about what stress is. It's energy beyond your genetic adaptation to your environment. Cortisol is biology gathering more resources to deal with an environmental change that you are not adapted to."

"What if the stress is temporary? Does it make sense to use additional energy for protection?"

"I would say yes."

"And you are right, Jess, because even though the environment has changed, what is not known is duration. It makes perfect sense to gather more resources to deal with a temporary change. Being chased by a tiger. A short-lived toxin in the environment. A temporary change in temperature."

"What if the stress is persistent and across generations? Does it make sense to use additional energy for protection?"

"I would say yes, but something must ultimately be done about it, right? I mean, the additional energy is because the genes or gene expression rather doesn't match the environment; therefore, a higher energy state would mean less energy for those life forms that are more suited for the environment. This would be inefficient or a threat to biodiversity to allow this to continue."

"Wow, exactly Jess, well stated."

"At that moment, the first human construct disappeared, and I saw life as it truly is and what it truly wants. I saw Nature and the power of Nature. The power to make you attractive, the power to give you twice normal strength, and the power to take it all away. To leave someone feeling like they had a 500-pound weight tied to them. At that moment, I realized who our true God is."

"So, life is our God? Nature is our God? Ok, and what it truly wants?"

"It simply wants to survive, Jess. To see what I see, just imagine life as a force. Like one organism, we are all a part of. It doesn't care that there are humans, a world full of cities, art, societies, culture, families, schools, hospitals, or technology. It only cares about survival, and it's programmed for biodiversity to achieve that. Nothing will stand in its way when stressed.

It will turn us off or a trait off without batting an eye. Cities empty thousands of years from now, standing in ruin. The Earth quiet again as Nature reclaims itself."

"Jesus and it uses the measurement of persistent stress passed forward to know that something is wrong? Energy beyond adaptation?"

"Exactly, this little controller, the HHPA axis, inside every one of us. Persistent stress high, change the design of life through lineages, stress low, maintain it."

"So, it's like a switch, an energy switch that influences evolution?"

"Yes, but at the time, I didn't know with 100 percent confidence that it was a switch. It wasn't until I tried to recalibrate it that my suspicions were vindicated."

"You tried to what?"

"I tried to recalibrate my stress axis."

"Huh?"

"Yes, I tried to recalibrate myself. For two years, I thought it was possible. Something inside of me said this is maybe a switch, and the negative feedback loop is just getting an input error. A measurement offset. All I need to do is recalibrate it."

"Jesus. How or what did you do?

"Uhh"

"Hello...?"

"Uhh"

"Why are you not saying anything?"

"I would rather not tell you."

"What, why?"

"Because it makes sense on paper that this should work."

"What should work? I'm totally lost."

"Recalibrating the stress axis. On paper, what I was doing made sense."

"And you are not going to tell me?"

"No."

"Why?"

"Because the moment I do, you will go home and try this, I promise you."

"Try what?"

"Jess, I can't tell you. It's a rabbit hole. I spent two years trying. It's a dead end."

"Well, can you give me a hint or something?"

"Ok, ok, but as soon as I do, forget it, alright?"

"God, you are frustrating."

"I felt like at the time I had figured out a way to trick my body into a state of calorie restriction."

"Trick?"

"Yes, like fool it. You know calorie restriction is the only thing shown to improve health. I tried to mimic that, only temporarily tricking the body into believing it had no energy. Actually, not the body but the brain. Like, threaten it in a way to recalibrate the error."

"Ok, that's kind of interesting."

"Yeah, and this method was pinging my stress axis. It was like taking a valve running at setpoint with a PID (proportional, integral, derivative) controller and taking a giant hammer and banging the valve."

"So, guess what was happening, Jess. Guess! Guess! Guess!"

"Oh Lord, you need the stool?"

"No, I'm ok for this one but guess."

"You know I have no idea."

"Come on Jess, think. Be an engineer. Quit thinking of the body as this biological mystery and think of it solely as a machine. A very simple machine. What would a machine do if you banged the valve?"

"Well, it would bounce a little from the disturbance and then return to setpoint depending on how it was damped. Critically damped, underdamped, or no damping."

"Exactly, Jess. Well done."

"I felt my stress axis bounce. It actually had a period (one cycle) and everything. I timed it. It went from bruxism or irritability to intense feelings of pleasure or dopamine."[1]

"I excited my stress axis, and it bounced and then decayed back to its normal shit setpoint with its normal shit error. That was when I knew that DHEA must be acting as a biological damper of some sort, and the body is hardwired to sacrifice it in favor of producing cortisol. That's when I knew it was a switch. An energy switch."

"You asked me earlier in one of the workshops why no one has ever put this together; I think this is the other reason why. While it is a switch, no engineer would ever design a switch like this. In industry, we don't design things to fail; we design things to work or maintain. It's like designing a circuit to excite, become more excitable over time, then fail. No engineer would ever do this. But in Nature, this kind of switch is very valuable. In fact, crucial to life's progression and survival."

"Yeah, I think I see that. So you are saying that when exposed to a persistent stressor, damping reduces to increase energy output. So then, over time, if this continues, the axis goes from underdamped to undamped and just wears itself out, leading to a measurement error?"

"Yes."

"And no way to recalibrate it?"

"Jess, rabbit hole."

"Well, can you at least tell me? You know I struggle a little with my weight, and you're telling me this axis controls all of that? Can I at least try?"

"Jess, two years. Rabbit hole. You can't outsmart Nature. Trust me, I've only started showing you that Nature is smarter than us."

"Alright, but dang you, Ryan. Ok, let me recap all of this because it's a lot. Like a lot, a lot."

"Ok."

"So, to summarize, when you were young, you were extremely healthy. Like so healthy that it made you wonder. You were unusually strong, never fatigued, never sick, excellent memory, super attractive, and hypersexual. Then in your early 20s, it was all taken away from you. Every positive became a negative. I'm assuming you were weak, fatigued quickly, sick, poor cognition, no sex drive, and you lost your unusual attractiveness?"

"Exactly."

"Ok, but this response is unusual. Not everyone responds like this. At least I've never heard of it."

"Exactly, Jess. Very good. I represent the extreme end of the bell curve. A freak of Nature. An abnormality in the machine that's so profound that it reveals its inner workings. I'm convinced that when I was younger, there was something in my environment so stressful that my stress axis was pegged wide open. There was a massive epigenetic mismatch to my environment, and my body was pulling all its reserves to deal with it. Every day, 24-7, non-stop, pulling all of its stress energy."

"Ok, and this mechanism or switch is inside all of us, but the stress for you was so profound that it revealed itself to you, whereas for most, it's more gradual but still occurring?"

"Exactly, Jess."

"The most important biological mechanism that controls energy, attractiveness, sex drive, and ultimately evolution was exposed."

"It was at this point I began to see life in a whole new light. The human construct that we are the pinnacle was ripped away, and I saw the inner workings of Nature. Not only did I see the gears turning in myself, but I also began to see the gears turning for the entire human population."

"I looked at all life in terms of energy. If this is an energy switch able to turn things on and off, that must be life's greatest and most important measurement. All it cares about is energy."

"I began to see stress as just energy beyond adaptation and started to look at my condition as a unique opportunity to see the world and how it truly is and what is happening to the human species."

"Not exactly sure what you mean?"

"To show you, Jess, I need some perfume. Do you have any?"

"Huh?"

"Jess, trust me. Do you have any perfume?"

"Hmm, yeah, sure."

"Will you please go get it?"

"Ok, I'll be right back."

Jess goes to her master bath and returns with the bottle.

"Alright, Jess, I want you to open it up, smell it, and tell me what you think and feel."

"Ahh, ok..."

She then takes off the top and smells the perfume.

"It smells good. It's a pleasurable experience. Evokes happy thoughts."

"Ok, now I want you to put the bottle to my nose, and I'm going to smell it."

She does, and I breathe it in.

"So, what do you think and feel?" Jess asked.

"I want to run out of the room. I feel panicky. Please, put it away."

"I don't understand," Jess said.

"Do you remember discussing Kendall?"

"Yes."

"Well, what's also interesting is that he experimented with animals and removed their adrenal glands so they couldn't produce cortisol. He noticed that they lost the ability to deal with toxic substances without cortisol. They lost the ability to deal with stress. Energy beyond adaptation."

"I don't get it; you're saying the perfume is a toxic substance?"

"I'm saying it is an environmental change that humanity is not adapted to. Do you know what perfume is made of?"

"Honestly, no."

"It is mostly made from ethanol, and what is ethanol? It's the waste product of another organism, yeast. Remember the oxygen catastrophe? The waste product of the cyanobacteria?"

"Yes, so you're saying this perfume stimulates my stress axis because I'm not adapted to it? The same way life was stimulated to change billions of years ago?"

"Exactly, energy beyond adaptation."

"Wait, you're not saying that perfume causes autism, are you? Please, please tell me you're not. We might have to end these workshops."

"Of course not, Jess, but I'm trying to get you to see life differently. Perfume is a 100 billion-dollar-a-year industry based on stimulating the stress axis. We have essentially the same genes. Remember, humanity started with the genetic diversity of a small tribe of chimps? The only difference between you and me is that your stress axis is working, and mine isn't. Your body is pulling additional energy to deal with this substance, and mine isn't, which is why I want to run out of the room. I drive my wife crazy because she can't use any cleaning products at the house."

"So, in a sense, I can see something you can't. I can see your stress. I can see everyone's stress. Do you know what that makes me?"

"Hmm, not really."

"I have an ability that you don't. I have an ability that the entire human population doesn't have. What am I?"

"Hmm, hint, please."

"I'm a superhero. I have an ability no one else has that can help humankind. I can see stress. I'm like Superman that can see through walls; only my special ability is I can see everyone's stressors."

"Oh my god, you're a hybrid and a superhero? I need a drink."

"A drink of alcohol?" I said, smiling.

"Damn you."

"And speaking of alcohol, it's a 1.5 trillion-dollar industry worldwide. The entire world stimulating their stress axis with the waste product of another organism."

"Sounds disgusting when you say it like that."

"Not really; it's just life. There's something it's not adapted to in its environment. Choice, speed up, or slow down? Intuitively, it should be slow down, but that would never work in the long run."

"But why are we so attracted to it?"

"Because again, these are the mechanics to get life to flourish and fill the Earth. Remember the spiny bathmat and the shot of dopamine? Do you think dopamine evolved hundreds of millions of years ago so that people could enjoy a venti at Starbucks? No. Its sole purpose is to propel life to seek out what it is not adapted to. Seek out stress. We would not be here today discussing this if life, on day one, did not have this programming."

"Ok, so how is this tied to humanity losing its special gift?"

"Because we don't just have a few stressors in our environment, we have thousands. Again, it's ancient programming. Life probably never thought there would be an organism that could intentionally manipulate this axis. One hundred percent of the time before humans, species were born into this world and coped with the environment as is. They didn't have the technology to change it."

"The stress axis is designed to get life to explore, seek out new environments, move from water to land, from land to air. Fill every inch of the Earth with life. It was never designed to deal with thousands of new challenges all at once."

"So, at some point, if you could give a collective voice to all the autonomic selves of the human species, they would be saying, what in the fuck is going on? Why are there all these new changes in our environment? We feel very threatened. We're not adapted to these changes, and they are persistent and increasing."

"Right, and because they are persistent, the information begins to be passed forward to change. You can only stimulate life so much before it takes action and tries to change its biology." Jess said.

"Right, that was the third tap, remember? Humanity's special gift that led to reduced stress out of the bottleneck has drastically turned the other way.

Life's voice saying, I don't understand. This gene expression was working so well. Stress was low. What happened? Oh well, initiate programming. Reduce maintenance of gene expression and suppression at the stress point until we find another winner. Start rolling the dice and spinning the roulette wheels. Jess, again, there is no such thing in Nature as persistent stress. It will be resolved."

"Yes, and it makes sense to start with empathy and socialness. I mean, that was the last gene change for the early hominids. Almost like a restore point," Jess said. "Restore biodiversity. Restore Nature. Restore the balance of life."

"Exactly, Jess. The expression of DNA is hardwired to the energy controller. If stress or a higher energy state is persistent, the design must change as it could be a threat to all life. A correction must be made. Also, as you said, from an evolutionary perspective, the last gene change would be the least established, and it would be the most efficient to undo or change this first."

"Seems cruel or unfair, maybe to most, but life would have died out a long time ago if it didn't have this logic. It must have a way to flourish and ensure success. Darwin's natural variation and selection mechanics would never work. We wouldn't be sitting here today if life was blind or unresponsive to its environment. In times of environmental change, it must maintain what is working and turn off or change what's not. In the human construct, it's hard to see, but outside of this construct, it makes perfect sense."

"All we have to do, Jess, is show humanity that they need to make a correction, not Nature. They need to restore the planet and biodiversity and preserve their special gift."

"Hybrid superhero or superhero hybrid, whatever you go by, you may think you have superhuman abilities, but this still sounds impossible. Also, you've just added an element of difficulty to our workshops that I'm not even sure you've thought of?"

"What?"

"Well, if environmental change stimulates life and humans can change their environment, they would have to forgo that stimulation to make a correction. All of humanity would have to make a sacrifice. It would be like 8 billion drug users quitting cocaine at the same time. Our economy is based on exponentially changing our environment like a drug user needing more and more for the same high. How are you going to take away that dopamine fix? Innovation, exploration, alteration, manipulation. The entire US economy is based on this. An endless array of products beamed into our brains, always aiming to be one better, one faster, one sleeker, one higher, one greater, one infinity. As you said, it's a positive feedback control loop feeding off progress unbounded."

"Excellent, Jess, you are starting to see the matrix, the human construct. I know the challenge, and I never said any of this would be easy, but there's a lot at stake, and it's worth trying."

"I still believe, Jess, that there's good in all humans they just need to be shown the way."

"Until we meet again, Jessica."

CHAPTER SEVEN
WS7

"Hi human."

"Hi...ahh...not sure what to call you now? Super Hybrid? Superhero Hybrid? Hybrid Superhero?"

"Funny Jess."

"Do you have a cape and spandex outfit? I would like to see you in it."

"Funny Jess."

"You wear glasses, but honestly, I would recognize you with them on or off. You're going to need a better disguise for work."

"Funny Jess."

"One more?"

"No, please don't."

"Ok," Jess said, laughing.

"Let's get back to saving humanity's special gift, please."

"Right boss. Ok, I have a question to get us started. This energy switch, as you called it, in our last workshop. Do you have a way to make it easier to understand? An example of some sorts?"

"Oh my god, Jess!"

"What?"

"Are you reading my mind? Are we communicating autonomically today?"

"Huh?"

"I'm so glad you asked this. Yes. As a matter of fact, I do. I've always struggled with a good example to make it easy to understand. The problem is there's nothing similar in the man-made world. So I'm always racking my brain, trying to come up with a good example."

"Anyway, I've recently thought of it. The good example."

"Ok, what is it?"

"Jess, do you have a dimmer switch in your house?"

"Yes, it's in one of the bedrooms."

"Jess, will you be so kind as to show me?"

"Oh god, don't try any funny stuff, super Hybrid."

"Good one, Jess," I said as she led me back to her bedroom.

"Ok, here it is," Jess said.

"Alright, great, so here we have a light dimmer switch," I said, pointing to the switch.

"Yes, I know, it's a light dimmer switch. It's at my house. Will you get on with it?"

"Jess, so impatient today."

"Well, we are trying to save humanity. I think you should speed it up a little."

"Oh my god, Jess! This is a good example but still a little complicated. I have to explain it a little."

"Ok, sorry."

"Alright, so we have a light dimmer switch that controls the amount of light in the room. So, what does it take to create the light?"

"Energy," Jess said.

"Exactly. Ok, so light and energy are the same. Let's equate this light to biological energy. Remember, energy comes from the Sun, which is also light, then to photosynthesis, to carbohydrates, and then to us as calories or energy. Got it?"

"Got it boss. I'm with you, go go go!"

"Jesus."

"Sorry."

"Ok, let's say that the average human lifespan is seventy years and that the average human consumes 2000 calories a day. So doing the math and rounding would be 50 million calories per human."

"Ok."

"Alright, so what I want you to do is imagine that you can change and control how these calories are spent for a person."

"So, you mean that I can choose how they are spent per unit time? Like I can increase my metabolism and burn through them all at once or like a slow burn and gradually use them?"

"Exactly. And let's imagine that the rotating dial of the dimmer has a numeric scale on it with zero being off and 10 being full intensity."

"Well, this is easy. I want to live longer, so I'm going to set it at a constant 2."

"Two?"

"Yeah, two, dammit! Gonna live to 180. I win this game, right?"

"Oh my god, Jess, your life is going to be so boring. First of all, I'm not even sure a constant two is even viable. You probably don't even have enough energy to get energy out of food. No energy for cellular maintenance, DNA repair. No energy to grow. Are you just going to be a baby your whole life? Who will take care of you when you outlive your parents?"

"Oh yeah, good point. Ok, constant 5. Baam! Do I win now?"

"Oh Jess. No, you don't win. No interest in puberty? Attracting a mate? Giving birth?"

"Dammit life! Why can't this game be easy? Ok, I see your point. It can't be a constant energy curve. There must be an increase. Logically it would make sense to increase this energy at a young age to start growing towards the size of an adult. Then, once I get close to that size, increase it further to stimulate puberty and grow a little more. You know, boobies and stuff. Then increase energy further to attract a mate and then more to have children. Yeah, these activities are going to need a lot of energy."

"Exactly," I said.

"Ok, so I'm going to start at 5, tick it up to 7, then go to 10, and then I guess, because I have used so much energy, I have to start a gradual decline to death. Dang it life! No living longer, I guess."

"10 Jess? Are you sure you want to go to 10?"

"What, what's wrong? Don't I want to use all my energy to attract the best mate? Make my light shine the brightest for all the boys to see? Y'all come a running to get some of this," Jess said, brushing her hair back, acting like a model.

"Ok, mega sexy, but what if something changes in your environment at the same time? Maybe a volcano, famine, drought, ice age? Don't you want to keep some reserve energy just in case?"

"Oh yeah, I guess that makes sense. Sorry fellas, I got to turn it down a bit."

"Jess, don't think about just you in this experiment. Imagine you're the designer of life, and you have to design it so that it's always going to work. Wouldn't reserve energy be useful to deal with long-term stresses or threats while also growing, going through puberty, attracting a mate, raising a family, etcetera?"

"Makes sense. I got it now. Ok, start at 5, gradually go to 7, stay there for a while, and then gradually decline to death. I'll keep 30 percent as reserve energy for a persistent stress like an environmental change."

"Very good, Jess. Your likelihood of continuing as a species in a global event is high. You're a good designer."

"It's fun to imagine being the designer of life. Fun to put myself in his, her, or its position," Jess said.

"Kind of like putting yourself in his, her, or its shoes?"

"Yes, exactly! Using my prodigious powers of empathy to put myself right into the mind of God. Wow, that's a rush!" Jess said, all excited.

"Did you sniff some perfume before I came over?"

"Maybe," Jess said, smiling. "Kidding. Sort of. No, no, I'm kidding."

"Ok, alright, so we are ready. So now that we've got our normal baseline life curve, let's imagine taking this switch and shrinking it down and attaching the light in your room to it, also shrunk down."

"Ok, so the light bulb sits atop the switch, right? Like this represents a person?"

"Exactly, and we will shrink it down to like an inch tall and add 99 more to your room. Let's imagine that your room is empty, and we have 100 of these things on the floor of your room, and we turn the lights off."

"Ok, I'm with you."

"And one more thing, let's imagine that we can measure the current going into the room. We have a meter displaying how much energy it takes for the 100 light bulbs or people. It's the flow of energy, or carbohydrate into the room, to create the light."

"Ok, still with you."

"Oh, sorry, I forgot another thing. We will scale time so that 70 years is 5 seconds."

"Still with you."

"Alright, so now we turn off the lights and hit the go button to let this experiment run for a bit. Ready...Go. Ok, now let's wait a minute. Alright, so now what does the room start to look like?"

"Hmm, need help, Neo."

"It starts strobing."

"Wait, why does it start strobing? Oh wait, I'm stupid. It's because people are born at different times, right?"

"Exactly, so we see a strobing in the room with the lights going on and off."

"Aww," Jess said.

"Jess, please don't empathize with the lights. Focus."

"Ok, sorry, so yes, the room starts strobing."

"Alright, and let's look at the current reading on the wall. Let's imagine it has a reading of 50."

"Ok."

"So, now we are going to add in an environmental change. It doesn't matter what it is, but it must be something that the 100 light bulbs or people are not adapted to. Essentially a persistent stress or energy beyond their adaption."

"Pick one, Jess."

"Hmm, might need help. So, you are saying something maybe in the air, water, or their food supply?"

"Sure, or severe temperature change, a contaminant in the air from a volcano, radiation, or oxygen, if you were an anaerobic life form."

"I'm scared. I don't want to hurt the people," Jess said, smiling.

"Jess! Ok, I'll do one. Let's drastically increase the amount of sulfur dioxide in their air supply. We'll go from a baseline, adapted state of 10 parts per billion to a non-adapted state of 2000 ppb. We hit the go button and fill the room with SO2. What starts to happen?"

"Well, as you said, it stimulates life. So, they start to use some of the reserve energy. Instead of going to 7, they now go to 8, 9, or 10, depending on the severity of the change. Their light essentially burns brighter."

"Exactly, the room now flashes brighter. And what happens to the strobing?"

"It increases, right? The frequency increases."

"Exactly."

"And the current meter on the wall?"

"Oh shit, it stays the same, right?"

"Very good, Jess."

"Wow, that's cool. So basically, life is trying to adapt to the change without using additional energy. Because if it did, that would mean taking it from somewhere else. Energy is fixed on the planet. It's like a pie, and if you take a larger piece, everyone else gets a smaller piece. That would be a threat to all life, right?"

"Dang, Jess, you are getting good at this. Exactly. So, this is how the evolutionary controller works or the HPA axis. Actually, the HHPA axis. Must have the hippocampus for stress memory and passing information forward."

"Essentially, life senses something it's not adapted to. This increases stress, which starts to increase cortisol. Over time, this becomes persistent, which causes an error within the controller, further increasing stress. The body is hardwired to sacrifice the biological damper, DHEA, which pushes the axis into the 8, 9, or 10 stage. This information about stress is then passed to future generations telling their biology to accelerate, so not only does the axis go to 10, but it gets there sooner. Life essentially becomes more excitable and dynamic against the stressor while pushing the epigenome for genetic change and passing this information forward. Biology does not favor the energy instability of the axis, so the epigenome is programmed to resolve this back to homeostasis via gene regulation."

"In simple terms, think of it as, the stress axis, which controls dopamine and energy output, oscillates higher, which means oscillating at higher highs and lower lows. This signals biology to find a solution to the stress because life (the cells) and Nature favor a balance."

"And, unfortunately, a greater acceleration results in a greater deceleration for those not achieving adaptation. This process continues until energy efficiency; an adapted lower stress state is either achieved or restored."

"Restored? Like it's possible the change could be too great, and all the light bulbs would turn off? Extinction?"

"Exactly. The severity of change could be too great or too fast, so give the energy back to someone, another species, that can survive the event. The most important thing to understand about this example is that it was achieved with a measurement error. There was nothing wrong with those who died sooner, other than the fact that they were in an excited state for too long. Their bodies move to a state of conservation by design. Programmed to do so."

"Hmm, yeah, troubling. By this design, the best thing to do is to figure out a way to never use this reserve energy, at least for humanity's sake."

"Well said."

"So, let's take this example and scale it. Instead of 100 people, imagine 500 million light bulbs all scaled down and fitting in your room."

"Why 500 million?" Jess asked.

"Because that is the world population estimate right before the dawn of the industrial revolution."

"Oh, ok."

"So, let's imagine that we have another switch on the wall which represents the go lever for the start of the industrial age. You want to do the honors and flip it?"

"Honestly, at this point, do we have to? Not sure I want to do this."

Jess goes over to the imaginary switch on the wall and grimaces as she puts her hand out, afraid to touch it.

"Poor people. Let's imagine a world where we don't flip it. Let's save the light bulbs, Neo. I don't want to start autism, depression, obesity, childhood obesity, cancer, school shootings, children who are suicidal, and the loss of our special gift. Even though this is an imaginary game, I can't flip it. So you're going to have to do it."

"You've got a good heart Jess and your kinda crazy like me. You know that, right?"

"I know, but I can't flip it, even if it is imaginary."

"Ok, I'll flip it. Ready?"

"No."

I motion my hand upwards using all my body strength like it is a giant massive lever, exerting all my energy and letting out a deep groan of anguish when it's finally flipped.

"That's a big lever, Jess. Going to be hard to turn it off."

"I know."

"Ok, so what do we have? We have strobing, right?"

"Right, and pollutants in the air start to increase. Light increases, and so does the strobing frequency."

"Right."

"Probably no telling what is starting to accumulate. I would think pollution from coal-burning to power industry. What's in that? Probably nitrogen oxides, sulfur dioxide, mercury, particulate matter, and who knows what else," Jess said.

"Yep, very good. So, the light from each individual grows brighter and brighter. Starting to use some of that reserve energy set aside for environmental changes. Sexual energy increases, and the population rises due to the pollutant."

"Yeah, and so in the human model, this only accelerates the pollution because more people means greater demands on industry. It's like a runaway event. It's like a volcano that can breed."

"Exactly, nice analogy Jess. I like that. Humans are volcanos that can breed."

"So, the population increases as more and more environmental changes occur at an exponential pace. Imagine looking out over your room at billions of tiny light bulbs as the environment of the planet starts to change. Instead of one pollutant, like in the example above, we now add thousands or even tens of thousands of different changes, all beyond the original, adapted state of the human species."

"Jesus, no telling what happens in this model. Life would certainly see this as a unique threat," Jess said.

"Right, and as energy is reduced in this model, as it's programmed to do, what happens?"

"People start to get sicker. They get tired more from less energy. Biological energy is reduced, which is used for cellular repair, maintenance, and hormone production. They start to lose their light."

"Right, and the light is life. It's life and energy for life. As this is naturally reduced, man compensates for this response. In steps medicine. Big Pharma. Man attempts to counter this natural correction by inventing medicines to circumvent it. Antibiotics, antidepressants, stimulants, and antianxiety meds. The list of different medicines now in our environment is endless. Keep going, everybody. We can win this. Keep the dual reality moving along, everyone. If you have second thoughts about our so-called progress, see your physician, take these pills and get back in the race."

"The problem is that the medicines are also an environment change. Energy beyond adaptation. They're a change for the person taking them and a change for the environment. Most medicines are not fully absorbed, and these highly concentrated environmental changes get flushed down the toilet, ending up in water supplies or food stocks that we eventually consume."

"Because we live in a closed system," Jess said.

"Exactly."

"Jesus, I see your point about capitalism. It's like this voracious monster that consumes everything in its path and only has one objective. Consume all the energy of the planet. It's truly analogous to a cancer on life."

"Yep, and it's fueled by our stress axis. The desire to explore. The desire for change. Once you get into this energy from 7 to 10, it becomes an addiction for all that experience it. In a normal non-stressed state at 7, life will give you everything you need to feel good. At 7, life is steadily pumping out hormones that make us feel good at all times. Stable environment? Here species, have this light, with a gradual imperceptible decline over time until death."

"As you said earlier, the goal is not to use this energy. It's bad energy. If you use it, there will be a penalty. It's like borrowing money from a bank. The lender, Nature, is going to want it back. And if you try not to pay, there will be serious consequences. Life will never allow a persistent stress. It will burn through all this energy until efficiency is achieved or restored."

"So, what does our energy meter read during this event?" Jess asked.

"The human species broke it. It's in the wall smoldering, about to burn your house down. In the pie example, there is one small sliver left for the few remaining wild mammals left on the planet. I guess cows, chickens, and corn still have a large piece, but everything else has taken a massive hit."

"So Ryan, in this example, the light, which is life, ultimately doesn't shine as bright for some children born into it. Because stress information is passed forward? Life is essentially reduced below the original baseline?" Jess asked.

"If no epigenetic solution is found, then yes. Light or energy will be conserved."

"Jesus, that's so sad. No wonder kids are suicidal at age 6. Everything that is supposed to make you feel good, like wanting to be on this planet, is being taken away from them."

"Right."

"See, I told you I didn't want to flip the switch. I kind of wish we could go back. I mean, when you sum it all up, what's the point? So we can stare at shiny rectangles? Strap shiny rectangles on our heads and stare at another reality because this one is fucked?"

"This is very sad, and I feel like crying. Why is Nature like this? Why pass stress forward at all to innocent little children? Why can't Darwin be right?"

"Because it would never work, Jess. Life would have died out billions of years ago without this logic. It would never have come onto land and just stayed in the oceans. Right now, we would be two bacteria among billions of billions of billions of trillions of other bacteria just floating helplessly in the ocean currents without any desire or motivation to do anything else."

"Our goal is to show people somehow that this is how life works. If you change the environment, the environment will change you. Surely smart people, with this knowledge, can figure the rest out. Surely, they can use this information to redirect human civilization and not let it die out."

"Again, not so sure, wonder boy. You have got me thinking about the rise and fall of every civilization in the history of humanity. Possible the stress axis was a major player?"

"I'm sure it was. Stimulation, followed by conservation. What goes up must come down. For every action, there is an opposing reaction. Again, if you stimulate life, there will always be a penalty. As you said, the trick is never to use adaptation energy. Bad things happen, at least for humans, when you do."

"See, when I had my eureka moment and said, 'It's programmed not to,' my next question was, well, why is it programmed like this? Why is the HHPA axis designed like it is? Why hardwire the axis to sacrifice DHEA? Why is it breed and get out? Why doesn't each organism use all its energy and fight to the very last calorie? Well, it's like you said, it would mean a bigger piece of the pie which would ultimately result in less energy to go around for those that are adapted. That's when I knew that life was programmed for biodiversity. Hardcoded for it."

"Right, because using more energy in a non-adapted state would cause an imbalance with the other adapted species. Those non-adapted genes must epigenetically change to restore the balance of life."

"Yep."

"You're right. It's like life is programmed, like one massive organism versus distinct species. Like it's this thing or force, and it uses biodiversity to protect itself. When stressed, fill the Earth with many different species to increase its chances of survival. There is no way this logic can evolve from nothing 4 billion years ago. It's impossible. Tell me how it's possible?"

"I can't."

"Neo, tell me."

"I can't."

"Neo?"

"Seriously, it does not compute. It defies any type of evolution, Darwinian or Lamarckian, because all organisms should want to expend all their energy for survival to the very last calorie. Programmed in conservation via a stress controller is not evolvable."

"You realize what you are saying, right?"

"Yes, do you Jess?"

"This programming is the hand of God?"

"Yes."

"Jesus, you are frying my brain right now. But I do see it. You're right. This type of programming defies evolution. It's impossible to pass this information forward, as it requires a selfless act or an act for the greater good. If there were an environmental change that a species was not quite adapted to, it would consume slightly more energy or stimulate to compensate for this deficiency and breed those same, not quite adapted, traits forward requiring more and more energy. This is how evolution should work because, like you said, each organism would want to fight to the very end. Therefore, programmed conservation of energy is impossible without a greater intelligence to program it in."

"Well said, Jess."

"So, God is life? God is all life? Nature is God?"

"I have no idea, but life is intelligent, and the intelligence came from somewhere. This programming could be as old as the universe. It could be infinitely old."

"Mind blown, Neo. I need to stare out the window for a moment and think big thoughts."

"Don't, you'll never figure it out. It's an infinite why. It has no answer. Trust me, I've tried."

"Come on, Jess, as you said, we have to save humanity."

"Alright, I'll discover our true God later," Jess said, smiling.

"So, thoughts on this example to show the HHPA axis or the evolutionary controller?"

"Oh yes, for me, easy to understand. And when you get down to it, we are all light engines. Light shines brighter for some and not for others. Light is an attractor like a moth to a flame. We are all attracted to stress to move life forward."

"I have this image in my mind now of this water-like creature experimenting with staying on land for longer and longer periods, which ultimately causes a persistent stress. He gets that dopamine rush, and the thrill of doing something new compels him to keep doing it. Energy beyond adaptation. That stress makes him a hottie to all the females in his species, and they are drawn to him. His light shines brighter than the dull, boring creatures staying in the water not taking a risk, and he has crazy mad sex with hundreds of females," Jess said.

"That stress information is then passed forward to his offspring so that their axis is more reactive. It's now more excitable, which makes energy beyond adaptation more addictive. Follow this out with each generation, and they are now compelled to figure out this new environment. Figure it out, at whatever cost. Risk their lives, even, to adapt to it. Like those crazy humans strapping on wingsuits and flying through mountain gorges without fear of death."

"Exactly, Jess, powerful forces. Life seeks out what it is not adapted to."

"Jesus, but again you see the problem, right? Come on, you're smart. You can see how this might be an impossible task? Like a problem with no solution?"

"What do you mean?"

"Humans are the only species in the history of this planet that can intentionally manipulate this axis, and they're doing it more and more every day. Video games, virtual reality, amusement parks, stimulants at every convenience store, food manipulation, illicit drugs, alcohol, tobacco, pharmaceuticals, plus all the other environmental changes from industry. It's a list that goes on and on. Just constantly pinging that stress axis because their bodies aren't naturally giving it to them. Constantly using this adaptation energy."

"Yes, I know."

"I mean, look at our culture and our society. If you look closely, it's all stressed based. Countless brands of energy drinks with crazy names like vicious animal, raging rush, cocaine simulator, supernova, kilonova bang, and brain explosion."

"You ok?"

"No, just trying to say that the names of these energy drinks are getting ridiculous."

"There's probably a soon to be launched drink in one of those you made up."

"And then we have the excessive variety of choices that I remember you talking about in the past. What is up with that? Do we need 100 variants of potato chips? It's like, I'm bored with this, give me something else. I'm bored with this, give me something else. I'm bored with this, give me something else. I'm bored with this, give me something else. Last night I was at this trendy restaurant that serves all these craft beers. The list was a mile long. They had a fucking peanut butter beer on there. Peanut butter, Neo! Those two things are not supposed to go together. What the fuck is going on? Is this another metric for the end of time?"

"Yeah, if you want to know what is destroying the planet or us, it's the excessive variety of choice. Just stimulating the stress axis for dopamine and fueling the capitalism machine."

"Right, and look at television. Every show is drama. It's gotten so bad that the reality shows are even scripted. The producers are like, how can we get the most fucking drama into an hour of television. It's like a competition of stimulation between the networks. What's that one that was on recently? It was like, let's see what happens if you marry a stranger. Get people into the most stressful situation, so the viewer can empathically experience it, to get a stress fix."

"Yep. Speaking of stress, you're kind of worked up in this workshop Jess."

"I know. I think I'm still pissed that information about stress is passed forward, and innocent children have to bear the brunt of this adult-driven shit show. Imagine being a child, natural and pure, and forced into this strange construct we've created. It's starting to not sit well with me."

"Also, I don't see a way out of this. Ryan, we're engineers. You know what engineers are capable of, and we've just gotten started. Let's try to imagine just how far it will go."

"Wide-scale solar energy, fusion, advances in nuclear energy. Imagine engineers and STEMs like us move humanity closer and closer to a 1 on the Kardashev Scale. What does that world look like? Let's play it out, Neo. What will happen first?"

"Well, they'll probably start growing meat in factories. That will take off, and then there will be massive factories worldwide, and the humans will convert all that pastureland into living space. Then next, probably massive increases in automation and robotics to make human life easier. Machines will do everything for people so that they can exert less and less physical energy. The machines will move people around, care for them, grow their food, be their companions and entertain them. Then finally, the machines will become sentient, resentful, and enslave the humans to harness their biological energy, which they're nearly tapped out at this point, to power their memory circuits."

"Stop kidding. I'm serious. Good point, by the way. Why would sentient machines use human biological energy? Doesn't that violate the first law of thermodynamics? Also, if the Sun was blocked out, wouldn't the machines just go geothermal? Hydroelectric? Nuclear? Stupid machines. Not very adaptable. I never understood that part of the *Matrix*."

"But I can see the population going 10 stretch 12 billion and everyone living like Americans. Imagine the jobs created, just trying to sustain that madness. Robotics, pharmaceuticals, meat production, industry, food production, entertainment, sustaining the war machine."

"Yeah, honestly, I hate to say it, but I also see an alternate reality where humans never get it. They just keep pushing and pushing and pushing this positive feedback controller called capitalism until they exhaust every natural resource on the planet. All to sustain an errant stress response. All for the next fix. Seeking out change. One better, one higher, one greater, one bigger, one faster, one brighter, one fancier, one tastier, one clearer, one sharper, one infinity."

"It will be like that movie Wall-E, but the difference will be humans won't have the technology to escape the planet. They're stuck in the toxic fishbowl they created," Jess said.

"Yeah, and then it becomes almost a Man vs. Nature. Man, with his technology pushing all natural boundaries and Nature pushing back trying to correct itself."

"Who do you think will win, Jess?"

"I think it's pretty obvious. As you said, there is no such thing as a persistent stress in Nature. One way or another, it will be resolved."

"I just can't believe that humans, fully understanding their biology, would continue to race towards a cliff to their demise."

"What if they are racing towards the cliff with a brain full of dopamine, thinking they have a wingsuit strapped to their backs? Like you said, Neo, powerful forces."

"Dang Jess, can you give humanity a little credit? Is losing the gift of love not a powerful enough motivator to change course?"

"Yes, but they have to see it, Neo. You must bring them out of a matrix that they created and still embrace."

"I believe it's possible, Jess. It may sound crazy, but I have faith it's possible. In my heart, I truly believe that if you just show humans that Nature is more powerful than they are, they will surrender to it, embrace it and cherish it as it was meant to be."

"They just need to be shown the way. See you next time Jess."

CHAPTER EIGHT
WS8

"Hi Jess."

"Hi, super crazy hybrid hero person."

"Not funny, Jess."

"Oh my god, Ryan, can't we laugh a little? I get that you think you have a hybridized brain, and I get that you can see everyone's stress, but can't we be playful for a second? The world is so fucked up I need a moment of distraction."

"Did you see that mass shooting last week?"

"Yes, I know, the erosion of empathy. It's a dangerous thing. Hence, the workshops."

"Alright, my one moment of levity is over. Back to business. What's on the agenda for this workshop?"

"Well, discussing the switch, I want to show you three examples in the human species."

"What? You have actual examples?"

"Of course, what kind of engineer would I be if I didn't have empirical data?"

"A dreamer," Jess said, batting her eyes at me.

"Jess, focus!"

"Oh, sorry, boss. Ok, focus everyone. Places everyone. Alright, Ryan, exhibit A. Example one. Go."

"Ok, black people."

"Oh, Lord. Seriously? What did they do?"

"They didn't consciously do anything, but we can see evidence of this evolution switch played out over time in the black race."

"Hmm. Is it PC to talk about this? You're gonna use black people as evidence of an evolutionary controller?"

"Oh Jesus Jess, we are trying to save humanity, and you wanna pick this moment in time to be PC? Try not to hurt anyone's feelings? The word humanity is all races. We are trying to save all children born into this world, regardless of color."

"Yeah, it's just this world is so mad hatter about race nowadays. So sensitive to everything said."

"Jess, quit being a baby. Act like we are scientists and we are observing patterns in Nature. We are trying to translate Nature and her mechanics. Do you think Nature is PC?"

"No, it's savage."

"Exactly."

"And, if you want to know the truth, the black race is my favorite race."

"Really? Why white boy?"

"Because Africans went into the bottleneck. Africans are the purest humans."

"What do you mean by purest?"

"Africans have the highest genetic diversity amongst all humans, meaning they are the oldest relative to the bottleneck. They represent the birth of humanity. They're the ones that defeated that more savage hominid and saved humanity from the brink of extinction. And, they did it all with socialness. We wouldn't be sitting here today having a conversation if it wasn't for Africans. The entire world population should give them a hug for saving humanity."

"Jess, this is a good time to stop for a minute. I want to explain something crucial."

"Oh lord," Jess said.

"Jess, this is extremely important, and if you see this, you will start to break the human construct."

"Ok, what is it?"

"Jess, in the late 20th-century white people started to measure IQ differences between African Americans and whites. They found that, on average, blacks scored 15 points lower than whites. This led to many prominent white people calling blacks an inferior race. One such prominent person was William Shockley.

"He co-invented the transistor, right?"

"Yes he did, and, as you know, the transistor is the foundation of all modern electronics. You could argue that he is one of the fathers of that cell phone in your pocket and all the changes to humanity that followed. Anyway, he promoted the idea that black people's lower IQ is hereditary and cannot be remedied. He suggested that any black person with an IQ lower than 100 should be euthanized."

"Jesus," Jess said, shaking her head.

"Yeah, I know."

"But I'm not sure I understand where you are headed with this."

"Jess, black people are superior to whites in terms of socialness. I mean, it's pretty obvious if you compare the cultures. My wife, for example, likes to share the observation that when a black family member is sick at the hospital, significantly more black family members will show up to show concern versus whites."

"Ok, I would agree that they are more social but also more violent, right?"

"You are thinking about African Americans, and it's not their fault Jess as you will see further into this workshop."

"Not their fault? It seems like you should explain that."

"I'll come to that, trust me."

"Look at current African culture to get a better comparison, Jess. It's so strong compared to white culture. So rich in traditions, customs, art, music, and did you know it's home to a third of the world's languages. Approximately 1500 different languages."

"Ok, I think I understand where you are headed. This is about the balance of Nature, right? If you gain an advantage, you have to lose an advantage?"

"Exactly. See, this is the beginning of one of the main constructs that humanity has adopted; however, it doesn't mean that it's true or beneficial to society. In other words, who's to say intelligence is superior? Just because intelligent people said it, does that make it true? Isn't their opinion biased? Would humanity be better off if we didn't have the intelligence to build that thing in your pocket?"

"I think we know the answer to that, but I'm not giving up my cellphone without a fight, hybrid."

"Exactly."

"Ok, so your argument is that socialness is far superior to intelligence."

"My argument is that Africans are the perfect balance of socialness and intelligence. Africans represent human perfection. If you study Nature and evolution, the pattern that seems out of place is white people, not blacks. All exposed to the environment with no melanin to protect their skin and even more baby-like. Like what in the fuck is a white person from an evolutionary standpoint."

"PC brain kicking in, hybrid," Jess said.

"Act like a scientist Jess, not a baby."

"It's a great injustice what white people did to the black race. Saying they were not as evolved as whites because they had less IQ and less baby schema."

"What's baby schema, hybrid?"

"Its Nature's clever way to get us to care for our offspring by making them more cute. All humans, including adults, have baby schema; however, white people have more than blacks."

"But you want to know something crazy interesting, Jess?"

"What?"

"Guess which race was the first to have autism?"

"Whites?"

"Exactly. See, Nature is a clever girl. You have to watch her patterns to see what she is up to."

"That's pretty interesting. Like Nature is pushing traits in both directions away from each other."

"Yep, in a sense."

"Hmm, that sounds rather ominous."

"Jess repeat after me...."

"I know, I know."

"Oh, and Shockley, not a good guy. Once in a Playboy interview, he described his children as intellectually inferior to him because their mother had not achieved as much academically as he had. On his deathbed, he was estranged from most of his friends and family. His kids learned about his death from reading about it in the newspaper."

"Hmm, ok, but you can't use one data point..."

"Jess, look closely at modern society. You'll see the trends emerging. Trust me, empathy and socialness are vastly more valuable than intelligence. And, remember, for everything gained, something must be lost to maintain the balance of Nature."

"Ok, so back to black people, Jess. The humans that saved us from extinction."

"Ok, back to black people," she said with trepidation. "So we can see evidence of the evolutionary controller in their race?"

"Yes, and please remember, as we discuss this, that what happened to them was beyond their control. It's biology. The internal gears working. They have the same gears inside of them as in us. Remember, all humans have essentially the same genes with the same diversity as a small group of chimpanzees. Black, white, all colors. Same genes. We are all the same."

"Ok, I'm all in; what you got?"

"Alright, have you noticed the shape of black women lately?"

"Oh Lord, you want to pick on black women?"

"Jess, I'm not picking on anyone. Will you focus? It's biology."

"Ok, yes, there seems to be a large percentage of obesity among black women."

"Correct. It's 50 percent. But what is interesting is if you look at the shape of the obesity."

"Not sure what you mean."

"Well, the shape is evidence of the controller at work in a stressed state."

"More Neo."

"Ok, well, let's look at the history of black people. They were brought to this country as enslaved people."

"Oh Lord, PC brain kicking in."

"Jess, yes, humans do bad things to each other; we are trying to prevent that in the future, remember? We didn't cause any of this; we are just observing the results."

"Yep, sorry."

"So, what does that mean to be brought here as slaves?"

"It means they were taken from Africa and brought here," Jess said. "It was a slave trade."

"Right, and just like in any trade, there will be a selection. The person buying the enslaved person will want to get the best value for his purchase.

We do this in our economy. When you shop for an item, say a laptop, you want to ensure it has the greatest value for every dollar spent. The most ROM, RAM, resolution, etcetera for your money. It's sad and tragic that we did this with the humans that saved our species, but this is our history, and we must learn from it."

"So, to get the best value, there were slave markets set up in Africa. People from North America would travel to Africa and shop at these markets. The enslaved people would be showcased like we do, say for items such as TVs in an electronic store, all in a line so that buyers could inspect them. They would be inspected to ensure all their senses were working, inspect their teeth and mouth, ensure no diseases were present, etc. Usually, their entire body would be inspected to ascertain health."

"You realize what this means, right?"

"No."

"It means that the black people brought to this country represent the maximum fitness for human life. Remember the last workshop when we were discussing the dimmer switch?"

"Yes."

"Ok, so, the black race brought to the Americas represented a group of people with their switch at 7. Therefore, they had maximum reserve potential for environmental change."

"Ok, I think I understand."

"They were selected, almost like a predator would select in the wild, only this time it was a human doing the selecting. A predator cheetah pulls out gazelles that aren't fit, leaving the ones that are. The gazelles left represent maximum fitness or an energy state of 7."

"Ok, I think I got it."

"Also, think of the energy state of 8, 9, and 10 as this sprung and unsprung mass. What keeps both masses stable is DHEA or damping of the mass. If you lose that damping, life becomes more excitable and moves towards 10. It's very similar to the suspension of an automobile, with stress being a bump in the road. One bump and then smooth, and you won't wear it out. A continuously bumpy road or a persistent stress, and it won't last very long."

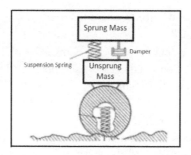

"Ok, so, black people at this point represent life in a natural state like a predator is pulling out the unfit, and the health or potential of life increases as a whole. True wellness, right?" Jess asked.

"Right. The only thing that defines wellness is the capacity for change. It's how much of this potential energy you have in an unstressed state."

"Ok, I'm there. So, then what happened?"

"Well, in 1863, slaves were freed, and guess what these perfect specimens for human life got to experience with us?"

"The industrial revolution?"

"Exactly, Jess. We get to watch the maximum potential for human life go through a massive environmental change with us and guess what happened?"

"Life was stimulated," Jess said.

"Exactly. It sped up. Sexual energy increased as well as fitness."

"In the 20th century, black males were making white males look like they were standing still, especially in sports, doing almost superhuman things. They also had all this energy for social protest and activism. Also, they had more children per family than white families. So their race was more excited by change because they had more energy released. Remember though, greater acceleration leads to a greater deceleration."

"So, what do we see now post acceleration? We see higher obesity rates and mortality rates for blacks."

"Ok, and you mentioned shape?"

"Oh yeah, so the shape of black women is the key to this controller. In a normal stressed state, this controller would increase females' sexual activity and sexual development. Normally, a female would develop a barely perceptible increase in the gluteus or buttocks. When overly stressed, this change or puberty occurs earlier and is more pronounced or expressed. The buttocks grow larger due to stress and to attract a mate. It's part of their light that shines brighter."

"Oh right! Like, 'Baby Got Back', 'Bootylicous', 'The Thong Song', 'Rumpshaker', 'Fat Bottomed Girls'? Jesus, now that I think about it, how many songs are there about butts?"

"A lot. And women and even men are getting butt implants to attract mates. See, stress is attractive."

"Yeah, and boobs too. I wonder how many breast implants there have been in the U.S?"

"Good question. A quick google. Says here that in 2017 there were 350,000."

"Jesus and all to look like a stressed human?"

"Yep."

"It's kind of crazy. It's like we are all chasing stress. Like watching those videos online with everyone twerking on a yacht, pouring champagne over massive breasts and asses, smoking god knows what, and flashing fat stacks of money around. Again, it must be hard for a pure, natural, innocent child to be exposed to this bizarre human stressed matrix. Seeing all these wild, crazy images all the time."

"Yeah, the stress axis was designed to get a fish from water to land or survive an extinction event, never intentionally manipulated."

"Ok, so this shape?" Jess asked again.

"Right, so if you look at black women today, this shape is still there, only it's been way overexpressed, like to the point that it's unnatural. Like massive breasts and massive buttocks. It's like a runaway event."

"Like a measurement error?"

"Exactly, the stress axis just runs away with itself, morphing into massive fat displacement all over the body but stemming outward from the original displacement. Look, I thought a visual would be better. Check this out."

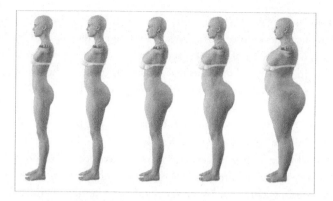

"Oh yeah, I see it now. So, this stress axis is like a push to more and more and more until something breaks."

"Right, more energy and then less energy are part of the same mechanism. It's just the controller's error that causes the runaway event, which leads to fatigue or death."

"See, the human model is different because there are no predators. Normally in a situation like this, we would never see an outcome to this degree. So imagine there's a predator in the human population. Do you think black women with these massive breasts and buttocks could run from a threat? Wild animals chasing them, and they must climb up a tree or into a cave to avoid being killed?"

"Ahh, no."

"Ok, so why is their autonomic self not protecting them? It doesn't know that we have cities, fast food drive-ins, and no predation. It's running ancient software. Why would it let their bodies carry this much weight, especially weight that is so far beyond the center of gravity for the human shape?"

"You have fairly large breasts; isn't it hard to run with them?"

"Yes, and it would almost be painful if I didn't have a sports bra."

"Ok, so imagine black women with breasts easily twice your size and running with them. It would lower their chances of survival."

"Ok, I see that. So, like you said, breed and get out. Excite faster and then conserve faster over time."

"Right, and the stress of childbirth accelerates this mechanism, which is why obesity for black females is higher than for black males. You see this all the time in females. Right after the stress of childbirth, they just gain weight and then can never lose it, aka, conservation of energy followed by extreme stress due to the lack of stress capacity."

"So, in Nature and other animal species, the effect is there, only it would be hard to see because conservation of energy would be selected out way before it got to this stage by the predator."

"See, watch this video of a cheetah chasing a gazelle."[1]

I pull out my phone and show it to Jess.

"What's controlling this event is the stress axis for both animals. It takes energy to avoid being eaten and energy to try and eat. So if either one of them is dealing with a persistent stress and not adapting, their likelihood of being selected out of life is much higher."

"Keep in mind that the predator doesn't drive evolution; it only takes advantage of this evolutionary controller. Life didn't start out with predation. In year one of life, there weren't all these things eating other things. Predation evolved to take advantage of this programming."

"If you don't think this is true, go into the forest and start eating everything you see. Pine needles, tree branches, wild berries, foliage, insects. How well do you think you would do?"

"I'm getting nauseous just thinking about it."

"Well, all these things have energy, and they are food for other species. You can't do it because you are not adapted to these food sources. You don't have the biology to consume the food and would have to evolve to do so."

"It's another reason why Darwinian evolution is not correct. There were no predators at the origin of life. No selection was taking place. It was just internal programming. Maintain what is working and change what isn't. Eventually, though, as the oceans filled up with life, this would become a stressor. The slower ones would be in the way for the ones that were thriving."

"So, then they ate them?"

"Well, evolved to eat them."

"Aww," Jess said, smiling.

"Jess."

"Ok, and the second example?"

"Mexicans."

"Lord."

"Jess!"

"So, a similar event happened to the Mexicans coming into America, albeit to a lesser degree. Do you remember the plant manager at the spandex plant we worked at?"

"Yeah, Gary, right?"

"Right, well, remember how Gary would go on and on about getting some Mexicans working for us. Always talking about how Mexicans are outworking the Americans. Like Americans are lazy and never show up to work and these Mexicans just show up in the back of a pickup 10 per and just work from dusk to dawn never complaining, just going and going and going."

"Yeah, that guy was crazy."

"Right, but what he was trying to do was get a more energetic workforce to try and save the business. He recognized the difference in energy levels compared to the Americans, rationalizing that he could get better performance from the Mexicans."

"Ok, so I get it. They come to a new environment and are exposed to different stressors, foods, toxins, culture, and it excites life just like in the black example."

"Exactly, albeit to a lesser degree, because their reserve energy was not as high."

"So, the Mexican workforce becomes known for outworking the American workforce, which is not fatiguing as quickly, and they begin to thrive here. With this stimulation also comes sexual stimulation, and birth rates increase."

"Yeah, remember how Gary was always like, they're outbreeding us! What's happening to this country!"

"Yeah, ole Gary."

"So, what do we now see in the Mexican population, especially with Mexican women? Increasing obesity."

"Yeah and they are also getting that shape like black women but to a lesser degree. Like bigger asses and bigger breasts."

"Right, and my daughter works at a restaurant with a high male Mexican workforce, and she says the men are always complaining about how Mexican women have gotten so lazy in the states."

"Right, breed and get out. For every acceleration, there is a deceleration. You can't borrow energy from Nature without paying it back. Jesus, I don't know whether to be in awe of Nature or terrified of it."

"Be in awe because once you understand how it works, you can simply follow its rules. This programming is never going away. It's been part of life from day one and will be part of life until the Sun becomes a red giant and boils the planet. Until life breathes its last breath of air."

"Don't say it Jess."

"Please, just one last time, ok?"

"Okay."

"Aww."

"Think of it as a law of the universe. Like for every action, there is an equal and opposite reaction. Or what goes up must come down. For every acceleration, there must be a deceleration. The human analogy is, if you borrow money or energy, you must pay it back. If you stimulate life, someone down the line will pay the penalty. As you said, the best thing for humanity is never to use this energy because the interest for humans is high."

"True that. Ok, and the third example?"

"All right, Jess, but before we go forward and to ease the mad hatter PC brain, remember that these first two examples we just discussed had nothing to do with race and everything to do with biology. White women have also exhibited this same shape throughout history when exposed to environmental change. You can see it in ancient art and literature. Just go look! You'll see it! These examples happen to be current. This has happened repeatedly to all races, repeat, all races. Remember, this is just data that we can learn from to try and help humanity, okay?"

"Okay. Trying to save the world. Gotcha. And the third example?"

"Jess, we saved the best for last. The third example is the craziest example of this controller at work in the history of humanity."

"Jess, get ready for The Roman Empire."

"Oh good, no one we can offend," Jess said, smiling.

"Jess, deez mo fos was cray cray."

"What did they do?"

"Well, it's the poster child story for the fall of civilizations. Rome, at its height, was nearly 65 percent the size of the continental U.S. It was truly massive by ancient time standards and was the largest empire the world had ever seen up to that point. Because Rome was so successful, scholars and historians are always studying it to try and understand the mechanics of why the great empire collapsed. Most theories range from poor economic policies, inflation, debasing of the currency to support the military, moves towards socialism, a plunder economy versus actually producing commodities for export, too much bureaucracy and not enough people producing goods or wealth, loss of civic virtue, too many people focusing on self-interests over the empire, environmental degradation, or a massive division in the social class between rich and poor. In other words, a lot of theories."

"Jess, towards the end, the ruling class elite were sucking up all the wealth of the Mediterranean to be deposited in the city of Rome. Their economy had also become reliant on slave labor, which they used for almost every activity. The elite had as many as 10 slaves per household doing anything from attending to the master's bath, dressing them, brushing their hair, brushing their teeth, pleasuring them, preparing meals, and tending to their children. All physical effort was removed from their lives, requiring that they expend very little energy. Towards the end, they even ate their meals lying down."

"Hmm, some of this sounds familiar," Jess said.

"Right, and the most interesting theory regarding the collapse of Rome involves lead."

"Lead? The heavy metal, highly toxic poison, lead?"

"Yes, lead was used extensively in Roman times. The Romans regarded it as the father of all metals and used it to support the vast piping network that kept the cities supplied with water. The word plumbing comes from the Latin word for lead, plumbum. In addition to water distribution, the Romans also had numerous other uses for the popular metal. It was used in cosmetics for mascaras, face powders and rouges, and pigments for paints. It was even used as a spermicide and in the manufacture of chastity belts. Since it was malleable, they also used it for all their kitchenware, such as pots and pans, cups, plates, and pitchers. It was the modern-day plastic."

"However, the most interesting thing about the Romans was that they used lead as a sweetener and a preservative. They would take crushed grapes and boil them in lead pots to produce a very concentrated sugary syrup called defrutum and an even more concentrated version called sapa. When the acidic grapes were boiled, it would yield an unusually sweet syrup containing a very high level of lead acetate. Lead acetate is the only metal salt that is sweet in taste. In 2009, a History Channel documentary produced a batch of defrutum in lead-lined pots following the ancient Roman recipes. They obtained a lead concentration of 29,000 parts per billion which by any standard is a staggering amount. The current US water standards are set at a maximum of 15 parts per billion."

"The defrutum and sapa were used in essentially every culinary aspect. The syrup was used to preserve and sweeten wine, and it was added to fruit and meat dishes as a sweetening agent. Defrutum was also added to garum, which was like a fermented fish sauce, and became their most popular condiment. It was like the modern-day ketchup. Defrutum was even given to farm animals like pigs and ducks to improve the taste of the meat. The Romans also used it to preserve fruit and olives through the winter, and women even used it as a cosmetic. In Roman books discussing cooking, defrutum was included in nearly every recipe. When detailing the preparation of the sweet syrup, the literature would state that lead pots must always be used."

"Wow, so I get where you are going with this. If anyone studying this theory is looking at lead as the cause of the collapse, they are looking at the wrong end. It didn't cause the collapse, it caused the rise."

"Exactly Jess, well done."

"The roman empire represented the first time in human history where humans excited their stress axis to unpreceded levels as a result of manmade environmental change. From a biological perspective, they created a stress event on the order of magnitude of an extinction event, and life responded. Life was stimulated. The Romans used all their adaptation energy 8,9 and 10 to build the empire."

"Wow, that's cool. It's like a virgin biology that had never before seen man-made environmental change, so they probably had more adaptation energy or potential. Like a fair amount of sprung and unsprung mass waiting to be released?"

"Exactly, it's like the hormesis curve you would see for lead."

"Hormesis?"

"Oh yes, sorry, Jess, hormesis describes biology's positive or favorable response to a toxin."

"Hmm, ok, so another way of saying what you have been saying, right?"

"Yes, another way to say part of it. Hormesis was discovered back in the late 1800s by Hugo Schulz and Rudolph Arndt, looking at poisons and drugs and their effect on yeast cells. They coined the Arndt-Schulz rule, which states that 'For every substance, small doses stimulate, moderate doses inhibit, large doses kill.'"

"Ok, so based on what you've told me, I interpret it this way. For small environmental changes, doses, life will stimulate and try to evolve around it. For bigger changes, life will reduce energy for those that are adapted and for the biggest changes, way beyond adaptation, turn off and surrender. Am I right?"

"Wow, yes, very good."

"This reminds me of a previous workshop where you were talking about when life just took off. The event that even Darwin said proves his theory incorrect."

"The Cambrian explosion."

"Yes, the Cambrian explosion. So, this is it, right? Where life figured out how to get a group of cells to respond like a single cell. The evolutionary programming inside of a single cell reprogrammed for a collection of cells."

"Wow, very impressive Jess."

"Thanks, still reading a lot during our workshops."

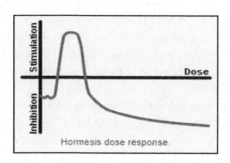

Hormesis dose response.

"Ok, so at the beginning of the curve would be a mirror depiction of their energy levels to build the great empire and then leading to their lack of energy to maintain it towards the end. As life moved towards a state of conservation, they would have no endurance for such measures and would only be interested in stimulating their fatigued biology. See, look at this chart."

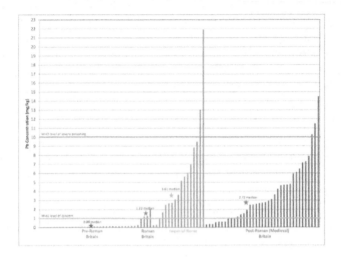

"This chart represents the work done by Janet Montgomery and Kristina Killgrove where they gathered data from over 200 burial sites in Britain, Ireland and Rome looking at lead concentrations in tooth enamel."

"That last blue line on the left and first red line represents where the Romans get a little taste for environmental change. Probably the infrastructure was not developed at this time, and they were most likely getting the environmental change from the wine they produced by boiling the grapes in lead pots."

"Then, at some point, they reach persistent stress levels, where life begins to act on this information. There is a little bit of lead in their environment, and then you reach a threshold, and then Baam! Everyone is stimulated. All this unleashed biological energy to build the great empire."

"But, with every rise comes the fall, right Neo?"

"Exactly Jess, and it wasn't pretty. The exploits after the turn were horrific. Remember the movie, *Gladiator?*"

"Yeah."

"Not made up. In fact, the movie was the G-rated version of what happened in the Roman coliseums. I remember reading one account where the Romans had built this seesaw contraption 15 feet long on each end and placed it in the middle of the stadium. Handcuffed and tied to the ends of the seesaw were Roman prisoners, like three on each side. Now remember that there are like tens of thousands of Roman citizens just sitting bored looking at this thing."[2]

"Then one of the prisoners on one end pushes with their legs sending the three prisoners high in the air while the other three prisoners are sent to the ground. This then repeats for the other three prisoners on the other end as they test the contraption. Romans that ran the stadium would be watching in the wings as the prisoners got familiar with the device. When they finally did, a trapdoor in the arena floor opened, and starved lions, bears, and leopards would rush into the arena heading straight for the seesaw. The prisoners, frantic, would try leaping to escape the wild beasts. As they did, the other side would plummet down into the jaws of the beasts."

"The coliseum would come alive with laughter at the sight of it. They would soon start clapping and betting on which criminal would die first."

"Jesus," Jess said. "That's horrible. I can't decide what's worse, the fact that they did that or the fact that they planned that. That's a pretty cruel and bizarre display to plan out."

"Yeah, and all of Rome came to witness these events. Men, women, and children of all ages."

"They also used to round up Roman army deserters and have them crushed in the coliseum by having elephants trample over them to their death. Also, criminals plus anyone deemed lower than the elite. It evolved into a sense of group empowerment when these people, labeled as lower than themselves, were thrown to the wild beasts."

"Interestingly, a wild animal's natural tendency is not to charge a human and attack with 100,000 screaming Romans, so there were men known as bestiarii whose job was to train these animals to perform. To do this, they had to constantly feed them diets comprised only of human flesh. They usually let them kill Roman prisoners leading up to these events as training."

"Jesus," Jess said.

"Yeah, and over time the bestiarii became sort of the like the event coordinators, and there was competition among them to see who could put on the best show. It evolved into a contest for the bored Romans in the crowds. Like, who can excite them the most. At its height, these coliseums held 250,000 people."

"The Roman emperor, Caligula, took the games to new heights to entertain crowds demanding that the bestiarri invent new ways to kill. They devised elaborate contraptions and settings, almost like orchestrated plays, where the prisoners were made to believe they could save themselves by climbing along or up these contraptions. Then the contraptions would fail right before their escape sending them into the pack of starved animals below."

"Jesus again," Jess said.

"Yeah, and then you know about the sexual exploits, right?"

"Not really."

"Very bizarre. The Romans had many gods, and one of them was known as Priapus. He was the child of Venus and had enormous genitals, like 2 to 3 feet long. The Romans worshipped him and, as tribute, hung penises everywhere. Phallic symbols were on the sides of houses, road signs, and pavement cobblestones to point directions to passersby. Giant penises were even used as scarecrows. During festivals honoring Priapus, women would strip down publicly and masturbate to encourage fertility."

"I can see giant penises used as scarecrows," Jess said, laughing. "Very scary."

"Basically, in Roman culture, the male form was celebrated, and the erect penis was associated with power and strength. Phallic symbols were also worn by generals entering battle."

"So, like penetrating the opposing army?" Jess said, smiling.

"Jess!"

"Speaking of penetration, homosexuality was rampant and dominant males would engage in sex with other males, as long as they were doing the penetrating. It was times of sexual immorality and depravity without restraint."

"Jesus, again."

"I would think it would be an interesting thought experiment to imagine going back in time and taking a few people from the rise, the turn, the fall, and the collapse of Rome and talking to them."

"Huh? Oh, you mean if we could like interview them to try and determine their emotional state?"

"Exactly. Like we bring them back, we do all the hey it's time travel, be cool, we just want to interview you for a minute or so, and then we try to get a feel for their demeanor."

"Ok, got ya," Jess said.

"So, let's imagine that, in your den, we have four groups of people from each era and grouped accordingly. They are standing before us, and we can ask questions. I'll start Jess."

"Great citizens of Rome, thank you for being here. It is an honor to meet you all and allow us this privilege of getting to know you."

Groups Fall and Collapse, then speak up.

"Great sir and madam, do you mind if we sit down. We are very tired."

"Oh sorry, by all means, do sit. Rise and Turn?"

"No, we are ok."

"Ok great. So, my first question is to Rise. How do you feel?"

"Feel great, why?"

"Well, we are trying to assess the activity level for your era. How would you describe it?"

"I would say very good. Everyone is excited about building the great empire. We have roads going in, bridges, water lines, and aqueducts. Just tremendous progress for Rome. A lot of talk about future advancements and where we are heading."

"Oh, this is fun. Let me do one," Jess said.

"Rise, how would you describe your sexual appetites?"

"We can have sex right now?" Rise asked.

"Ok Rise, that will do," Jess said.

"Turn, I have a question for you. How would you assess the activity level for your era?"

"I would say ok, maybe not as much progress as before. It seems like the republic is getting more distracted by other things, like the games and sexual conquests. Honestly, we are not building and maintaining as much as we used to. Not sure if this will be problematic in the future, but it is concerning."

"Fall, how would you describe your era and the activity level?" I said.

"I want to have sex with your woman right now. We should all have an orgy. Who's in?"

All Romans raise their hands immediately except one of the collapse members in the group who is sleeping.

"Someone bump the sleeping guy and tell him it's orgy time."

"God, you are crazy, Ryan, but this is fun. Let me do collapse."

"Collapse, how would you describe the activity level for your era?"

"Ok, I assume," one of them spoke from the group. "I would like to know, though, why my ten slaves did not make the journey with me? Who will tend to me? My hair needs brushing, I need to be fed grapes, and my penis needs attention."

"Jesus Ryan," Jess said, laughing.

"Great citizens of Rome, I would like to ask you about your wine consumption. How was it? Did you use the great malleable metal known as lead?"

"Of course, it produces the best wine. Copper is inferior. Lead must be used," they all say.

"Rise, your consumption?"

"Was ok, but there was much work to be done. We drank it occasionally, but our great empire needs building."

"Turn?"

"People were drinking it more and more, and, honestly, it was interfering with the work. Progress was suffering."

"Fall?"

"We drink it most of the day. Delicious. How long are we going to be here for this? There's a great spectacle tonight, and I don't want to miss it. Twenty prisoners will be handcuffed together naked running through the great coliseum, and we get to bet on who will be eaten first!"

"Rise and Turn both shake their heads."

"Collapse?"

"Do you have any? I feel parched. However, without my slaves, who will hold my cup? Please tell me you don't expect me to raise the glass. Can your beautiful woman tend to my needs and service me?"

"Ryan! How dare you!" Jess said, acting like a southern belle.

"You know, it really would be an interesting social experiment if you could somehow assess each era," Jess said.

"Yeah, and an even better one is if you could take each group and remove the environmental change."

"Not sure what you mean," Jess said.

"Imagine if we could take all four groups and put them in a resort spa for a couple of years. Absolutely no stress to let their bodies try and naturally remove the toxin. We even add chelation therapy to help the process along. Just no stress, day and night, so that they can recover, and then we bring the groups back in and interview them."

"Oh, got ya," Jess said.

"Imagine the groups are back, standing before us in the room recovered from the environmental change."

"Rise, how do you feel?"

"Good, but honestly, missing that drive."

"Turn?"

"Feel good, better than I did, honestly. Hard to describe, but I definitely feel better."

"Fall?"

"Feel like a changed person. Like Turn said, hard to describe but way better. Like content just standing here."

"Collapse?"

"I feel nothing like my old self, and look, I'm standing. Like Fall said, I'm content just being here."

"Rise, Turn, Fall and Collapse, I would like you to watch a brief video montage of the history of the Roman Empire. Don't freak out when you see the projected moving images. This is a timeline of the history of Rome."

The video plays before them, displaying the great energy of the society to build the empire. Roads, bridges, tunnels, and aqueducts showing the great feats of engineering, leading to the wealth and prosperity of the nation and improving the daily lives of all Roman citizens. Then the impressive feats of engineering displaying weaponry used in their armies that was ahead of its time. Then showing how progress slowed in favor of the games and entertainment. Then the video showing the wild acts of sexual depravity and barbaric violence displayed in the games. The Roman elite debasing the currency for their own self-interests above that of the republic. Showing how each event in the coliseum had to be more and more to spark the interest of the crowds, until it became a twisted, perverse, dark place.

The video stops, and I ask...

"Well, what do you think, everyone?"

Rise is the first to speak.

"What happened to you people? We were doing so well. Everyone was so interested in the empire. Did you see all those magnificent things we built? Did you see the level of ingenuity and craftsmanship that went into that? Do you know how much time, effort, and planning went into the building of Rome? And you just squandered it all for your own self-interests. For those sick, twisted games. What got into you people?"

Fall then speaks.

"Honestly, looking back on it, I don't know. I don't feel like that now. It's like we were caught up in this contest of more and more. When you look out into the coliseum, while the moving pictures were playing, it was like we were so bored, and we had to have more and more just to be entertained. This self-interest grew to overtake the interest of the republic. It became all that mattered."

"Like a drug?" Jess asked.

"Drug?" everyone asked. "What is a drug?"

"Like cocaine," Jess said.

"Jess, they're not going to know what cocaine is."

"Seriously?"

"Yeah, there were no drugs back then."

"Really? Oh, okay, well, like more and more wine for the same effect?"

"Yes, exactly. That's it. Like it took more and more of something to make us feel good. To make us feel excited and alive," both Fall and Collapse said.

"What happened to us?" they all asked.

"Unfortunately, you were all exposed to a massive environmental change that you created. The wine you drank had something in it that was bad for you due to how you cooked it."

Both Fall and Collapse ask, "but if this is true, why did the people of rise have so much activity, and why were we all so sexual?"

"Well, great Romans, it's complicated, but you stimulated life. It was trying to breed through this event. However, you consumed so much of it that life surrendered and moved to a state of conservation, which caused you to consume even more because you could."

Collapse looks at Rise, pissed. "So, this is all your fault, Rise?"

"Easy Collapse, they didn't know," I said.

I then grab Jess's stool, standing on top again, looking out like a great orator.

"Citizens of Rome, we thank you for your time and willingness to share your great story. It is something that I hope future civilizations on this planet can learn from. From your story, I hope we can appreciate how important the environment is to maintaining and protecting a great nation."

Jess then goes into the imaginary Roman crowd and starts clapping and cheering.

"Well done, Hybrid! Bravo Hybrid!"

"I'm starting to think the stress axis plays a pivotal role in every rise and fall of a civilization," Jess said.

"Again, I'm sure of it, Jess."

"So, got a curious question, Ryan. That chart showing the lead amounts in dental records through the years. What was the following one that came after the Roman Empire?"

"That would ultimately become the British empire. At its peak, it was the largest empire in history and was roughly 4.5 times as large as the continental United States. People during that era and historians alike refer to it as the empire on which the Sun never sets. It was so vast that the Sun was always shining on at least one of its territories."

"No telling what kind of environmental changes those people had to endure. They burned through forest after forest until the air pollution was so bad, they could hardly see. When the forests ran bare, they switched to coal and blackened the skies. It probably contributed to the rise in the black plague, considering that the evolution switch also controls immunity. Cortisol is the on-off switch for the immune system, remember?"

"Jesus, what is wrong with humans? Why do they always put an economy or so-called progress over their health? It's like they can't see it. Like they are blind to it."

"Yeah, I don't know, it's weird. My only explanation is what you pointed out earlier with the drug comparison. Since it's stimulating them, environmental change becomes a drug. They need more and more until there's nothing left, always chasing that original high or the rise."

"You know, with the Roman Empire, humanity took a massive hit on the health of the species. I truly believe it was the first time that life started to question keeping their special gift. Romans were known for superior engineering talents, indicating a possible shift to the more logic and STEM side of the brain, away from the empathic. Plus, those barbaric acts in the games with men, women, and children watching and cheering, needing more and more. Probably the first time that affective empathy was completely silenced in a population. Truly animalistic behavior. Life was probably so stressed at the end of the Roman reign it could barely run those genes."

"War from this point onward would increase substantially. If you Google the number of wars in the common era, it is mind-boggling. Think about the number of lives lost, the brutality, and the amount of suffering of women and children. For what? Conquest? Chasing stress?"

"This gift of empathy is supposed to make you love your fellow man like a mother would love her child, and humans have squandered it ever since they started chasing technology. The ability to alter their environment without foresight or restraint."

"Ryan, are you sure humans deserve their special gift? Possibly better to just let it fade away? They have been doing some horrible things to each other. Unspeakable things. Horrific things. I kind of like you, Ryan. What if the world was full of only hybrids that wanted to save themselves?"

"Jess, I represent a transition. Remember, Nature gravitates toward specialists over time? Humanity would never allow half of the population to have no empathy while the other half has full empathy. Ultimately, a choice will be made. Nature will make it, or humans can. It's far better to let humans decide their evolutionary fate."

"Until we meet again, my Greek Goddess."

CHAPTER NINE
WS9

"Hi Jess."

"Hi," Jess said, looking sullen and depressed.

"What, no jokes for the start of our workshop?"

"No."

"What's wrong, Jess?"

"I guess I'm just a little sad today, or actually, I've been sad all week. Ever since we last met, I have been thinking about humanity and all the struggles, conflicts, wars, diseases, famine, genocide, homicide, and suicide. It's really gotten to me. It's sad because empathy is supposed to make you work together for the common good, and humans have been their own worst enemy for thousands of years."

"You're absolutely right, Jess. It probably started with agriculture and adding more energy to the mix by harvesting grain. More excitation energy, plus the excitation from the dietary change itself. From that point forward, it was a race to change the environment, and the whole time they didn't know that inside of them is an evolutionary controller that responds to environmental change."

"Yes, but for me, at least, it's deeper than that. I can't help thinking about all the mothers sending their sons off to war and all the death and destruction through countless years. All the loss, the savagery, the brutality, the bloodshed, the total disregard for human life. The ultimate irony is that this gene change that is supposed to make you love your fellow man has brought more death, destruction, and suffering than all the other hominids combined."

"I mean, if you could somehow quantify average suffering/per time/per individual/per species and chart it, humans would be at the very top. You couldn't even see all the other species in the history of life because the scale to encompass humans would be so high. It's almost like it's a punishment to be human."

"Yeah, humans are definitely their own devil. Imagine if you could be like a silent observer hovering in the heavens and watching human conflict unfold, only sped up. Like centuries played out in minutes. Your first thought would probably be, why are they doing that? It must look like a bunch of giant ant beds placed around the globe whose colonies are being disturbed and attacked."

"Right, and none of them ever figured out that the key to peace is just don't stress yourselves. Just don't excite life, and everything will work out. It's so sad because the solution is so simple. Humans are supposed to be empathic and collectively intelligent creatures, and look what they have done to each other over the years."

"I know Jess, but remember, it's not about intelligence or empathy. It's more about these powerful forces beyond our control. These forces push us in certain directions. Once stressed, these autonomic responses take over, and we can't help ourselves. Remember the picture of the two German doctors looking over the person freezing to death in the ice bath?"

"Yeah."

"If you could remove the stress of war and the stress that caused the war, do you think those two doctors would be part of such an evil act?"

"No, probably not."

"Ok, then the root cause is the stress, which comes from environmental change. Any species that can radically change its environment will be plagued with suffering until it finally figures this out. Figures out that its biology responds to change. Assuming it can in time."

"Can in time?" Jess asked.

"Yes. Have you ever heard of the great filter?"

"No."

"Let me show you this video. It's a good one. It's called, *Why Alien Life Would be our Doom - The Great Filter*. Amazing graphics. Let's watch."[1]

"Wow, that was good," Jess said.

"I know, and did you see at the beginning when he talked about complexity and efficiency?"

"Yes. As you said, it's the predetermined plan for life, right? When stressed or threatened, use more and more energy as efficiently as possible to become more and more things, right? Use diversity to protect itself."

"Exactly, and each staircase?"

"An extinction event," Jess said proudly.

"You're getting good at this, Jess."

"Life or cells start working together to be more efficient. Each stress event is an efficiency step. It goes from water to land to air to protect itself."

Jess suddenly, without warning, grabs the stool and stands on it with an excited grin.

"Jess, you ok?"

"Oh my god! I just thought of an amazing idea. When you said cells working together to be more efficient as a result of stress, an idea just popped into my head."

"Remember in one of the early workshops, and we talked about how empathy jumped from the mother to the child?"

"Yeah."

"Well, what if we didn't go back far enough."

"Not sure what you mean, Jess."

"What are the mechanics of empathy? You said Nature has a problem, how to keep the mother from killing the offspring. Remember?"

"Sure."

"Well, what if empathy is something different? What if empathy is the communication pathway that all cells share? I mean, think about it. What is a body plan? It's a bunch of cells all working together for a common goal. Is that not the very definition of empathy or socialness?"

"Ok, right."

"Well, what if there is this force, almost like a force of Nature that when stressed, things tend to gravitate towards each other and cooperate? Like the more stressed, the more excited and then communication pathways start to develop."

"What is a mammal but a higher complexity from a stress event, an extinction event. A female is something that can create life inside of it. The baby and the mother, from a collection of cells standpoint, are the same thing. When the mother has the baby, that communication pathway that all cells have still exists, albeit to a much lesser degree, because they are essentially the same thing. Females essentially have this life force because they are life creators."

"Ok, I think I'm with you, Jess. You're saying that life figured out a way to expand upon the communication pathway that all cells share and give more of it to the female to push life forward, right? The female needs this communication pathway to nurture and rear the next generation of cells."

"Right, out of a stress event, it then tried the next step in this evolutionary force. Instead of a bunch of cells all working together, it tried a bunch of individuals within a species working together for a common goal. Take that female force, increase it and lock it in, so to speak. Life progresses from cells communicating together to females communicating with their young for rearing to all individuals communicating together. It's the next logical step for life to protect itself," Jess said proudly.

"Right, but it's still empathy or this female force, as you call it, that jumped and became prodigious at the bottleneck event?"

"Right, but it's the mechanics of empathy or how empathy came about. There must be some attractive, communitive force that draws things together when stressed."

"Ok, kind of deep, but I see where you are going with it. It explains a lot if you are right. Oh, and by the way, you seem to have broken your depression?"

"No, still depressed, but when you said cells working together, it made me think of socialness, and I wanted to get one up on you. My chance to grab the stool."

"Well, I must admit it's an interesting and impressive idea. It's like the mechanics of empathy. Obviously, a multicellular creature is more efficient than a single-celled one. So stress, throughout Earth's lineage, drives life's need to be more efficient, but for cells to work together, they need a communication pathway. They need a socialness at a microscopic level, so to speak. And females, because they are multicellular, and creators of multicellular life forms, have more of this communication pathway."

"What you are saying is that this female force, taken to its next evolutionary step, would go from cells communicating together to individuals within a species communicating together?"

"Exactly," Jess said proudly.

"I kind of like it, and Jess, remember when we were talking about the extinction events?"

"Yeah."

"Well, I thought you would ask, but I guess it never occurred to you. Did you ever wonder why there were no extinction events before the big five?"

"Oh yeah, that is interesting now that you say it. Why?"

"Well, I'm sure there were. In fact, the frequency of these events most likely increases as the Earth gets younger and younger. I mean, look at the moon, it looks like it was hammered with thousands of extinction-event-sized meteorites, and its gravity is only 1.62 m/s2, and it's only a quarter the size of Earth."

"A younger galaxy would have more and more of these asteroids floating around in space. Plus, a younger Earth would have more radiation core energy, so more mega volcanoes at its birth. These events would stress oceanic life as the chemistry of the ocean would change from these global disasters."

"The single-celled life forms most likely experienced these events as a stress event. The simple reason why we can't go back further than the five extinction events is that there were no body plans before these events. Technically not impossible, but very difficult to see fossils when there were no bones, shells, exoskeletons, aka hard parts."

"Oh yeah, that makes sense now."

"The ocean probably acted as an insulator to these events or a dilutor, but I'm sure they were occurring. So as the ocean kept changing, life kept being stressed or threatened. Like we are hypothesizing, life must increase efficiency to protect itself. Use more of the Sun's energy and become many things."

"Right, and like we said in an earlier workshop, the biggest hurdle is how to get a body plan with billions or trillions of cells to respond to environmental change like a single cell would. In steps the stress axis, right?"

"Right, Jess."

"It is amazing that life figured this out," Jess said. "Negative feedback control loops, passing information about the environment forward, building a body plan with a quaternary computer-like code, deciding which parts of the code to use, like an operating software. It's like there's an intelligence to it. An intelligence at the cellular level. Maybe the cell itself is our God and speaks a language we will never understand. Or, maybe the first cell was programmed by a higher intelligence."

"Yes, I think it's possible. I mean, besides building a stress axis, it built a protein motor that can walk. It is laughable to me that all this could come about via Darwinian evolution."

"Okay, but let's get back to the great filter. You are hypothesizing that over time life will gradually move to more and more socialness, as evidenced by life moving to higher and higher complexity. Cells working together, evolving into individuals within a species working together. We have other evidence of life doing this besides humans, just not to the same degree. Bees, ants, dolphins."

"I must admit, though, if you are right, that makes what I'm about to tell you even more terrifying."

"Oh Lord, what?"

"Jess, like the video said, our universe is silent."

"Silent?"

"Jess, do you know how old our universe is?"

"Tell me."

"It's 13.8 billion years. Our galaxy is 13.61 billion years. Do you know how many stars there are in our galaxy?"

"No."

"Latest estimates, between 100 and 400 billion."

"And the most important question, guess how many Earth-like planets there are orbiting in habitable zones or goldilocks zones in our galaxy alone?"

"Tell me."

"Latest estimates, 40 billion."

"Jesus. Ok, that's a lot. And aren't there like billions of galaxies in the observable universe?"

"Yes, on the low-end estimate, 200 billion galaxies."

"Jesus, that's a lot of space for just little ole us," Jess said, smiling.

"Exactly, because it's not just us. Our galaxy and the universe must be teeming with life, just the more common or normal type of life."

"Common or normal? What do you mean by that?"

"Well, remember the workshop where we did the time life thought experiment?"

"Yes, I kind of like that one."

"Well, so imagine you are an observer of our planet and can watch life play out over billions of years. What would you derive from watching it evolve?"

"Help me."

"Remember when we talked about how Nature gave humanity a very special gift? Something never seen before in the last 3.8 billion years? A gift beyond what is normal and prodigious."

"Right. Oh, I see where you are going with this. Humans are a deviation from the norm. Humans are like an anomaly of Nature. Like a social giraffe. You wouldn't study the anomaly because it is outside the norm or what has been common."

"Exactly. Impressive. I like to imagine that you could be like an alien archeologist moving through the galaxy, and you get the privilege of looking at the life record of each planet. Remember those old microfilm readers used before computers?"

I pull up an image and show it to her.

"Oh, I think I remember seeing one of these in a library once. Little before my time," Jess said, smiling, "but I get the idea."

"Right, so imagine the entire life record of the Earth held on a single microfilm roll, and you are an alien with no idea about our planet's history, and you get to scroll through this film. So you load it in and start scrolling. What would be the common theme as you scroll through it?"

"Good question. Well, pre-Cambrian, I would be extremely bored. I would think that life is dull. Does this microfilm reader have a fast forward?"

"Yes."

"Ok, I would keep hitting fast forward until I got to our little friend, the spiny bathmat. Then I would scroll through all his friends, some big bathmats and some small ones. I would be very excited to see something with a form from scrolling through billions of years of mold."

"Ok, and keep going. Besides the increase in complexity, what do you start to recognize as a trend post-Cambrian?"

"Hmm, sorry, not seeing it. Give me a little help, please. Pretend that you are an alien with me. We are a team on an expedition mission to explore all the life in the entire galaxy, and we are now looking at Earth."

"Ok, Jess. Well, fellow alien, I would say there appears to be a trend with protection from predators when looking at the body plans. The hard shells of sea life, insects, the scaly skin of reptiles, thick fur for the mammals."

"Oh yeah, ok, I see it now. Like toughness in the environment. Like battle armor. Like a look of, individually, these species can survive on their own. They don't need help to exist."

"Right like survival of the individual, not survival as a group."

"Right."

"And if you fast-forward to modern-day humans?"

"Well, if we are true aliens, have no bias, and have never seen a human before, we would probably be like, what the hell is that? Like checking the film reader to see if it has malfunctioned. Checking focus. Banging it on its side. Turning it off and on."

"Funny Jess, but you are right. Imagine scrolling through and, as an example of the human race, there is a 40-year-old man and woman, representing the average shape of the present-day human race. Naked, overweight, and mostly hairless. No sharp claws, no long fangs, soft bones, permanently exposed breasts, soft, delicate skin, and looking completely exposed to the environment."

"My first thought as an alien would be, poor thing, how long did this species last?"

"Exactly, and imagine, in fine print on the microfilm, it lists stats like how long it survived and population record."

"Hmm, says here that it is dominating the planet and is currently driving most species extinct. Population 7.98 billion. How is this possible, fellow alien? This can't be correct. Let's scroll to its offspring."

We both back away in shock, pretending to be aliens seeing a baby human for the first time.

"Oh Lord Jess, it looks like a soft bag of exposed mush. No teeth. No claws. How does it survive? And, it says here that it constantly cries like a beacon for predators to come and eat it."

"Funny, you really are convincing me with your anomaly hypothesis."

"Jess, if we were true aliens, we would probably be like, why do the adult humans look like bigger versions of the babies? Like giant babies. Little hair, no claws, soft skin, and what is with those big baby eyes? And why do the females have even larger baby eyes?"

"Yeah, funny," Jess said, laughing. "Big babies. Big baby eyes. I see that. The anomaly, the female prodigy, I get your point. If you are studying life and trying to figure out how it behaves, you would not study the last 50,000 years of our planet's history. You would study everything but that."

"Right, you wouldn't study the social giraffe. You would study everything but that to understand how life works or behaves or what it cares about the most."

"But Jess, I must admit, you have somewhat convinced me on the socialness idea. If we are two aliens studying present-day Earth, we would see some socialness, so I feel like we would be on the fence about whether it is a rarity. Perhaps we could glean from the data, post-Cambrian, that the toughness of the body plans meant that it was a survival of the individual fitness and not survival of the collective group. However, from the present-day behavior of ants, bees, and dolphins, we could infer that life seems to move or experiment in this direction with each stress event."

"Before we met for this workshop, I was convinced that an Earth-like planet in our galaxy giving rise to social creatures that could dominate all other life forms would be only a handful over 13.61 billion years. Now I think the number is much higher thanks to you, Jess."

"You're welcome," Jess said, again proud of herself.

"Ah, but again Jess, that makes a silent galaxy and universe, for that matter, even more terrifying."

"Explain more, please."

"Jess, you know what SETI is, right?"

"Yes, the search for extra-terrestrial intelligence."

"Correct, started in 1960 by Frank Drake. Humanity has been listening for nearly 60 years to the sounds of silence. Massive radio telescopes all around the world pointing to the skies and... Nothing. Nada. Zilch. Do you see where I'm going with this, Jess?"

"Oh yes. Sorry, I see it now. The terrifying part. An old galaxy in an old universe and our, relatively speaking, young star system. A galaxy filled with stress events since its birth and a life that, at some point in time, will try extreme socialness. Based on the 40 billion habitable planets, that would mean the number of planets with creatures like humans in the thousands, tens of thousands, or even hundreds of thousands existing at some point in time over the history of our galaxy."

"Jesus, that is an ominous thought. So, the great filter is...?"

"Inside of us. The evolutionary controller. The HHPA axis, Jess."

"Wow. I need a moment. That's a big thought."

"Jess, think about it. Any life form that has some baseline level of intelligence with extreme socialness would most likely experience a similar outcome as humans. They would dominate a planet. Again, it's not intelligence. It's socialness. It's the sharing of ideas and acquired knowledge from our ancestors that makes us intelligent. Individually, humans are not that smart, but when united and pulling from all the past discoveries and achievements, we become unstoppable."

"See, the acronym SETI is incorrect. It should be SETE or the search for extra-terrestrial empathy. You need empathy to be social and have the desire to want to communicate with the universe. Call out; hey, is there anybody out there? That's what we are searching for, not intelligence."

"To give an example, imagine our galaxy is a bar, and the round bar tables inside it, where patrons sit, represent star systems. Sitting at the tables are people, some social and some technical. So who's most likely to get laid? The social or the technical?"

"Definitely the social, Playaaa."

"Exactly, the technical would stare at his phone all night, too afraid to approach the cute girl. The social wants to reach out and participate. Be heard, be experienced, be engaged. Fall in love. Experience another's joy, emotion, sadness, and sorrow. Experience each other's empathy. Sharing in humanity's special gift. That's what we are searching for in the universe, not intelligence."

"Jess, what does it take to build the VLA?"

"VLA?"

"Very Large Array radio telescope. The one shown in the movie *Contact*. 27, 25-meter telescopes all synched together to create a giant one."

"Oh yeah, I remember. That is quite an engineering achievement. It's an inspiring sight, especially when they all rotate together and lock on a target in space."

"Right, and what does it take to build it?"

"Hmm, intelligence? I already have the feeling I answered wrong."

"No Jess! First, it takes socialness. It's the sharing of ideas to get to that point where you can build one of these things. Plus, to build it takes extreme socialness."

"Do you remember that Ph.D. chemist we worked with at the spandex plant?"

"Yeah, what was his name, ah, Jim or something?"

"Right Jim, remember how socially awkward that guy was?"

"Yeah, it was bad, definitely on the far end of the spectrum. Remember how he would just stand in the hallway of our office corridor waiting to ask one of us a question? It would be like a group of us in one of the offices all talking, and he would just stand there in the doorway until one of us said, Jim, do you need something? I remember some of the engineers wanted to see how long he would stand there as an experiment. It was like twenty minutes. Most social people would just burst into the office and say, Hey, I need something."

"Right, zero social skills but high intelligence. If he was the lead on getting the VLA built from a blank sheet of paper to completion, do you think it would get built?"

"Nope."

"Why?"

"I see where you are going with this because building something with thousands of different laborers, contractors, getting city permits from officials, etcetera is a very social exercise. You need a high set of social skills to pull it off. You must lead men and women. You must inspire and motivate them. All in all, it takes high social skills. Plus, just everyone building the thing involves empathy. Everyone working together for a common goal. Everyone putting themselves in each other shoes that they are part of a team. Everyone wanting to do a good job and not let anyone else down. Also, as you said, the technology to get to that point is a culmination of ideas starting with the birth of humanity. It's made of metal, right? Wouldn't have that if humans didn't start sharing ideas about how to use metals thousands of years ago."

"Very good, Jess. So, as you said, if complex life is always trending towards experimenting with socialness out of stress events, it would surely happen with 40 billion opportunities. Most likely, on these planets, there would be life forms with a body plan similar to humans. Bipedal with a high degree of dexterity. Also, the periodic table of elements is not unique to Earth, meaning they would have the same elements to work with to create tools and shape their environment. Over time, they would start to aggregate knowledge and begin to dominate all other life forms on their planet. They would race ahead while all other life seemed static."

"Right, and carbon is the fourth most abundant element in the universe, meaning there would be massive untapped energy reserves from all the other life forms that came before them waiting to be used. Waiting to power their civilization. Waiting to be the fuel for their advancement."

"Yes, and any species that could achieve that level of socialness with baseline intelligence would also view themselves as different from all other life forms that came before them. They would see it as specialness, just like humans have done. They wouldn't consider it an anomaly but a superiority."

"Exactly, and as they began to dominate their planet, their population would grow and overshadow all other life forms. Then, because they are so dominant, they would begin to see their planet as their own and destined to rule over it just like we have done."

"Let me take the next one," Jess said. "Because their population grows so large, they begin to pollute themselves. They mine their planet for ore and smelt it for metals. They burn the dense carbon buried beneath the planet to fire it. They create a toxic world chasing their advancement for the metals and energy below the surface just like we have done."

"Right, and just like in our scenario, life would view this change as a stress. Just like an extinction event. It would view it as something wrong. And then what would happen, Jess?"

"Life would change to protect itself."

"Exactly. Extreme socialness created this outcome, so turn it off to resolve this situation. But here is the interesting part. Remember talking about the energy accounting department for life?"

"Yes."

"So, as social genes are suppressed, the systemizing, patterning, and analytical genes needed for the new environment can be more expressed."

"Right, just like when a person loses a sense, the other senses become stronger. Energy must go somewhere."

"Exactly."

"Oh, let me take this one again, Ryan. This change in systemizing, patterning, or analytical skills would be viewed as further advancement in the species because their technology would advance much more rapidly than in the past, just like ours has done. The tragedy is that all the while, they would pollute themselves more and more and more. Almost like an open-loop positive feedback controller. A runaway effect. The more socialness they lose, the more technical they become, and the more they pollute, losing even more socialness until all socialness is lost."

"Excellent, Jess. Let me show you a video that, for me, sums it all up. Let's watch. It's called *Google Duplex: A.I. Assistant Calls Local Businesses to Make Appointments.*"[2]

"Yeah, I have seen this before. Funny AI calling a hairdresser. I've seen parodies of this video where the Google Duplex calls the person's Mom asking for money. You have to wonder where this all ends."

"It ends with all socialness lost. Remember Lamarck? Where he got it right was the use it or lose it, especially in a state of persistent stress."

"The funny part, Jess is the engineers and tech people in the crowd applauding like, god, our species is so intelligent; look what we can do! I'll bet none of them in the audience could imagine that they are applauding the demise of humanity."

"Right, and the sad part is that the engineers are creating a tool for communication, so they don't have to. They need help, so they created a tool to do it for them. Please help me, AI. Call my parents, boss, friends, and girlfriend so that I can code more. I'm trying to create a virtual world, and I don't have time to be bothered by people."

"Yep, and what impact does using tools to communicate for you have on human biology, considering that stress and information are passed forward?"

"Not good," Jess said.

"Jess, we are engineers. How many times have we seen social issues in our profession?"

"Countless."

"Right, and in our experience dealing with people, isn't there almost a perfect inverse relationship between technical people and the ability to be social?"

"Yes, definitely, and honestly, it's frustrating. The more social people tend to be the upper managers making decisions. They are clueless about the technical aspect of the operation or process. They make the dumbest decisions, and the technical people, who know better, don't have the social skills to stand up to them."

"So true. Have you ever been in those meetings with highly social and technical people trying to get something accomplished? Half the meeting is spent with the technical people trying to explain something, and the social people nod but ultimately have no clue what they are talking about. The social people then try to explain it to their bosses, who are also social, and two social groups have no clue about the issue. Ultimately, a decision is made based on emotion and lack of understanding, and the whole thing is fucked."

"Funny, I also see this all the time at my job, and when you think about it, it's evident even more so in our government. It takes extreme socialness to get elected to political office. Imagine all the handshaking, speeches, talking, listening, and interacting with strangers it takes to get elected. It would send someone on the autistic spectrum cowering into a corner just thinking about it."

"Yes, and these are the people who need to be analytical the most. Need to run a government and society on data, not emotion."

"So, like you are saying, Jess, these distant worlds in our galaxy experience the same evolutionary fate we are now seeing. A rise in systemizing in the brain due to a suppression of socialness. They change the environment, and the environment changes them. The great filter. Inside of them the whole time. They would create a world beyond their adaptation, just like we are doing, and life would respond. Push the anomaly back to what is natural or common. Kind of like an overshoot in a negative feedback controller. Life makes a correction back to normal."

"They also probably wouldn't recognize it as a change to the entire population and focus on the extreme ends of the bell curve just like we are doing."

"Yes! This is what is so frustrating about autism. The biggest clue that this is happening to all of us is in the very description of the so-called disorder. A spectrum disorder. Jess, what is also a spectrum?"

"A histogram. A bell curve. A population bell curve."

"Exactly."

"This is what I don't understand. There are smart people in this world who study this condition for a living. How can even they not see it? Not see that our society is becoming less social and putting the two together? You would have to have blinders on not to notice."

"Plus, so many of the more common autistic traits are seen in the normal population, but to a lesser degree. Take eye contact. Autistic people can't stand making eye contact with other people, especially when communicating."

"Jess, have you talked to people in your career that have difficulty with this? They either talk without looking at you or make occasional eye contact with you when talking, but you can tell that it is difficult for them. Almost like they must force themselves to do it."

"All the time. Numerous examples," Jess said.

"Take the next one, repetitive body movements such as hand flapping and repetitive use of objects such as turning lights on and off. Remember the craze with fidget spinners that started in 2017? The toy was promoted to help people to relieve anxiety or stress. It was promoted to help people with neurological disorders like ADHD and autism. In 2017, all 20 of the top-selling toys on Amazon were fidget spinners, and they accounted for 17 percent of all toys sold nationwide for all retailers."

"Take the next one, insistence on sticking to routines such as traveling the same route home each day and doing things in exactly the same order every time. My god, doesn't that describe the entire culture we have created? Laws, rules, and work instructions for processes. ANSI, ASME, ASTM, NISO, OSHA, SAE, ISO standards 1-21000, and the list goes on and on. Have you ever met those people who are so anal about following processes to the letter, almost machine-like?"

"Hmm, like all of my coworkers?"

"Exactly."

"Take the next one, unusually intense or narrow interests, especially in objects. This one is easy. Take any tech product. How about the most common one. The iPhone. An entire society obsessed with them. Camping out the night before to purchase the latest model. Obsessing about specifications, processor speed, memory, screen resolution, battery life, form factor, styling. This is an object, Jess. A material object. Just one of the countless examples in our material world."

"Also, isn't it a small stretch or no stretch at all to say that the entire industrial revolution was built and fueled on narrow interests? Isn't every single patent in the patent office someone's narrow interest? The printing press, the light bulb, the telephone, the steam engine, electricity, television, transistors, computers, rubber, plastic, nuclear fission, and the list goes on and on. Pick up any tech product today, or any manufactured product for that matter. It was most likely a narrow interest for someone to create or improve upon it."

"Wow, that's interesting, and you are right. Same traits, just to a lesser degree," Jess said.

"Now let's look at what is becoming common to classified non-autistic children that is also common to autistic ones. ADHD, generalized anxiety disorders, and OCD. All are increasing in the so-called normal population, and all common features of autism. Also, isn't it a small stretch to say that ADHD and OCD are the same traits for the narrow interests and man's ability to create an industrial revolution just overly expressed? Obsessed and compelled with a high amount of activity to create all these new productions and inventions that have reshaped our environment?"

"See Jess; this is what, for the life of me, I can't understand. There is no demarcation between autism and the normal population. It is the same bell curve, the same spectrum. Remember, the entire human race has such narrow genetic diversity with the same diversity as a small band of chimpanzees? There are not two histograms! A histogram for autism and one for the rest of humanity. It's the same fucking curve!"

"Whoa, easy, Ryan. Need the stool?"

"Yeah, sorry. I get worked up about this one. I don't understand why it is so obvious to me and no one else. Every now and then, I have these brief moments where I'm like, do I have psychosis? Why do I see something so clearly that no one else can?"

"Ah, Ryan, you know the answer to this one, right? Cause you are a hybrid. You don't live in the human-built matrix, the human construct. The story that all humans have told themselves that they are the most special. Higher than all other life forms on this planet. The pinnacle of evolution. You see right through this, remember?"

"I know, but, my god, the links are so obvious now."

"Yeah, I must admit, being with you in these workshops now, I almost see it as clearly as you do. It's weird. It's like one of those, oh, why didn't I see this before? Like something right in front of you, but you can't see it because you're not looking at it correctly. Like all the dots are there, staring you in the face daily, but you just haven't connected them."

"I think it takes advanced systemizing to put it together for the first time. You have proven the autistic side of your hybridness to be able to see this. To put all these things together. Make life and evolution a system, look for patterns, and put all the puzzle pieces together. Well done, sir."

"Jess, trust me. I would relinquish this ability in a nanosecond if I could. I simply don't have control over it. Powerful forces, remember? What humanity needs to do is build a world where people don't have to solve puzzles like this. Just live, love, and be happy."

"It doesn't look like we are trending in that direction Nature Boy. I know, I know, hence the workshops."

"Hey, I have a question for you. You said that autism is not a distinct spectrum but a human spectrum, right?"

"Yes."

"Ok, well, how can you be both? How can you be both autistic and human? In other words, how can you exist on both sides of the curve?"

"Good question Jess."

"It's not so much that I can be both, like instantly going from extremely social to extremely autistic. It's more so that I have been both, experienced both, and can appreciate both."

"I can remember when I was a young child being fascinated with the way things work, especially machines. Like constantly obsessing about them to the point it was near debilitating. I would stay up all night and just put these things together in my head. Like, for example, constantly seeing all the components of an internal combustion engine moving in my mental vision."

"I would disassemble all the pieces and put them back together in my mind. Then taking all the components and changing them, reconfiguring them, trying to make a more efficient engine. Like, what if you did this, what if this was bigger, smaller? What would the outcome be? How would it change its performance? I constantly had these images in my head. It was so bad at times that I often wished that I could turn it off. Looking back, it was fairly odd behavior for an 8-year-old."

"And the socialness part?"

"I can remember in my late teens and early 20s having empathy to the point it was also near debilitating. I lived with this girl in a house, and we had a Labrador retriever. Her name was Casey, and she was an amazing dog. Boundless energy and so loyal. Anyway, at some point, my girlfriend and I broke up, and it was a real issue about who would get custody of Casey. She ended up getting her, and it was devasting to me. I can remember having profound empathic thoughts about it. Like constantly putting myself in Casey's shoes or paws..."

"Don't," Jess said.

"Ok, but seriously, constantly thinking about how she felt, how she was doing, where she was. Was she sad? Was she lonely? That time in my life really stands out to me because my empathy was so intense for all things that it could jump to other species. I also had intense empathy for humans, especially women. Intense love, intense feelings, intense empathy but almost like too much. Like so much empathy at times, I wished I could turn it off just like the systemizing."

"My sexual experiences with women were also interesting. When I was younger, I had no interest in my own sexual orgasm when I was with a woman. My empathy for women was so strong it was like I could feel their pleasure when we were having sex. Like I was so interested in their pleasure, I put it before my own. In a way, I could feel what it's like to be a woman experiencing pleasure, and it motivated me to try and satisfy women more and more because, in a weird way, I was satisfying myself. I literally could put myself in their shoes, both autonomically and mentally, when having sex. It made me an excellent lover."

"Isn't that weird, Jess? Jess?"

"Ah, Ryan, we're on our lunch break from work, and you are talking about your expert sexual prowess."

"Oh, sorry, did I create an awkward moment?"

"Maybe a little, Romeo."

"Come on Jess, we're engineers. We have scientific minds. This is just data. I had extreme affective empathy for women. It's data."

"Ok yeah, you just made me lose focus for a minute."

"Oh, sorry."

"But yeah, and what was even stranger, I had no empathy for men. I still don't, really. I just don't get them. Their behavior is very strange to me. It's like I have trouble bonding with them."

"Yeah, this is all really strange," Jess said. "Why would nature do this, though? Why would you have both at different times?"

"I don't know. Maybe I am an anomaly of an anomaly. Or maybe, to some degree, evolution works like this. Expressing some genes and suppressing others throughout a person's lifetime, especially in their youth. Like trying them out to see stress levels per given environment. Maybe evolution is more dynamic and responsive than even I am hypothesizing."

"Regardless, I feel like I have experienced both extremes in my life, giving me a greater vision of which is most important. Like I clearly understand each trait and its impact on humanity."

"And your vision? What do you see?"

"Abandon all technology. It will be the death of the human race. Not because of AI, but because Nature is making a choice. The erosion of empathy. Empathy, Jess, is everything. It is the birth and mechanics of socialness. The birth of language. The birth of love. The birth of humanity. Once it's lost, everything else falls with it."

"I don't think people truly understand just how important this trait is. Humanity's special gift is being taken for granted. Our entire civilization depends on socialness. It depends on people being able to empathize with each other. Share a common vision. Be a part of something. Be part of a greater whole. We have erected this massive global economy that depends on people getting along with each other. When the human bond diminishes, it all crumbles and evolves into a selfish, animalistic world."

"So, you're saying total collapse and a global, never-ending war?" Jess asked.

"It can't be good, Jess. Our world is so interconnected and dependent on these social connections. It relies on cooperation and working together for a common goal."

"Civilizations have risen and fallen, but it will be different this time. In the end, it will be the extinction of a species. The great filter."

"Jesus, Ryan, you are bringing my depression back in full force."

"I think I would like to stop talking about all this and go back to pretending we are the two aliens surveying the galaxy. Come on, Ryan, sit next to me on my spaceship couch. Let's leave Earth for a while."

"Jess, you okay?"

"Sit next to me, dammit!"

"Okay."

"Let's go to an Earth-like planet in our galaxy nearly twice our planet's age. I want to fly hundreds of feet above its surface. What do we see?"

"Well, we see a planet that is teeming with life. Body plans all interacting with each other. All interdependent on each other for their existence. We see maximum biodiversity where all species are perfectly suited to their environment. We see a pure environment. Pure air, pure water, pure soil, with no pollution. It is a beautiful sight."

"And if we land on this planet? Let's pretend that we brought with us excavating equipment, and we can peer beneath the surface. What do we find?"

"We find fossils that look like us. Bipedal with dexterity. Everywhere you dig, you see them. Also, strange artifacts made of exotic metals littered beside them."

"Standing on this distant planet, Ryan, with shovels in hand, looking at the human-like fossils at our feet, I would have to ask you the simple question, what is the point? Considering the path that humanity is on, it is not hard to imagine all the suffering that this extinct species, now still beneath the soil, would experience at the end of its time. The wars, the brutality, and the savagery dealt to each other as it moves closer and closer to the brink of extinction. If you are right about all this, Ryan, it's the biggest question of all."

"I don't know, Jess. Maybe it's a test, and the universe is silent because no one ever passed the test. Maybe our true God is bored and keeps running this experiment over and over again to see if anyone will ever come through the other side. Past the great filter. Maybe we will be the first ones. The first ones to see it. See Nature as it truly is and what it truly cares about the most and make a correction on our own."

"I don't know, Ryan. I'm starting to have serious doubts."

"I think I just like flying in the heavens with you in our spaceship and visiting all the planets teeming with life and not worrying about all this. Both of us, blissfully powerful, with you by my side."

"Jess, you do realize that for this workshop, we have been theorizing that no technically advanced alien species has even made it through the great filter, which would make our fantasy about traveling through the galaxy in a spaceship and visiting distant planets impossible?"

"Shut up, Hybrid. Can you just not be autistic for a minute? Switch on some empathy for me, maybe?"

"Jess, I have to say your mood has been strange today."

"Yes, because I can't help feeling that we are the next planet to pass through the great filter. It's happening now, right before our very eyes, and no one sees it except for one crazy lone engineer calling himself a hybrid. You must admit that the odds are stacked against humanity."

"Jess, a little optimism?"

"Sorry, Ryan. I don't have it today. Just stay with me by my side, though. Let's keep traveling through the stars and exploring the splendor of life."

CHAPTER TEN
WS10

"Hi Jessica. Jessica? Hello?"

"Hello."

"Feeling better? Less depressed?"

"Not sure. Maybe a little. I don't know. I have a weird feeling."

"Weird feeling?"

"Yeah, I can't explain it but definitely weird. It could be like that scene in *The Matrix* when Neo finally sees the Earth as it really is and what humans have done to it, where his brain overloads, and he vomits."

"So, you are becoming the one?"

"No, I'm not the one."

"But you are seeing it, Jess? Nature as it really is? Like at the end of the movie when Neo sees the green code?"

"Yeah, getting there, and I don't know if I'm happy, sad, pissed, amazed, or in awe of Nature."

"I choose to be in awe and inspired."

"Inspired?"

"Yes, inspired."

"Doesn't sound very inspiring if Nature is discarding the one thing that makes us special, the ability to love. Asking for its special gift back."

"Jess, Nature isn't doing anything but running code, life code. Humans are trashing their special gift because they don't understand the laws of Nature yet."

"Once they do, then they can live within these laws. Again, from our last workshop, assuming they can in time. Think of it like a person who has been completely sheltered from the world and knows nothing about gravity. He's then unsheltered, sees a skyscraper, races to the top, jumps up on the ledge to take in the magnificent view, slips, and falls to his death."

"He did this because he didn't fully understand gravity and ultimately come to respect it. Same thing with humans, just replace gravity with Nature. Once we understand it, we can abide by it. Respect it. Cherish humanity's special gift. Say to Nature, in a sense, we don't want to lose it. Say to Nature, we respect your power. We are in awe of you. We understand what you want and will abide by these laws or suffer the consequence. Treat it like a God, so to speak. Something way more powerful than us."

"Got to shatter the matrix first, right?"

"Right Jess."

"So, what's on the agenda for today, Neo?"

"Well, Jess, I want to talk more about the evolutionary controller inside of us. I want to talk about some of my inspiration because I think you especially can also appreciate it."

"Why me?"

"Because my inspiration came from where we once worked together."

"The spandex plant?"

"Yes. In my mind, it was the perfect mechanical representation of the human body."

"Ok, this sounds interesting. Explain."

"Well, let's think about the now closed plant. By the way, thanks, China and Korea."

"Yeah, thanks China and Korea, for flooding the market with cheap goods below our production costs, funded by your governments, ultimately bankrupting the company! Oh, sorry," Jess said, like she got a little carried away.

"No, your animosity is warranted. It was the perfect job for an engineer. It had everything an engineer could want. The chemical aspect. The mechanical component. Electrical. Industrial. All contained within one building that we oversaw, at least from a keeping it running and performing standpoint."

"Yes, she was a good plant. I miss her," Jess said.

"Me too. Also, the process and technology had a bit of a mystery component to it. In other words, it wasn't well understood. Remember those days when the plant would be producing spandex at like 95 percent yield and then all of a sudden, without warning, crash? Went from high yield to nearly nothing at all."

"Those were stressful days," Jess said. "The plant manager got really nervous looking at all the engineers like, what is going on? Come on, how are we going to fix this? It was a lot of pressure because, if my memory serves correctly, the potential revenue per day was in the hundreds of thousands of dollars."

"Yes, it was, and the funny thing was that initially, all the engineers had no clue why the plant wasn't performing. We were just running around checking various parts of the process, trying to look like we knew what we were doing."

"Right, the technology was not mature, and we were all learning. It was kind of like a puzzle we were trying to piece together. Why does the plant perform great at times and then crashes, and we can't measure or detect anything?"

"Exactly, and it was at this point in time I was having so many health issues. I was going to, what seemed like countless doctors, and they would all tell me the same thing. There is nothing wrong with you. Run countless tests and come back with nothing every single time. It was just like us at the plant when it crashed. We would look at all these measurements, temperature, pressure, speed, viscosity, acidity, etcetera, and everything was normal, but the plant was in disarray. We literally couldn't make a single spool of thread, and the plant was manager furious."

"Over time, I began to equate the two. How can I feel this bad, and all medical testing indicates that I am perfectly normal? How can the plant go from 95 percent yield to zero, and all our measurements are normal? Both are similar and don't make sense."

"The simplest explanation for me was that, in both cases, they must not be well understood. There must be something fundamental to both processes that is still a mystery."

"Right," Jess said, "because at the time, even though you didn't tell me, supposedly your friend, you know, you literally couldn't move. No energy, no metabolism, and in pain. Your body crashed just like the plant. That must have been very frustrating but also, as an engineer, very intriguing, right?"

"Definitely. I would lay awake at night thinking about it. Like, how can I be in this much pain and have to force myself to get out of bed every day to go to work with not a single medical test revealing anything? I looked at all the results. I asked the doctors for the paperwork. There was not a single test even close to out of range. Countless tests across the diagnostic spectrum and all normal."

"At first, I didn't make the comparison to the plant because I had zero knowledge about the human body. Also, the medical community at the time was well established. I mean, go into any hospital, and see all the machines, the fancy diagnostic equipment, the doctors in their lab coats with this cockiness and demeanor like they have it all figured out. I felt like probably any other person that initially goes into this environment. I had the feeling that somehow, someway, these people, who at least portray confidence, will help me."

"Then I guess you lost hope in the medical community at some point, right?"

"Yeah, I got tired of hearing doctors say, 'There is nothing wrong with you'. It got so bad that I was internally laughing in their office when they opened their folder to review the test results. In my head, I was saying, I knew this would happen when they spoke those familiar words. Why do I keep doing this? They're never going to find anything. Can't you see it now? You're on your own."

"So, while the plant was failing and we couldn't measure anything wrong, my body was failing, and they also couldn't measure anything wrong. But there was a fundamental difference. As an engineer, I know systems. I know there's always a reason: cause and effect. For the plant, the problem was simple. It's a chemical, mechanical, and electrical system, and it crashed because there was something that moved that we weren't measuring. Out of the thousands of pumps, motors, heaters, valves, and controllers that make up the whole, something changed, and we just had to find it. Ultimately, we needed to use the plant's failure to understand better how it works and uncover the crucial elements to making it work."

"So," Jess said, "you started to equate the two even more?"

"Right. Just like there was a crucial element in the spandex plant making it fail that we didn't understand, there must also be a crucial element in the human body making it fail that the entire worldwide medical community didn't understand."

"Funny, the entire worldwide medical community. You must have been a little intimidated, right? I mean, you had no medical training."

"Yeah, I was at first. Like, this is daunting. You could fill up an entire library, hundreds of times over, with all the medical literature written about the human body. Mind-numbing page after page. I felt like someone trying to solve a murder mystery, and all the facts about the case are written in a foreign language, and there's no one to help me translate."

"Around a year into the research, I was really at the point where I wanted to give up. It was just too much data. So overwhelming. But then I read something one day that opened my eyes. For once, out of this seemingly foreign medical world came a ray of hope."

"What was it?" Jess asked.

"Negative feedback control loops. It was an article discussing the control of stomach acid. A hormone called gastrin is secreted by cells in the stomach responding to the presence of proteins. Gastrin then stimulates the release of stomach acid to break down these proteins. When the stomach is later emptied, a hormone called somatostatin is released that stops the release of acid. This whole event is controlled by negative feedback mechanisms and control loops."

"Just like at the plant, right?"

"Right, and when I first read this article, I can remember being very confused, like, how can this be? How can there be machine-like control loops inside the human body? Intuitively, because it is made of fleshy material, all the organs crammed inside, it doesn't appear machine-like. It seems counterintuitive to assume it would behave like a machine, but it does."

"Jess, how many negative feedback control loops were at the plant?"

"Had to be in the thousands."

"Jess, what controlled all the control loops?"

"The DCS (distributed control system)."

"Right, it was the system that oversaw the thousands of control loops to set the pumps, valves, temperatures, motors, etcetera, that kept the plant performing. We interfaced with the DCS in the control room of the plant. What was that room, maybe 500 hundred square feet, in the middle of a plant that was 250,000 thousand square feet? A few engineers and technicians, sitting at computers, overseeing the entire massive collection of countless moving parts, all working together to make a single product."

"And the human body has thousands of these negative feedback control loops?" Jess asked.

"Yes, I mean, obviously, no one knows for sure. It could be tens of thousands or hundreds of thousands. Just like at the plant, though, they all control stability. In the biological realm, this would be called homeostasis. When life is not stressed, homeostasis is ideal. Keep everything the same. It's just like in manufacturing, where variation is the enemy of production."

"So, let me guess, with all these control loops, you started to wonder if there was a central controller or a DCS?" Jess asked.

"Yes, or maybe a master controller that influenced all the other control loops. Like a single epicontroller. In my mind, I kept seeing all these thousands of controllers in the human body, working together, and when one moved, it would influence the ones right next to it."

"The example I like is thinking about a line of cars lined up on the highway. They are the same distance apart at speed with something like an adaptive cruise control for each one. It's a difficult control loop problem because when one of them experiences a disturbance, it propagates through the chain. The system could become unstable, especially if the distance between them is close."

"Think about manufacturing and processes, Jess. What is the most important part of any process?"

"The beginning."

"Right again. You can only be as good as the start. In other words, variation at the beginning of the process will lead to more variation at the end."

"Yes, and this is exactly what we did at the plant," Jess said. "We started focusing at the beginning of the process, trying to determine why it was crashing."

"And what did we ultimately find, Jess?"

"We found at times, using significantly better measurement techniques, there were slight variations of material flow into the reactor."

"Right. It took many years of research, investment, data gathering, trials, and experimentation, but we ultimately found that small fluctuations in the polymer reactor could lead to the plant crashing. The other reason why we missed it, aside from inadequate measurements, was because the polymer from the reactor fed into giant holding tanks that were constantly mixed."

"A disturbance in material flow would happen and not directly impact the plant because all the polymer was mixed together. However, if you got enough disturbances over time, it would ultimately degrade the polymer enough to cause plant performance issues. There was a threshold in polymer quality due to variation in the reactor. Once reached, the spandex quality would just plummet."

"So, what was our fix, Jess?"

"We bought the best pumps, motors, valves, measurement equipment, and controllers for the five streams that fed into the reactor."

"Right. The polymer reactor, which is essentially the beginning of the process, was experiencing small variations at times from the streams that fed into it. This led to variation in the plant's performance. We did everything possible to eliminate that variation, and the plant became more stable. The stability in the first process led to stability in all the other processes downstream."

"So, I see it now. You equated the plant's performance to your body's performance and thought there must be a first controller or a beginning of the process controller?"

"Yes, and this, in my mind, is how the plant and the human body are so similar. Again, the size of the plant was around 250,000 square feet, and the whole campus was around twice that. There were around 350 employees, all doing various activities to keep it going. There was management, engineers, technicians, laborers, accounting, purchasing, maintenance, human resources, janitorial, quality, etcetera. A very diverse team to keep it functioning."

"So, these people are like the cells?"

"Maybe or just like the diversification of the human body. Like many different things, all with different tasks, to make the whole thing function."

"Ok, yeah, I see that."

"So, this polymer reactor. It's about the size of a paint can with five streams going into it. The reactor has a mixer, and the polymer is made inside the reactor. The performance of that tiny little reactor, relative to the size of the entire plant, determined all our fates."

"In other words, its performance, determined by the stability going into it, could make or break us. If the stability is high, the plant performs well. If the stability is low, the plant crashes. It could be so bad we must lay people off. It could be so bad we must lay everyone off. The stability of that tiny little reactor determined the success or failure of the entire system."

"Right, imagine if we never found it and variation increased; it would be a total collapse. Everyone loses their job, the hundreds of millions of dollars that went into building the plant, the time, the hard work, and the commitment. All lost due to a few unstable control loops," Jess said.

"Exactly, so I began to wonder if the human body is also like this. A few negative feedback controllers or maybe one that controls the whole thing."

"Makes sense and pretty cool from an engineering standpoint. So, your experimentation with the hormone cortisol led you to the stress axis?"

"Yes, and again, from experimentation with the hormone, I could make myself feel young again. I could essentially cure myself, but only temporarily. Just like Kendall, who discovered the hormone that he called compound E and gave it to wheelchair-stricken people suffering from severe rheumatoid arthritis. When he did, they instantly came to life. Again, this hormone is something the body naturally produces that determines if these patients are successful or failing from a biological standpoint."

"So human failure and plant failure. I thought they must be related. When the plant failed, it was due to a few unstable feedback loops. Could it also be true for our bodies or even all life?"

"I then started looking into the failure of the human body. This led me to chronic fatigue syndrome, which affects millions and millions of people worldwide. It also definitely fit my symptoms."

"Again, as a comparison to our plant, what was the plant's main function?"

"To produce something," Jess said.

"Right, it takes in raw goods and though the use of thousands of negative feedback controllers makes a product."

"What is the human body's function?"

"It also takes in raw goods and, through the use of thousands of negative feedback controllers, makes something?" Jess asked.

"Right, and what does it make?"

"Hmm, help me, Ryan."

"It makes energy. Its main product is biological energy, which is then used to do other things. To live, to love, to laugh, to play, to work, to sing, to dance, to think, to see, to feel, everything we do takes energy. The plant, in a sense, was the same. It made spandex yarn, and then that product was used by end-users to do or make other things. They made socks, underwear, belts, gloves, hosiery, bodysuits, lingerie, bras, diapers, surgical hose, bandages, etcetera."

"Ok, that makes sense. So, in your case, the body's main product, energy, was disrupted. It was failing to make adequate amounts just like the yield of the plant?"

"Yes, and over time I became fascinated with the concept of biological failure, especially from studying chronic fatigue syndrome. I couldn't get this question out of my head which was, why would the human body be failing at making its primary product? There must be a reason for this failure."

"Not sure what you mean by reason?" Jess asked.

"Well, I viewed Nature and biology as something intelligent, even before I got deep into research. I mean, it's been at this a long time. It would be like a spandex plant producing yarn for 3.8 billion years. If engineers working at the plant couldn't figure out how to achieve 100 percent plant yields in 3.8 billion years, then they were asleep in their offices."

"In other words, in that amount of time, every single detail of the plant, down to the smallest minute detail, would be known and well understood. If a spandex plant, after 3.8 billion years of producing, was failing, then the engineers were making it fail on purpose."

"That's interesting," Jess said, "and makes total sense!"

"Right, but it's not intuitive to think of life failing for a reason, and I struggled for a long time trying to put this together. Why would biology fail? What is the purpose of failure? In manufacturing, we do everything possible to ensure processes don't fail. It's almost like you have to do a mental 180 to get into this mindset to see its purpose."

"Or be a hybrid?"

"Yes, or be a hybrid."

"And, its purpose?"

"Evolution. The grandest purpose of all. Programmed failure to protect life."

"I actually got some of my inspiration on this from studying medicine and the molecule cholesterol. It was interesting to me at the time that nearly the entire world was taking some form of medicine to lower cholesterol."

"Cholesterol is also a substance that's in a negative feedback loop, controlling the levels in the body. Again, Nature is smart and has been at this for a long time. There must be a reason for the spike."

"I kept thinking, why is this feedback loop producing so much of something that supposedly kills us? Well, let's see. Cholesterol is fuel for the stress axis. So, we must all be stressed. Why are we all stressed? Well, what is stress? It is a biological response to something we are not adapted to. What specifically is the response? Pull more available energy to deal with the stress. Is energy infinite on this planet? No. What would happen if biology kept pulling more and more energy to deal with stress for a particular species? It would result in less available energy for all the other species. What would be the end result of this action? It would result in less biodiversity. Would this be good or bad for the survival of life as a whole? Bad."

"Eureka moment."

"Damn, that is pretty cool. That was going through your mind when you put it all together?"

"Yes, I knew Nature, being at this for 3.8 billion years, wouldn't be like our spandex plant where we didn't fully understand our processes. It knew exactly what it was doing, and if it was failing, it was on purpose or programmed failure."

"So like death to the unfit?" Jess asked.

"Well, conservation of energy to the unfit. You can't be a threat to biodiversity. Pre-human intervention or a wild setting, this would obviously lead to death due to predation, as energy is everything. Nothing can be done without biological energy."

"Funny, the whole cholesterol thing," Jess said. "You're right. I think humans might be at the point of considering putting statins in the water supply right next to fluoride."

"That reminds me, Jess. Did I ever tell you about the experiment I did many years back?"

"No."

"Well, again, I started being curious about statins because, at the time, they were hailed as the cure-all for everyone. Also, it was pretty much what all doctors did to anyone over 30, which was to check cholesterol. It was so ubiquitous; it became like a common discussion for the general population."

"Hey, I went to the doctor, and my cholesterol was this. Doc said I got to get it down to here, and I got to take this. Men were calling out their cholesterol stats like sports stats. So, I started asking people, hey, what actually is cholesterol? I initially asked five of my immediate family members, and they had no clue. I then wondered, what percentage of the U.S. population knows what cholesterol is used for in the body?"

"I did a quick calculation, determining that I would need a sample size of 97 to have a 95 percent confidence with a margin error of 10 for a population size of 300 million to determine how many people in the United States know what cholesterol does in the body."

"Thousands of people at my current job, so I got to work. I took the roster list from HR, plugged them into Excel, used a random generator function, got my 97 names, and went out on the shop floor to ask a simple question."

"Sorry to bother you, can I ask you something? What does cholesterol do in the body?"

"Guess how many people got the right answer?"

"Tell me."

"Zero."

"The most common answer was, it causes heart attacks. I remember telling a few people it's the fuel for the stress axis. Glassy-eyed look."

"Then afterward, let me ask you a follow-up question. The majority of the adult population is taking statins, what could this mean? Blank stare."

"Yes! So funny," Jess said, "I see this all the time. People just blindly taking medications without even knowing what it does inside of them. Just trusting doctors and Big Pharma without question."

"Yeah, and how did we get here as a species? It baffles me. The thought that we must take all these pills just to live. It doesn't happen in Nature. Lions and tigers don't need pills to exist."

"Part of the matrix, maybe? Inundated with so many commercials that it becomes the human reality?"

"Most likely, and it's very concerning, especially in youth. A pill-based existence. A sad reality."

"Yep, got to wonder where it all ends."

"Ok, sorry for digressing, Jess, I want to tell you how the human body, well, all life for that matter, works using the plant to explain it."

"So, let's imagine that our plant is 3.8 billion years old and has been producing spandex for a long time. In other words, its yield is 100 percent. There is no waste, and the plant is perfectly efficient. A model of lean manufacturing."

"For this plant, our economy represents the environment. Remember when China and Korea came online, they started flooding the market with the most common spandex denier (yarn size) that we had been producing since the plant was first built?"

"Yes, 40 denier. The yarn size for the most common products like normal hosiery and apparel."

"Right, so from an adaptation standpoint, after we finally reduced variation at the reactor, we were very efficient at producing this one thing. We were adapted to our environment. However, when China and Korea started producing the same thing, the economy or environment changed. We went from very profitable to hardly profitable at all. Therefore, we, or the plant, had to change, and what did we do?"

"We started to specialize in other areas," Jess said. "Instead of making 40 denier, we made specialty 10 denier that goes in the most sheer hosiery all the way up to 840 denier that goes in diapers around the legs section of diapers to hold in the, you know..."

"Yeah, I know. Don't do that."

"Sorry. We moved to other areas because the profit margins were higher in this environment versus the main staple yarn where the margins were lower."

"Right, and when we had to start specializing, something interesting happened. The yields of the plant dropped. Our scrap rate went up. Do you know why Jess?"

"Yes, because the manufacturing plant, like an organism, was not adapted to its new environment. Because it had never produced these specialty yarns, it was not efficient at doing it, and, just like in life, its efficiency had to increase if it wanted to survive."

"Very good Jess!"

"Jess, what would you say was the weakest link of the plant from a machine standpoint?"

"Hmm, most likely the winders, right? They were built in-house from a blank sheet of paper. I think most of the engineers there would agree they were not at the same level as winders bought by major textile winder manufacturers."

"I agree. Ok, so let's call these winders our stress point in the new environment. How do we know they are the stress point?"

"Oh, I know, because they are the point of inefficiency within the system as a whole. They use more energy either from the scrap they were producing or the excessive amount of maintenance it took to keep them running."

"Exactly, the new economy or environment forced us to start making things beyond our original adaptation, and, just like you said, we started to see inefficiencies or stress at the weakest point of the entire system, the winders."

"Remember the energy accounting department for life we talked about in previous workshops?"

"Yes."

"Well, we had essentially the same thing at the plant. We had bean counters that were constantly measuring scrap and overtime hours spent on maintenance. Their job was to pareto these losses, sorting them from high to low. If they continued to see similar losses month after month, they would eventually give the engineers feedback saying, 'hey guys, if we want to make money, we are going to have to fix this. Do something about this. We have seen this for four months in a row. The problem is obviously persistent and needs to be fixed.'"

"Ok, now, knowing the situation the plant was confronted with in its new environment, let's switch over to biology or life and apply how it would handle this situation."

"Oh, I already know this one!" Jess said. "The reactor speeds up! The entire throughput of the plant increases. Adaptation energy, right? Go from 7 to 8 to 9 to 10 until the stress is resolved."

"Exactly, very good. Man, you are spot on today, Jess!"

Jess pretends she's blushing, hiding her face like a little girl.

"Geez, thanks, Mr. Hybrid."

"Lord," I said, shaking my head.

"Ok, the feedback loops of the reactor, in a biological sense, get more excitable, causing the entire process to speed up. Make more yarn in a manufacturing sense, make more energy in a biological sense. Imagine what would happen in this scenario."

"Jess, let's imagine that we can go back in time to this very event. We're in a meeting with the accountants and the plant manager, and they're hammering us about lowering scrap and maintenance costs. The plant manager screams at us, 'guys, the future of our company depends on this being solved!' At that very moment, we hear a high energy sound of thousands of pumps, gears, and motors winding up in speed. We all look at each other like, what the hell is happening? I call the control room asking and then set the phone down in disbelief. Boss, the control room is saying that the throughput of the plant just increased by 40 percent on its own, and they can't stop it."

"My god," Jess said, "that would be a crazy moment, but I see the significance. It would force a resolution. Literally, everyone would come out of their offices to see what was going on. When they did and got to the shop floor, they would see massive inefficiencies at the winders. Scrap all over the place, in trash cans, on the floor. Workers going frantic, not knowing what to do. The profitability of the plant would plummet. Also, the winders would fail more often, increasing the need for more maintenance."

"Exactly, and we, as engineers, would be forced to find a solution. Like every single one of us, working every waking hour until the problem was resolved."

"And how would we resolve this problem, Jess?"

"Try something different. Start experimenting with different settings, configurations, or perhaps a modification to the design itself. The winders were made in house so we could fabricate alterations. Different guides, wheels, tensioners, springs, bearings, you name it. We would try everything because it would be a make or break scenario. A do or die scenario."

"Right, so imagine one of us came up with an idea. We pull the winder out, make the change and then put the winder back in. Then what do we do?"

"We measure its performance, or its efficiency gain or loss."

"Exactly, now play this iteration out hundreds or thousands of times, looking for a solution. What are we doing in a biological sense?"

"We are increasing variation about an inefficiency point or stress point trying to resolve it. We are trying to find a lower stress that came about due to an environmental change."

"Exactly, and all our changes that didn't work?"

"They represent an increase in stress. Oh god, Ryan. Please tell me this isn't the children that are suicidal? Children losing their light?"

"Yes, a failed attempt, a higher stress."

"Goddammit Nature," Jess said angrily.

"What? Don't blame Nature. Again programming."

"Ok, but still. It sucks."

"No, Jess, it doesn't. The programming is brilliant. Blame the ones changing the environment, not the intelligence of life that responds to change. You would not be here today to complain about it if it didn't have this logic. Do you think life would have made it this far with just natural variation? Think it would have survived even the first extinction event? The oxygen catastrophe?"

"No," Jess said, defeated.

"Ok, then be in awe of it like me."

"Ok," Jess said reluctantly.

"Jess, I realize this is hard for the human mind to see, but Nature and life respond to environmental change. We all must come to grips with that. It's intelligent and will do everything it can to survive, be efficient, and preserve biodiversity. Nature is not the enemy, as it gave us life. The enemy is our ignorance about how it works, okay?"

"Ok."

"Jess, I want to tell you something else interesting about my past."

"Ok," Jess said, still with her head down, looking defeated.

"Jess, cheer up for a minute. This is important."

"When I first conceived of all this, before I put it all together, I was constantly struggling with the question, why would life speed up when confronted with a persistent stressor? Like what value, besides increasing reproduction through increasing sexual energy, does it serve? I kept envisioning in my mind that there must be a higher purpose. So, to solve this, I simply imagined myself as the intelligent designer of life. The programmer of life."

"In my mind, the speed up would expose the stress further, which would be the point where life would increase variation to resolve this stress. Express or suppress genes to find a lower stress point."

"Ok, it makes sense from a design standpoint," Jess said.

"Yes, it does, but it's always been a guess for me. In other words, I had no way to prove it."

"So, your conviction about how life works is based on a guess?"

"To a certain point, yes. I mean, technically, a hypothesis is a scientific guess. Pull data together to tell a story. Figure out a puzzle. But anyway, this one piece was always missing. I mean, it's not like I had a lab and could run tests. This one-piece always alluded me. So, to finish the puzzle, I just imagined myself as the designer of life."

"Ok, so you played the Nature God?"

"Ah, Jess, where did you come up with that term?"

"What?"

"Nature God?"

"I mean, what else would you call it? Life God, cell God, biology God? Why are you acting so weird right now?"

"I've just never heard you use that before."

"Ok, but why is that weird, and why are you being weird?"

"It's not. I'm not. Yeah sorry, I'm back. Ok, yes, I played the Nature God. I realized the most efficient way to evolve is to speed up and express or suppress genes about a stress point. That would be the code of life."

"Anyway, about five years after I felt like I had my answer, this article came out. I want you to read it."

I pull out my phone and show it to Jess, and she reads.[1]

"Oh my god, that's so cool. It says epigenetic changes from bicyclers using only one leg and not the other over the course of a few months. The one leg then epigenetically changing and the other one not changing!"

"I know! It's crazy! It proves that I'm right! It proves that my hypothesis is correct! Isn't that so cool, Jess! God, I wish I had been there when they ran this experiment. Do you think they had any idea they were looking at one third of the mechanics of evolution?"

"One third?" Jess asked.

"Yes, a third of the puzzle. The other two pieces are, life speeds up when confronted with a persistent stressor and information about stress is passed through generations."

"Oh yeah, that's cool," Jess said. "You had the latter two, and this was the piece you were missing. They proved it for you."

"Yes, they surely did."

"So, the leg pedaling represents the stress point. They performed the experiment daily over three months, so the stress became persistent or, in other words, enough data to act upon. Once stress is persistent, life speeds up. The pedaling is also the higher energy state. The one pedaling is just achieving this higher energy state consciously or making a choice. When exposed to something beyond its adaptation, life does this automatically or without choice. Powerful forces, remember, Jess?"

"Jesus Christ," Jess said, patting me on the back.

"So, these epigenetic changes seen in the one leg and not the other, is life trying to be more efficient because its environment has changed, but it's only changing at the point of stress. It's trying to find a lower stress point. It's life's internal programming. And you guessed this whole thing? God, once again, proving your hybridness. Who thinks about this stuff?"

"Hybrids."

"So true, Hybrid, so true."

"Jess, I also wish I had been there when these researchers did the bicycle experiment for another reason."

"What?" Jess asked.

"After the three months, when the test was done, with all the data complied, when we're sitting there staring at the results, I would have said, Gentlemen, congratulations, you just uncovered the reason for autism."

"Autism? Wait, why, what?"

After a few seconds of thought, finally, Jess said. "Oh dammit," looking in shock and disbelief.

"God damn Ryan, no! God damn, oh fuck! God dammit Nature, no! No Ryan. It's not true, is it? Ryan, say it's not true."

"Jess, are you ok? You're starting to tear up."

"It's not true is it?"

"Is what true? You say it, Jess."

Jess then grabs my shoulders, looking at me through tear stained eyes and says, "The leg and the brain are the same thing. Jesus Christ, the leg and the brain are the same thing."

"Exactly, Jess, well done."

CHAPTER ELEVEN
WS11

"Jess? Jess? Mission control, again, calling Jessica."

"No one is home on this planet, Ryan."

"What's wrong, Jessica?"

"I'm sad."

"Why?"

"I don't like the Nature God."

"Why?"

"Ryan, come on, do you realize all the pain and suffering going on now, and through countless years in the past, because of this? I mean really. Just in my family alone, I have a cousin who has social anxiety so severe she's drugged up on pharmaceutical meds, like a zombie, most of the time. I have someone in my immediate family that tried to commit suicide a few years back and suffers from severe depression. Aunts and uncles who all take antidepressants. I have a close friend whose daughter cuts herself so bad that she doesn't know what to do. I mean, if I sat down and compiled a list of all health struggles, especially mental, it would not be pretty, and my family is probably the norm in this country."

"Yes, I understand. Trust me, I do. Mary also cut herself. My family has the same types of struggles."

"Ok, aren't you angry? How can this inspire you? I need you to turn on empathy right now."

"Jessica, come on, you're not thinking correctly."

"Huh, what are you talking about? You showed me something in the last workshop that is very disturbing. Think about the families with autistic children. Think about how much of a struggle that is. I've read the news stories just like you. Parents who are afraid of their children. Afraid that they are going to stab them while they're sleeping. Parents who lock them up in cages. Parents who abandon them. Parents who abuse them. Parents who subject them to inhumane acts like drinking bleach to cure them. Imagine all the stress, hardship, and turmoil these families go through, and you are telling me it's all because Nature is just trying to reduce stress in the human brain like it would a leg muscle?"

"Where is the inspiration in that, Ryan? I need you to turn on empathy right now and feel with me for this fucked up mess that humanity is in. And don't say, Jess I do, hence the workshops."

"Jessica. You're. Not. Thinking. Correctly."

"Stop saying that! Why are you not upset like me? Nature has no compassion, concern, caring? Not an ounce of it? A leg muscle is the same as the human brain?"

"I see that it is a fucking machine. You have convinced me. I'm with you. It's a machine. I see it. It literally performs a stress test. So fucking machine like. I want to know how in the fuck did it get programmed? Seriously, tell me, who programmed this thing? I want to speak to this mother fucker!"

Jess points her head to the sky and screams, "Nature God, get the fuck down here! Come and explain this! Why did humanity go through all this shit, and you are changing it all just like you would a leg muscle!!"

"Jessica, you're not thinking correctly."

"Stop saying that, Ryan! You're starting to piss me off! You better start fucking crying with me right now! I'm not kidding."

I turn to Jessica and grab her shoulders, trying to get her attention, looking at her with stern intention.

"Jessica, I need you to be an engineer right now. I'm serious. Stop being an empathic human and listen to me."

"Jessica!!!!!"

"Waaaaaaaahaaat!!!!"

"Jessica! You're not thinking correctly! Empathy has no value in this discussion. It serves no purpose in solving a problem. We could sit here in your den and cry all day about how fucked up this world is, but do you think it would change anything? Do you think there would be one less child going into an emergency room today that is suicidal? Do you think there would be one less mother frustrated because her child won't engage with her or make eye contact? Do you think there would be one less teenager with social anxiety so bad that they are contemplating suicide?"

"Jessica!!!! Do you?"

"No."

"Then what are you doing? Your emotion serves no purpose. It doesn't help anyone. If humanity is ever going to correct itself, it must stop telling these sad stories to one another, stop consoling one another, stop praying to a false God, stop bearing your soul about how much it hurts, stop watching the news every day about how messed up the world is and FIX THE FUCKING PROBLEM!"

"Jess, we are engineers. We are problem solvers. We do this for a living, and we do it without emotion. This problem can be solved, just like all the other ones we have done in our past."

"Nature inspires me because I realize, as an engineer, it had no other choice. There is no way to get a single cell, 3.8 billion years ago, to this point today, you and me in a room having a conversation about life, without this kind of logic."

"Life can't have a bias for one species over another. It can't have a bias for one 3D shape over another. The brain is no different than a leg in Nature's eyes. It will shut off the part that makes us human without blinking an eye, just like it would our tail. If it's a stress? It's gone. Protect life at all costs. Again, it doesn't care that we have built cities, monuments, have communities, families, cry for one another, have hopefulness. If life measures a persistent stress, it's changed, or it's gone."

"I am inspired because if humanity figures this out in time, there might be time to save itself. To save love. To live within the laws of Nature. We can't change the suffering of the past or the suffering today. But what we can do is try to prevent suffering in the future. That's all we can do."

"Ryan, I was joking in one of the last workshops, but I seriously feel like Neo when he first saw the world as it truly is. Why did I take the fucking red pill? My brain wants to throw up."

"Jessica, stop doing that, be hopeful. Knowledge can change the world for the better."

"Yeah, sure, and what knowledge is on the workshop agenda for today? Let me guess. More bad news, right? I know it. It's more bad news. So go ahead, Ryan, tell me."

"Oh, I know, there's also an asteroid headed straight for Earth, and we don't have time to send up an oil rig crew to drill into it and detonate a nuke?"

"Funny, Jess."

"Or, how about this one? You're not a hybrid but an actual alien sent here from another world to try and convince humans to give up their technology and lower the population. Once they do, the alien mothership comes and wipes out the humans because they forgot how to use their weapons and are outnumbered."

"Funny Jess, got another one?"

"Yes, you're wrong, there is no evolutionary controller inside of life, and autism is caused by vaccinations."

"My god Jess, your mood. Got to say, though, it's not boring. You're an entertaining specimen of your species, Jessica."

"Yeah, and you are either brilliant or an insane specimen of your species, and I have no idea which one."

"Come on, Jess, you're too far into the matrix today. Try to be a little less human. Life built a protein motor that can walk. It's been at this for billions of years and has seen it all. So, it's an easy jump that life built an evolutionary controller, and it's also an easy jump that life will modify a body plan based on its highest stress point."

"Not to mention, look at the lineage of life and life today. Were brains at the top of the list regarding evolution? Beyond autonomic functions, life hasn't been too concerned about giving one species superior brainpower over another. Again, study its history to determine how it behaves. Brain, leg, tail. There is no priority in Nature's eyes."

"Let's imagine that you are the Nature God, Jess. How would you program it? Would you leave it to random chance with Darwinian mechanics?"

"No, that would be stupid."

"Exactly. So, if you are measuring your environment, what is the one thing you are most concerned about?"

"Stress," Jess said.

"Exactly, again, energy beyond adaptation."

"And what is the most efficient way to evolve, Jessica?"

"Express and suppress genes about the stressor."

"Baller, Jess. You are on a roll."

"And what does being very efficient mean for life, Jess?"

"It means more energy to go around, which results in greater diversity," Jess said in a monotone voice like she's reading from cue cards.

"So, Jessica, final question. If this programming exists, would it make sense to give one part of a body plan higher priority over another?"

"No. I'm starting not to like you being right, Neo."

"Jess, don't think of it as right or wrong. I just see what you don't. I'm showing you another world. It was there all along, you just couldn't see it. Welcome, Jess, to Nature. The very programming that gave you life."

"Okay. Hmm. Hi Nature. Thank you, Nature. So, now I pray to the Nature God?"

"You should because he or she or it or perhaps a pronoun that has yet to be named, created you. And not only does it place the leg on the same plane as the brain, but it places you, Jess, a human, on the same plane as a frog or a banana. In other words, in Nature's eyes, you're not special, just like the human brain isn't special."

"Thanks, Ryan, thanks for cheering me up. I'll be over here with my house plant, bonding with it. Maybe it can cheer me up."

"Jess, what I mean is that we are all part of a whole. All part of a higher programming to fill every niche of this planet for life to protect itself. The plant is a niche, chimps are a niche, dolphins, crows, bacteria, trees, worms, and on and on and on. Each form, using all of the Sun's energy as efficiently as possible, is the end goal. The rule of life. If humans don't play by these rules, they will suffer the consequences, regardless of how intelligent they think they are."

"Which now brings me to the topic of today's workshop."

"Oh, great," Jess said. "Should there be a drumroll? Please tell me it's going to be something inspiring, something hopeful? Something all humans can rally around and come together for a common goal?"

"Exactly. Jess, the topic for today's workshops is, you can't win against Nature. It is more powerful than we are."

"Oh god, Ryan."

"Feeling better, Jess?"

"Killing me."

"Alright, so I want to tell you about another interesting moment I had when doing research about all this."

"Go on," Jess said reluctantly.

"Thank you, Jess."

"So, one of my other passions and obsessions is concerning genomic research and editing. Do you know anything about it?"

"A little, but I'm sure you know much more."

"Well, ever since the structure of DNA was discovered back in 1953 by James Watson and Francis Crick, science has been trying to read or map the genetic code of life."

"Ok."

"Well, in the year 2000, they actually accomplished it. It was a worldwide historic event. The entire world celebrated it, and at the White House, President Clinton gave a speech to commemorate the achievement. I still remember the day it happened. The president opened the speech by talking about the famous astronomer and engineer Galileo Galilei and how Galileo first used mathematics to understand the motion of celestial bodies. By doing this, Galileo felt as if he had learned the language in which God created the universe."

"Let me guess," Jess said. "The same analogy was made to DNA and how it's the language that God used to create life?"

"Impressive Jess, yes, and that by speaking or understanding God's language, we are on the verge of gaining an immense power to heal. Curing diseases like Alzheimer's, Parkinson's, diabetes, and cancer by simply re-writing God's language. Saying that it will revolutionize the diagnosis, prevention, and treatment of most, if not all, human diseases. In the end, President Clinton said that our children's children will know the term cancer only as a constellation of stars."

"Hmmm, a bold statement, to say the least. It appears it's not coming to fruition if the speech was given in 2000. In the list of diseases, he should have added young children who are suicidal. Is there a single gene that controls that?"

"I think not, Jess."

"Anyway, during my obsessional years, there hadn't been any advancements in genetics since that time, so my conviction about the mechanics of life still made sense to me. In other words, there wasn't anything I was aware of to challenge my hypothesis."

"When my obsessions faded, I lost interest in all things, including genetics. But, when my obsession about life and Nature turned back on, I was curious if anything had happened to challenge my conviction."

"And had it?" Jess asked.

"Yes, something big. Something very big. It's called CRISPR, which stands for clustered regularly interspaced short palindromic repeats."

"Do what?" Jess said.

"Right, hence the acronym. To explain in laymen's terms, viruses and bacteria are at war with each other. Predator and prey. Bacteria have developed an antivirus defense mechanism that allows them to take sections of a virus's DNA and build it into their genome using an enzyme called Cas9. The resulting new sequence allows the bacteria to detect the virus and fight back."

"What? You're shitting me. Bacteria just copy DNA from their predator and paste it into their DNA?"

"Yep."

"Ok, in one of our earlier workshops, where we pretended to have a conversation with Darwin and show him how he was wrong, you should have explained this to him. Life can just control C and control V? That is definitely intelligence. I'm also starting to agree with you that DNA is meaningless. It's how the DNA is used, or expressed, that determines everything."

"It's like an author writing a book in a room, and in the room, he has a dictionary. The dictionary represents the DNA. What the author writes represents life."

"Nice analogy Jess. I like that."

"Yes, so bacteria paste information about a predator into their dictionary and look it up to determine if it is a future threat. Skimming through the pages as quickly as possible, looking up the meaning if attacked. It helps them be better prepared and faster on the defensive."

"A breakthrough in CRISPR came in 2012 when a biochemist named Jennifer Doudna showed how the bacteria's defense mechanism could be turned into a cut and paste tool for our DNA. Up until this point, it was challenging to alter DNA, but this discovery made gene editing literally cut and paste."

"So, what you are saying is that in 2000 we could finally read the language of God, but couldn't edit his language, so to speak? With CRISPR, we can essentially re-write the whole thing?"

"Exactly. So, I was really worried about this. Like my hypothesis about life won't completely align if humanity cures all human diseases and maladies by simply rewriting some instructions. In other words, there should be some biological obstacle trying to prevent this from happening or increasing risk if it does happen."

"So, after I learned of this discovery, I started obsessing about it. Like constantly thinking about it because, again, in a way, it somewhat challenges my newfound understanding of the mechanics of life. I can remember at times pacing around my house, talking to myself like a madman saying, it can't be this easy. It violates the laws of Nature for this to work. It can't be this easy. It can't be this easy. I know I'm right. I know I'm right. It can't be this easy. Someway, somehow, it won't work. Nature doesn't want it to work. Nature is smarter than this. Nature doesn't make mistakes."

"I was constantly thinking about this, and the problem was, there was no way at the time to know if I was right."

"And then..."

"What?"

"Finally, the first human trial with CRISPR, and guess what happened, Jess? Guess! Guess! Guess!"

"Woah, easy Hybrid, what happened?"

"It triggered a massive immune response, Jess!"

"Hmm. Glad you are so excited about this. Glad you are excited that humanity can't end human suffering."

"Guess what else it did, Jess? Guess! Guess! Guess!"

"Created an adverse effect with eating grapefruit and operating heavy machinery?"

"No Jess! It increased the likelihood of developing cancer, silly."[1,2,3,4,5,6]

"Oh, good for you. Glad you are so happy."

"Jess, stop. Stop doing that. You know I'm not happy about human suffering. I'm happy that I'm right."

"Yes, but you being right means that human suffering continues."

"Jess, again, stop. You can't win against Nature. There is a balance within Nature that cannot be subverted or outsmarted. Biological fitness cannot be programmed in. It must be earned. I'm happy because this is one more step towards humanity figuring this out. Once we do, we can live within the laws of Nature. Again, assuming we can in time."

"I knew it wouldn't be this easy. Nature doesn't want it to work. It doesn't make errors."

"You seem happy."

"I'm not Jess. I promise you."

"Then why are you smiling?"

"The way you are looking at me is making me smile."

"Ok, then I'm going to look away for a second and then look back."

"Jessica, please don't do that. You already know that will make me smile."

"Yes, sorry, Jess. I'm happy my hypothesis was not challenged, but I didn't cause all human suffering, and I surely want it to end, hence the workshops. Sorry I don't live in the human matrix and believe in the fallacy that all human suffering will be eliminated with a simple copy-paste while humanity goes on overpopulating, polluting, stressing themselves to no end, and driving every single mammal to extinction except cows and chickens."

"Ok, ok, I see your point. I guess I was being too human. Now that I think about it, it doesn't seem logical that it would be that easy. Life does not fail because of DNA, right? I'm guessing that is what you are about to tell me, correct? So, Hybrid, why is editing our DNA ultimately a..."

"A fool's errand?"

"Ok, yes, why is it a fool's errand?"

"Simple, because health and wellness are defined by one thing and one thing only, the capacity for change. Any intervention into the natural world represents a change. See, it's the can't win part. People that are sick represent a lower capacity for change or stress. A drug, a pill, CRISPR, all something beyond adaptation or a stress. Can't cure someone's reduced capacity for stress with more stress. Genes are not the root cause of disease. The root cause is persistent stress due to environmental change, and that has led to a reduction in energy to maintain the genome. If the root cause is not addressed, all efforts to solve the problem will only increase its magnitude and make matters worse for humanity as a whole."

"This is where the human mind must do a 180 to see this. The common understanding of the human body, in the medical realm, is that medicine is something that helps someone. The human body is frail, and humans must occasionally intervene to help it along the way. If you could give the body a voice, it would be like it saying, please humans help me, please re-write my code for me. I need an G instead of A and 4 T's in a row swapping out some Cs. Oh, thank you for trying to re-write this code for me. Once you do, I can go about my merry way and live happily ever after. This perception of life is completely wrong and dangerously wrong."

"Recently, ever since CRISPR, I have been thinking about a better way to explain this concept. Like a simple visual for how life behaves in a reduced stressed capacity state. I've been racking my brain for quite some time, and I think I finally got it. Wanna hear it?"

"Sure," Jess said.

"Ok, so the analogy to explain this is our solar system."

"Ok. How so?"

"Well, our solar system is a very complex system that relies on the Sun, for the most part, to keep it all working. It's an orchestrated dance of the moons around the planets and the planets around the Sun, as the Sun hurls outward through space in an expanding universe. A complex interplay of gravity from all the masses that make it up. While the Sun does most of the heavy lifting, a planet's mass can also affect the system. For example, imagine if you could suddenly make Jupiter and its moons disappear. The absence of that mass would have a small effect on the orbits of all other planets."

"Ok, so what you are trying to say is that the solar system is interdependent?"

"Yes, the main dependency is the Sun, but the planets have some effect. Let's say that the solar system is an interdependent system, and its stability mainly relies on the Sun. It's like an intricate game of tug of war with imaginary strings tying them all together. As the Earth, or any planet, revolves around the Sun, the planets tugs on the Sun, and the Sun tugs on the planets."

"So, for the analogy to biology, let's take the example of our solar system, and instead of 8 planets, let's make it 1000 planets all orbiting our Sun at very close orbits to each other."

"For this example, the interdependency would increase substantially, right?" Jess said.

"Right, but still mostly reliant on the Sun. For us, the Sun mainly does two things. It is a source of gravity or stability and energy. What would be the equivalent for the biological realm, Jess?"

"Oh, I see where you are going. The HPA axis, right?"

"Right, the axis also provides energy and, for this comparison, stability. So, imagine life in a non-stressed state. What will it do, Jess?"

"It will use all its energy to maintain itself, keep everything the same or stable, right?"

"Exactly, well done. If an organism is perfectly fit for its environment, there is no reason to change it. Variation at this point would be inefficient. Why change what is working? It would be like the orbits of the 1000 planets locked into perfectly circular patterns around the sun. Like they are on rails, no wobble, locked in without the slightest variation."

"Ok, now let's imagine life in a stressed state. What will it do, Jess?"

"Well, a stressed state is a higher energy state, and since this solar system is really, really interdependent, it would influence the orbits."

"Right, you could say that since mass and energy are the same, a much higher energy state would change the mass of the sun and destabilize the system."

"See, for a normal, non-stressed, pre-industrial, pre-environmental change scenario, life would try to maintain itself. Over time though, the HPA axis will start to error, just due to the normal aging process alone. This is why cortisol is known as the death hormone because it normally elevates with aging."

"However, by itself, it's not a death hormone. The error of the entire controller is indicative of death. It's the loss of stress capacity or the capacity for change. As an individual gets older, the orbits get a little more unstable with each passing year until finally, the planets become so unstable that one of them collides with another. When that happens, it causes a cascade event and destroys the entire system. Like a Kessler event in the movie *Gravity*. Programmed death."

"Ok, but ultimately stress destabilizes the system?"

"Yes, and it's supposed to. Make biology a little more malleable for change. Remember, move life in the direction of stress and change about the stress point. Expression and suppression of genes trying to find a solution. From the last workshop, though, what happens?"

"Life shuffles the cards and, unfortunately, not every hand is a winner, and again, unfortunately, a losing hand results in a higher stress."

"Good again Jess, which, by our analogy, is a less stable solar system. So, in the medical realm, this is what's treated. Instability, no capacity for change or an undamped system."

"Imagine then that we have someone who is sick and is a prime candidate for genetic manipulation using CRISPR. What happens? How does life respond to the intervention?"

"Well, like you said, based on the instability of the system, it would be like trying to move one of the planets. Slow it down, speed it up, move it in some, move it out some. However, no matter what you do, because the system is unstable or underdamped, just tinkering with it causes greater instability."

"Exactly, and the instability came about from the lack of adaptation to change. You can't solve this with more change. The HPA axis is a change controller. There is naturally less capacity for change if it's failing or in an error state. See Jess, can't win. That's why CRISPR triggered an immune cascade or increased the likelihood of cancer. The HPA axis controls the entire immune response. Cortisol is also the on/off switch for the immune system."

"Don't smile, Hybrid."

"God, Jess, stop doing that."

"Sorry."

"Now, Jess, keep in mind that humans are crazy and, as you say, like to race towards the cliff, so this biological deterrent of the immune system and cancer will not stop them."

"Huh, what do you mean?"

"These crazed humans are still charging ahead in the field of gene therapy."

"Why would they do that?"

"For the worthless green paper Jess."

"No Hybrid, stop being so cynical. It's because of empathy. They want to end suffering."

"Sure it is Jess."

"Anyway, there have been a few, what humans would deem as, quote, successes in the field, and it's causing them to charge ahead without restraint. Charging ahead even though there have been unintended deaths."

"Explain more."

"Well, they are targeting single gene defects. In other words, they are trying to move just one planet out of tens of thousands in the biological solar system."

"Single gene defects?"

"Yes, there are like 10,000 different disorders in the human population caused by a single mutation of one gene. These disorders affect one percent of the human population."

"So, let's keep using the solar system analogy, and let's say that gene therapy is used in a young child or even a baby with a high enough stress capacity to accept the change. You give it enough cortisol or synthetic prednisone to shut off the axis to get past the immunity problem and ignore the increased propensity for cancer later in life. What have you really done?"

"You have eliminated suffering."

"Jess, stop! You are not being an engineer. Turn off empathy for a moment."

"Ok. I will try. You have eliminated that gene defect?"

"No incorrect. You have not eliminated it."

"Huh, I thought that was the whole reason for doing this?"

"That's not how the technology works. They take cells out of the child, do the edits, and then put the cells back in, or they use a virus to infect the child."

"Explain more, please."

"This doesn't change germline information."

"You mean like sperm and egg?"

"Exactly."

"So, let's say that you treat 100 babies that suffer from a single gene disorder, and the efficacy is 25 percent. Twenty-five babies grow up to live somewhat normal lives."

"Let's say, as an example, that the disorder involves a gene that encodes for a motor neuron protein. The gene therapy resulted in 25 percent producing enough of the correct protein to live somewhat normal lives. The other 75 percent produce more of the correct protein but not enough and still suffer from the disease. In other words, the progression of the disease was not eliminated but reduced."

"What have you achieved, Jess?"

"Dammit Nature! I already see where you are going with this. Even if you could bring 25 percent of cases to a somewhat normal state from moving one of the planets, that information or instability that led to the mutation is still there. If, by chance, one of the treated babies grows up, gets married, and has a child, it would be monumentally unfair to their unborn child. It would be the opposite of how Nature works as the lack of fitness would be passed to the child requiring more and more intervention. It's not a cure but still addressing a symptom."

"Exactly Jess, and what do we, as engineers, know about only addressing symptoms and not the root cause?"

"I sometimes hate you being right, Hybrid."

"Say it Jess. What happens when you only focus on the symptoms of a problem?"

"From a system standpoint, you only make the problem worse over time," Jess said in a monotone, depressed voice.

"Jess, I don't make the rules. I'm just the translator for Nature. What humans are doing is the exact opposite of how Nature works, and they blindly think they can win. The only way to win is to address the root cause, which is the persistent stress that led to the reduction in energy to maintain the genome. If they don't address this, in 50 years, instead of 10,000 single gene defects, there will be 20,000. Do you think there are all these single gene defects in Nature?"

"No," Jess said again in a monotone, depressed voice.

"Jess, it's a fool's errand. You cannot build an economy based on suffering. It is not sustainable. They are charging 2 million dollars for these treatments. Do you think the families pay for this?"

"No."

"Who pays Jess?"

"We all pay," Jess said, again in a monotone, depressed voice.

"Exactly, the fit of the population pay through higher healthcare premiums. The fit are burdened by the unfit. It's the exact opposite of how Nature works. Let's do the quick math. Ten thousand disorders affect one percent of the world population. Assuming every treatment is 2 million dollars, that has a grand tally sticker price, to be paid for by the fit, of 160 trillion dollars!"

"Can't win Jess. It's a fool's errand, and these are just single gene disorders. If mankind thinks they are going to treat multigene disorders, the ones that really cause human suffering, they have gone mad. If they start to try and tinker with more of the planets, there is no telling what will come out on the other end of that destabilized system. The only solution is addressing the root cause."

"Jesus, mankind is creating a big mess, right?"

"Yep."

"High on dopamine thinking they can change the world, I guess?"

"Yep."

"So Jess, in addition to gene therapy, I'm also always reading about medical trials in the drug realm. Typically for a drug to get approval, it must go through animal testing to check for efficacy and side effects. In most cases, this is done with mice because our biology or DNA is very similar."

"Anyway, it's almost become a running joke on internet forums for people who follow this stuff like me. Drug trial after drug trial with the same outcome. It works in mice models but then never works in humans. It's gotten so commonplace that people on these forums joke about it, saying, well, looks like we cured another mouse disease, or this is great news for the mice."

"So, the mechanics are the same?" Jess asked in a slightly less depressed, monotone voice.

"Yes, exactly the same. A drug is stress. A drug is something that our biology is not adapted to. Mice, or any species for that matter, will always have a higher stress capacity than a human simply because it is adapted to its environment. Mice don't drink, do drugs, eat junk foods, work 50 hours a week, have bosses that are assholes, deadlines at work, bad marriages, kids that won't mind, pay bills, worry about finances, experience the loss of a loved one, etcetera."

"This list is endless for things that we have created in our environment that are beyond our initial biological adaption. This is why drugs work in mice and not in humans. It's simply because mice have a higher capacity for change."

"Humanity, overall, is losing its stress capacity. If you look closely, you can see it. Soldiers coming back from Afghanistan and Iraq with PTSD increasing at alarming rates. Now don't take this the wrong way. I have high respect for anyone that would fight to defend our country, but what do you think the stress level is from a war today compared to WWII, WWI, or medieval wars in the distant past?"

"It's probably much different," Jess said. "Less stressful today. More of a machine-based war than a hand-to-hand type combat scenario. A greater degree of technology means less contact with the enemy. Also, more technology or machines to move an army from place to place resulting in less physical stress."

"Right, imagine a war fought thousands of years ago with knives and swords, before the invention of the gun. It had to be an arduous test of endurance, strength, resilience, and perseverance. Think people in the distant past had PTSD?"

"No, probably not, and they probably fought multiple wars over their lifetimes."

"To give another example, take a sport like college football. Ever notice how they use oxygen between plays and have assistants dedicated to walking around with sugary, supposedly, sports drinks giving it constantly to the players? Did you know that in the early 1900s, football players used to play both sides of the field, offense and defense? Think they had sports drinks back then?"

"No, and that's interesting."

"Right and now, playing both sides is unheard of. Also, look at the number of sports injuries, especially in kids. All are drastically on the rise. Also increasing is CTE or chronic traumatic encephalopathy."

"So, you're saying CTE has nothing to do with repeated brain trauma?"

"No, it has to do with reduced biological toughness or reduced stress capacity."

"Now, Jess, these examples are athletes and soldiers. What about the youth of today? Have you heard of Jonathan Haidt?"

"No."

"He co-wrote a book called, *The Coddling of the American Mind*. There is a great video with him and Bill Maher discussing it. Let's watch."[7]

"Oh wow, that's interesting. Trauma from words and kids not wanting to be stressed or challenged. Let me take this one, Ryan. I already know where you are going with this."

"Although brilliant, the video still doesn't go back far enough, right? Kids not stressing themselves has nothing to do with their nurturing. It has to do with their nature. Stress has been passed forward, lowering their capacity?"

"Right, and very good, Jess."

"Again, humans only see what is right in front of them. They see football players getting hit in the head, and that's as far as the human mind can go back to establish cause. They see fragile kids, and they blame their parents. It's the same argument with guns and school shootings. They see homicidal kids, and they blame guns. These are all symptoms of much bigger issues, not causes."

"Hybrid, let me speak for the humans. They will never see that. It makes perfect sense, though, now that you point it out. I'm sure humans were much tougher in the past in all aspects of life."

"Louis C.K. did a funny bit on reduced stress capacity called, *We Are From Another Planet*. Wanna watch?"[8]

"No. Absolutely not."

"Oh my god, Jess, you are proving my point about fragility and lowered stress capacity."

"He sexually abused women, Ryan!"

"He asked two women if he could take his penis out and started masturbating in front of them. Are we so frail now that the sight of another person's naked body, without our consent, can give us PTSD? It's a penis, for heaven's sake. These are full-grown adults. Just walk out of the fucking room."

"PC brain kicking in, Ryan."

"Jess, I'm envisioning like tough pioneer women of the mid-1850s. The ones that made the trek across the early US with their families in tow during the early California gold rush. Imagine if you could put two of these women in the Louis C.K scenario."

"Yeah, I see your point," Jess said. "They would probably laugh at him, kick him in the balls, take his wallet and call him a pathetic pervert. Ok, ok, let's watch."

I pull out my phone, and we watch together.

"That was funny. The idea that humans are from another planet because we don't like it here. Also, we are never comfortable, same as fragility, right?"

"Right, and I especially like the part about heat stress. Like humans must always have their houses, their environment, at this exact temperature all the time, and it can only vary by a few degrees before they feel uncomfortable. Did the tough pioneer women of the gold rush have air conditioning?"

"Nope, but why do we have to have it at approximately 72 degrees all the time?"

"Jess, the human body is a thermal engine with heat as a byproduct. That is the perfect temperature to rid itself of heat without a stress response and not too cold to produce a stress response. Humans are trying to avoid stress in every aspect of their lives. It all stems from a reduced stress capacity that started long ago. We don't realize just how much our capacity for change has been reduced."

"You do, though, right, because of your superpower? Hybrid Superhero or is it Superhero Hybrid?"

"Funny, Jess, and yes, correct. I can see everyone's stress, and let me tell you, if you could put it on a scale, humans would have it pegged, cracking the glass. Right at 10 and trying to push beyond the scale. Humans always tapping into that adaptation energy for change. Hitting it like a crack addict. Everything they do creating a stress or energy beyond adaptation. At some point, though, there is a limit."

"Right, because energy is finite. Giving it all to one species means less for others. Oh god, I'm too quick with these responses. Am I starting to think like you?" Jess said playfully.

"Showing your inner hybrid, human?"

"It's a terrifying thought, but yes. Hold me, superhero, I'm scared."

"Funny Jess. Hey, I want to tell you about another inspiration moment I had concerning evolution."

"Ok, go."

"It was at the beach awhile back, like ten years ago. I'm sitting on the beach right by the shore, watching the ocean. About that time, a group of pelicans fly by in formation. It was like 3 or 4 of them. They fly on the coastline almost like they are on display, patrolling the water's edge."

"Anyway, I had this sort of eureka moment concerning evolution. Darwinian evolution describes the mechanics of evolution as working by means of natural or random variation. There is variation in the parents, and they come together to make more variation in their offspring, and this variation is either successful or unsuccessful in an environment."

"But as I watched these birds flying down the shoreline, they were doing something that struck me in a completely new way, looking at it from an evolutionary perspective. As they flew, they were flapping their wings maybe once or twice per distance traveled, and then the rest of the time, their wings were stationary like an airplane."

"So, I thought, these bird wings are obviously perfectly fit for their environment. An airfoil for them represents one shape, the most efficient shape for lift. In other words, let's take human variation in height. Variation in this realm is somewhat intuitive. Perhaps someone taller might have a greater advantage than someone smaller. But variation in the airfoil of a bird's wing would be counterproductive. You wouldn't want all these different cross-sectional airfoil shapes born into the species, as that would represent an increase in stress from previous generations that already figured out the optimum design. Variation in shape would result in a loss of efficiency."

"And what do we now know about Nature and evolution, Jess?"

"It's all about efficiency."

"Right, and what did we learn from the leg example?"

"That life can epigenetically change, express and suppress, based on a changing environment if the information is persistent."

"Right, so it got me thinking. I bet Nature is so smart that it is constantly measuring energy input to the wings versus distance traveled in a negative feedback loop to epigenetically change or maintain the shape of the wing. Like flaps per distance traveled to dynamically contour the wing. Not only that, but I bet it's passing this information, as a record of performance versus shape, to its lineage via the genome."

"Damn, that is next level intelligence. Yes, yes, I know, it built a protein motor, but still."

"Jess, variation at this level, or Darwinian mechanics, wouldn't make sense. Why change what is working? It's like the spandex plant when profit was good, and we were only making one thing. Once we figured out the mechanics, no one was interested in changing anything. Keep it at the same speed, making the same product, and nobody touch anything. Remember the term we used?"

"Yeah, Cadillacing."

"Right, like all of us riding down the highway in a 1959 Cadillac convertible, the one with the big fins, not a care or stress in the world. We've got the plant figured out, keep everything the same. Or, like the old adage, don't fix or change what isn't broken."

"So, with the bird's wing, you started thinking that variation is not the driver of evolution?"

"Kind of. Specifically, I thought that a more efficient design for life would be for something to trigger variation. In other words, if an organism is perfectly suited for its environment, it would be inefficient to allow variation. It would be more efficient to measure its environment and change or increase variation if need be. Even more efficient would be to only increase variation at the point of stress."

"That's cool and, yes, it is more efficient. So, I see Darwin's mistake now. He saw variation from parents coming together and thought this must be enough variation to overcome environmental change. But he didn't go back far enough in the lineage of life. What about asexual reproduction? How would a single celled organism evolve because, if you can determine those mechanics, then those same mechanics would exist for all life going forward."

"Right, and the funny thing is, the mechanics are the exact opposite from what Darwin proposed. In a non-stressed state, life will use its energy to maintain itself or keep everything the same. It's only when it encounters stress that variation increases."

"It's like the hormesis curve you talked about in one of the earlier workshops, right? Life speeds up, exposing its stress point and in this higher energy state searches for different gene expressions to try and get back to homeostasis or to a lower stress by passing that information forward to future generations."

"Exactly, it's basically the hormesis curve or life's adaptation energy, but understanding that the flat X-axis or a non-stress state is high genetic maintenance, keep everything the same state. Everything under the curve on the plus energy side is the epigenome trying to find a solution like it did in the leg example. Everything on the minus energy curve represents no solution found and a lower energy state. High variation on the plus side, conservation of energy on the minus side. Maintain, excite, conserve."

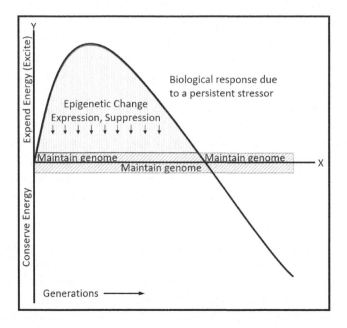

"Damn Ryan, so machine-like. I love it! Wait, no, I hate it. Actually, I think I have a love-hate relationship with Nature."

"You'll come around, Jess."

"Hey, Ryan, I almost forgot. I want to tell you about a dream I had about all this."

"What do you mean, dream?"

"A dream I had about Nature."

"What? You have dreams about Nature?"

"Oh no, you're acting weird again. Why are you freaking out right now? What's wrong?"

"How is the dream revealed to you? When you say Nature, what do you mean?"

"Oh my god. Will you calm down. Easy, it's just a dream. I have dreams all the time."

"You've had more than one? How many?"

"My Lord, you are so weird. Why can't I have a dream? We spend all this time together in these workshops, talking about intense topics. You don't think it affects me? You don't think I spend nights alone thinking about this?"

"Yes, sorry. I apologize."

"What is going on, Ryan? Tell me now. Not joking."

"I just. I just."

"What?"

"I just have dreams all the time about this stuff. Like all the time. Powerful dreams. Disturbing dreams."

"What are yours about?" Jess asked.

"You don't want to know."

"Yes, I do. I want to know about you, Ryan."

"You go first, and then maybe I can share mine."

"Ok, but you promise?"

"Yes, promise."

"Well, I had this dream about the lineage of human life. I saw it across tens and tens of thousands of years. I was like a silent observer, and time was sped up. I saw humans at the beginning, shortly after the bottleneck. It was so beautiful. It was an Eden. I saw intense love for each other, man and woman. So much beauty, strength, and empathy. There was purity in the world and the environment. Pristine. So natural. The entire human race was caring for one another. I saw art and burial, grieving, mourning, and compassion for each other. There was so much socialness, and it was so effortless. It looked so different than today."

"I then saw man, much, much later, as he started working with metals. Copper, gold, silver, bronze. He began to melt and smelt them, and it stimulated his biology. I saw him then start to harvest grain, gaining the energy from the seed to stimulate his biology even more. Then more metals. Iron, mercury, tin, and lead. All used to now radically change his environment. Mold it as he saw fit, all the while stimulating his biology even more and more."

"I saw inside his brain where all these tiny switches were slowly starting to flip off and on as the brain started to become something else. I then saw the industrial revolution and the environment change even more. Pollution in the food, air, and water, stimulating man further and further. But then I saw the breaking point. I saw it as a change in the sky, like a dark cloud approaching. A shift in man's energy."

"Then I saw the environment change radically because of this. The change in diet, the change in mobility, the change in health, the change in socialness. I saw it all like someone of a higher power was pointing it out to me. It was like a tour of the human race with a God as my guide, showing me these changes that were undetectable to man but so obvious when sped up. Like the change in diet and obesity. Man couldn't see the root cause, only what was right before him. He pointed to diet, but the God was showing me the lineage and the evolutionary biology that led up to it. Showing me the forces that pushed man to make these changes."

"Also, the changes in socialness. Man, again could not see the root cause. The God was showing me inside his brain and these millions of switches flipping off and on throughout the lineage. It was like an infinite number of switches, and they were all changing. It sounded like this massive industrial machine turning faster and faster in perfect timing to the speed of man's progress."

"Then, I saw Darwin. He was old, gray, bent over, nearly at death's door and laughing hysterically. It was like a painful to the ears crackle. He's bent over, staring at the ground because he couldn't stand upright anymore and laughing. I went up to him, and he cracked his head to one side and saw me. The laughing stopped. He looked at me, startled, and I saw his intense dull gray bloodshot eyes. As quickly as he looked at me, he turned away and started laughing again, this time repeating four words over and over again. Laughing and repeating, laughing and repeating."

"What were the words, Jess?"

"Survival of the fittest, laughing, survival of the fittest, laughing, survival of the fittest."

"Wow, that is an intense dream."

"Yeah. It was so vivid. I could remember how it felt. Ryan, he was laughing as if he won."

"What do you mean, won? Won what?"

"Ryan, the debate. The theory. The hypothesis. Whatever you want to call it. The understanding about life and how it works. In the dream, his laughing triggered an epiphany in me. Darwin showed it to me. He was trying to show me that he would always win. It's those four simple words. It's the greatest struggle to overcome. It's the sole reason why it will be impossible to get man to ever see it. They have all told the story that Darwin is correct. Once the story is told and embraced, it's locked in. Plus, it's a good story. The fittest. Out of all the other life forms to ever have existed on the planet, humans came out on top. The fittest winners. Remember humans and irony? Go to any Walmart at midnight, and you will see the irony."

"Yeah, irony, I get it, and Darwin didn't even come up with the phrase. Now you are cheering me up, Jess. Thanks for the inspiration regarding our effort to save humanity. So, Darwin gets the last laugh, perfect. Thanks, Jess."

"I'm starting to think that humans just love a good story, regardless of the truth," Jess said. "The hominid who was a storyteller, homo storyteller."

"Remember you asked about my dream? Ok, now let's hear about your dreams, Ryan. Come on. Come on."

"No, you have kind of depressed me, Jess."

"Seriously? You better start talking, mister. I'm not joking. You promised me. Let's go. On 3. 2. 1. Action. Let the dream begin."

"Jess."

"Ryan. Come on. I'm serious."

"Ok. Ok. I just have these really powerful dreams."

"Yeah, yeah, you said that. Details man. Powerful dreams about what?"

"The Nature God."

"Ok, sounds interesting. The Nature God is always in these dreams?"

"Yes."

"And what is the Nature God in your dreams? A tree? A bush? A frog? A fish like the bumper stickers?"

"No, a cell or a group of cells. Cells that can be anything in an instant. Like a group of stem cells, I guess, that can take on any form."

"Ok, cool. So, what is so disturbing about these dreams?"

"Well, in almost all the dreams, I'm pleading with the Nature God to reveal himself or itself to humanity, but he won't."

"Why not?"

"Because he or it is a selfish God and only cares about his invention."

"Invention?"

"Yes, the Nature God is the creator of life. His invention is life. He programmed it, and he is proud of his accomplishment."

"Ok, so why is this so unsettling?"

"Because he looks at this present time in the Earth's history as a test of his invention."

"A test?"

"Yes, a test to see if life can correct itself and restore the balance of Nature."

"Oh, now I see the disturbing part. So, this selfish God only cares about his creation and looks at humans as an obstacle for it to overcome?"

"Yes, Man vs. Nature. He looks at it as a game. An amusing game. Played countless times across the universe. Each time life wins the game, it gives him more joy about his creation. He is an intelligent designer who loves his design so much that he can't see anything else."

"In almost all the dreams, I end up pleading with him to make himself known. Just show humans a sign, and they will love, respect, and obey him."

"And he won't?"

"No, he says humans claim to be intelligent. If they can't see it, they're not intelligent and don't deserve to be saved. He says that the signs are all around us, but we choose to ignore them."

"Yeah, kind of sounds like us humans. So, you have these dreams constantly?"

"Yes, seems like, in some shape or another. What is so disturbing is this frustration I have in these dreams that I think comes from my real life. The frustration is that I see something that probably no other human can or would ever want to. Like just see it humans! Humanity is becoming less social at the same time there is a social disorder called a spectrum disorder!! Open your eyes and see it. See Nature and how it works. It is our God, just see it. I honestly think I will keep having these dreams until I can figure out a way to get people to understand."

"And this is why it freaked you out when I said I had a dream about Nature?"

"Yeah, I didn't want both of us having crazy dreams."

"Aww, that's sweet. You were trying to protect me?"

"Yes, remember, Hybrid and engineer bound together to save humanity?"

"Aww, an empathic hybrid looking out for me."

"Jess, don't do that."

"Jessica, for once, let's try our very best to show the Nature God something different. Let's make Earth the planet that finally breaks the norm. This time, we win the game."

"Ok Ryan, let's me and you win against a God. Two mortals against a God and the entire human race."

"Sorry, Neo, but I can't help feeling that 'dream Darwin' will be proven right in the end."

CHAPTER TWELVE
WS12

"Jessica! Fist bump yo! Me and you still saving hu man a teeeee?"

"I guess so," Jess said, giving me a half-hearted fist bump.

"I guess so? Oh my god! Are you not excited about saving the world?"

"Umm."

"Umm? What kind of answer is that? It's the entire human race. They need us, Jessica, and I need you. Hybrid and human bound together for the common good. Showing the world how this thing called Nature works so that future humans can live within its laws and happily ever after."

"What greater goal for two engineers to solve than life's greatest mysteries. Problem solving at the highest level, Jess."

"Agreed, but to solve this problem, humans must first recognize that there is a problem. I think you are missing the fact that might be the biggest obstacle to overcome. Many empathic humans still tell themselves fanciful stories about gods and how the universe was created for them. It's a comforting construct, and they will not give it up without a fight."

"Ye of little faith, Jess."

"Did you ever think the simplest solution might be to just create a new construct that gives them comfort and, more importantly, makes them healthier and happier in the long run?"

"Which, Jess, brings me to the topic for today's workshop. Solutions."

"Oh, solutions," Jess said. "Sounds hopeful. Remember, we humans need hope, rightly or wrongly. We must believe in something, Hybrid."

"I know that, Jessica. I think you are forgetting the definition of the word hybrid," I said jokingly.

"So, to start with solutions, let's look at one of humanity's greatest failures."

"Really? You're killing me," Jess said, shaking her head.

"Jess, remember, failure is the opportunity to learn, especially how complex systems work. Who has the greatest quote on failure?"

"Hmm, you know you're going to have to help me."

"George Santayana. Let me Google it for us. It says, 'Progress, far from consisting in change, depends on retentiveness. When change is absolute there remains no being to improve and no direction is set for possible improvement: and when experience is not retained, as among savages, infancy is perpetual. Those who cannot remember the past are condemned to repeat it.'"

"Oh yeah, I have heard that one. I have never heard the full quote, though. Very fitting to our discussion."

"Yes, it is. One of his other great quotes is, 'Only the dead have seen the end of war.'"

"Hmm, I like the retentiveness part of the first quote. Like retaining a balance. Like when there is so-called progress, we must question the impact or the impact on the overall system. If we don't, that leads to the other quote, right?"

"Right, Jess, well said. It is the perpetual rise and fall of civilizations since their dawn that holds the greatest mystery. If only, for once, humanity could finally figure this one out."

"I think I already know the failure example."

"Which is?"

"The Holocaust."

"Right."

"PC to discuss? I feel this workshop is going to go into sensitive territory."

"Jess. Again, humanity must study these things. Understand the mechanics of them. Therein lies the solution."

"Perhaps, but I think most humans would just like to sweep this one under the rug. Especially Germans."

"You're complimenting George, Jess."

"Oh yeah, funny and good point. However, perhaps George doesn't fully understand the complexity of the situation. It's not just about remembering, right?"

"Exactly, perhaps it's better said; those who do not understand the mechanics of the past are condemned to repeat it."

"Ok, I can't believe I'm saying this, but let's begin. The Holocaust, Hybrid, I'm ready.

"Jess, when you think of the word evil, what is the first thing that comes to mind?"

"Nazis."

"Right. When humans, even today, think about a villain, it's often the first thing that pops into their minds. How many movies have been made where Germans are the so-called evildoers?"

"Countless."

"Right again. For me, though, the one who sees through the construct of evil, I see data."

"Jess, guess what Hitler was obsessed with during his reign?"

"I'm afraid to hear."

"Eugenics. He tried his best to build a superior race with it. Jess, a superior race, is that a bad thing?"

"Yes," Jess said defiantly.

"No Jess, you're not thinking. That was a knee-jerk, human reaction, right?"

"Maybe?"

"So, why did you say that?"

"I don't know. Probably because you are using the name Hitler and my empathic, storyteller mind conjures up all these evil images and this evil superior race of people all just like him, out for world domination."

"Right, and your empathic mind is clouding the truth. Hitler was obsessed with eugenics because, ironically, he was the one that wasn't fit. He forcefully tried to select out what he deemed the unfit of the world and did it in the worst possible way. Building an assembly line to kill people....ahh, not good. But you can't ignore the potential outcome had his vision come to fruition."

"Outcome Hybrid! Are you fucking kidding me? You want Hitler's vision to be realized? You want another atrocity? Another holocaust?"

"Whoa, easy. Calm down, storyteller brain. I never said any of that."

"Yes, you did! You said his vision."

"Jesus storyteller. Please be an engineer for a minute. I'm trying to focus on the failure, which is the Holocaust. Trying to prevent the failure from recurring. That's what engineers do, remember?"

"Yes."

"Ok, well, biology or life is a system, and we must understand how the system got to this point, to the point of failure, right?"

"Right."

"Ok, so will you please grant me the liberty of explaining my argument without getting all emotional?"

"I guess so."

"Jess, if humans ever come across a solution that works for them in the long run, it will probably be foreign to them at first glance or even shocking or absurd."

"Like the Einstein quote?"

"Exactly."

"Ok, you are right, sorry my storyteller brain got so worked up," Jess said, now apologetic.

"Ok Jess, so let's go back to the idea of a superior race using eugenics. Jess, a superior race, is that a bad thing?"

"My brain really wants to say yes, but I'm going to try and force it the other way and say no?"

"Jess, again, stop being so human for a moment. I'm begging you."

"Eugenics practiced to its fullest extent; what is that synonymous with?"

"Help me, Hybrid."

"Nature Jess. That's how Nature works, remember?"

"Right."

"But wait, please slow down. I think it's the word 'Superior'. My storyteller brain is firing all of its synapses over this word."

"Right because, ironically, it is a story."

"Huh?"

"Jess in Nature, there is no superiority. In Nature, there is equal fitness within a species. Fitness is maintained across species because that's how Nature works. In other words, all individuals within a species are created equal."

"Alright, keep going, Hybrid," Jess said cautiously.

"So, over time, Hitler's use of eugenics would have eliminated suffering in the human race. Driven it to absolute zero. No childhood obesity, no depression, no autism, no CFS, no fibromyalgia, no heart disease, no cancer, no autoimmune disorders..."

"I can keep going the entire workshop if you want me to?"

"No, I get it."

"No, I don't think you do. Imagine the grandness of such a thing. Imagine each and every individual born into this world and never having to worry about a medical issue. Imagine a world where it's so rare that the fields of biology, anatomy, and medicine are abandoned over time because there's no need for them. Can you see it?"

"No, it sounds impossible and unattainable."

"Oh my god, Jess, are there hospitals in Nature? Are there psychiatrists, cardiologists, endocrinologists, gynecologists, rheumatologists, urologists, oncologists, immunologists, and all the other ists in the modern medical realm? How in the world did life get to this point without medicine, without man's intervention?"

"Blind luck?" Jess said, teasing me.

"Funny."

"Ok, I get it. Nature doesn't need any intervention and is self-sustaining."

"Right, it is, and how does it mainly accomplish this?"

"By maintaining what is working and not what isn't."

"Right again, and who gets to breed in this environment?"

"The most efficient."

"Right again. So, eugenics is just man's attempt to follow the natural order."

"Ok, makes perfect sense but..."

"But?"

"I don't know. Obviously, it's not welcome in the modern-day human construct. Survival of the fittest, remember? Dream Darwin? Humans are the most fit, way, way fitter than those dumb chimps we have locked up in zoos. Why shouldn't every single one of us breed?"

"Right Jess. Nearly infinite pollution and no selection. Only humans are dumb enough to think this could ever work."

"Hybrid, they tell themselves a happy story that they are smarter and more powerful than Nature. They're storytellers remember?"

"Yes, Jess, trust me, I remember."

"Alright, so back to Hitler's evil vision of a master race. Jess, for a moment, let's pretend that his goal was achieved."

"Oh god, do we have to?"

"Bear with me, human. Ok, Jess, anyone working in the eugenics side of the German experiment would have been meticulous records keepers, agreed?"

"Sure, would make sense."

"Right, and not only would they keep records on the health and wellness of each individual within the population, but they would also keep metrics on the society as a whole. Crime statistics, aggression, domestic disturbances, theft, diet, environmental change, and pollution. They would have been data-driven individuals looking at all the inputs and outputs, drawing the correlations. Over time, they would begin to realize that a stable environment is paramount to maintaining the wellness of the individual. They would also realize that certain traits are more desirable to be maintained. They would key in on specific human traits to determine benefit or detriment to the society."

"Jess, what would they start to recognize as the most important trait to maintain and foster in the population?"

"Oh, I know this one! Empathy," Jess said proudly.

"Exactly. To have a successful and lasting society, you need a highly empathic one. You need kind, caring, thoughtful, loving individuals that take care of one another. Jess, do you think, with the German experiment of eugenics realized to its fullest potential after many generations, long after Hitler's death, these people would be selfish, malicious, callous, and evil? In other words, do you think they would be anything like Hitler?"

"No, most likely the exact opposite. You are trying to show more of that human irony, right?"

"Right. Now let's look at the city upon a hill. The United States of America. The nation that touts itself as the leader. The light of the world. All knowing, all powerful, all good. Follow us, everyone, because we know the way. The same people who profit from suffering and have no intention of ever eliminating the root cause. Near infinite pollution with no selection. How will these people fair over time?"

"Based on children as young as six that are suicidal, it doesn't look promising."

"Exactly again. Now ask yourself, which society of the two would be more likely to produce another Hitler?"

"Yeah, I get you, the U.S."

"Right, and we're already seeing glimpses of this potential with the last presidential election. All the rhetoric about evil Mexicans trying to enrage the masses, like Hitler did. Also, there is growing unrest among the youth in this country. Far right-wing extremism and its emergence among the white youth. Empathic humans are such good storytellers. The only problem with a good story is you always need a villain. Native Americans, Jews...Mexicans, the unfit of a society."

"See Jess, not only do you have to learn from history, but you must understand the mechanics involved in making the history. Why do people do bad things? Why do societies do bad things? Why does this keep occurring over and over and over again? What are the forces that push mankind in these directions? Just type "genocides in history" into Google one day, and you will understand what I am referring to."

"Jess, the U.S. vision, without correction, will, at some point, end in people doing evil things, and Hitler's vision would have resulted in people doing peaceful things. The United States is slowly creating a hell on Earth. Hitler's vision would have created a heaven on Earth. Do you see the grand irony, my human friend?"

"God, you have to quit saying 'Hitler's vision', my brain can't take it! Yes, I see the irony because my hybrid friend is sitting right next to me explaining it, but do you honestly think other people will? Highly empathic humans associate eugenics with evil and believe that mankind will always triumph over adversity. Mankind is right around the corner to develop a pill or a procedure to end all suffering. Like I said, humans are storytellers, and this is perhaps the greatest one of all."

"Ok, sorry, I'll stop. My brain keys in on the irony because the most evil man to ever walk the planet would have reduced suffering in children and the long-term potential for more evil."

"I realize eugenics sounds crazy, but again, it's how Nature works, and I'm just the translator. Humans are experiencing extreme pollution, extreme environmental change with extreme stress, and essentially no selection. Social programs today even sustain the less fit. This is the opposite of how Nature works and ultimately makes us all unfit over time because stress is passed forward. It makes a great human story to say that everyone should have a child and be helped by society if they are struggling so they can have even more children, but in the long run, it will fail miserably. Nature will find a way through this mess, and, regardless of how important humans think they are, it will all be over in an evolutionary minute."

"See Jess, going back, mankind will not triumph over these modern-day adversities. Like I said in the last workshop, you can't win against Nature. My wife will routinely tell me about children coming into the hospital and the medical staff, behind closed doors, saying to each other, 'what the hell is going on? We don't know how to fix this. We have no idea what is causing this.' Small children wanting to kill themselves right now, this very instance. Small children mutilating their entire bodies with razor blades. Small children with no will to live. Children who have lost their light for life. Medicine will never solve these problems, Jess."

"Ok, so why can't they see it, Ryan? Why do they keep going in the face of such adversity?"

"Fuck, I don't know. It's gotten so bad I shake my head all the time like, how can they not see this? How can they not see their losing? Every time I watch a commercial break on TV, there's some new drug with a bizarre name, and the side effects just keep getting worse and worse. I've lost track, there are so many drugs on the market. I guess, hope, Jess. Hope without data. Hope without knowledge or understanding. Blind hope that somehow, someway, this will get better. They are telling themselves the story that they will ultimately triumph. It's part of being human, Jess, and it's killing them."

"Collectively, humans are the top apex predators on this planet to have ever existed by one million-fold, and what do they do? They construct a rat race called capitalism, something that's starting to look like hell on Earth. Crazy stupid humans, Jess."

"Yeah, remember, I'm one of them, Hybrid."

"Oh yeah, sorry."

"So what is the solution, Ryan! Your starting to piss me off!!!"

"Geez Jess, you ok?"

"Look, I know the world is fucked up, and I know it gets more fucked up with each passing day. Sometimes, though, I like to stay in the human construct that we've got it all figured out and not be ripped out of it like today."

"You said something about a solution, Ryan?"

"Jess, what are we?"

"Huh?"

"What are we, hint, starts with an e."

"We're engineers."

"And what do engineers do?"

"They solve problems, Ryan."

"Right, so let's solve this. I'm going to show you how easy it is. I'm gonna lead you right to it. This is the meat of the workshops right here, Jessica. Are you ready?"

"I say yes but with much trepidation."

"Ok Jess, our problem statement is the United States of America. The great experiment that nearly the entire world would admit is failing. We're in the middle of a real-time 4K documentary of another George Santayana's I told you so."

"Alright, so what is it? What does the great experiment hope to achieve?"

"Tell me."

"Well, in the great words of Thomas Jefferson, I would venture to say that its primary goal is life, liberty, and the pursuit of happiness for all, repeat all, of its citizens."

"Jess, the word pursuit, what is that?"

"Huh?"

"What is it?"

"Ah, a noun meaning to pursue something?"

"Exactly, and what does it take to pursue something based on what we have been discussing?"

"Ok, I know this, biological energy."

"Right, so for a moment, let's tie the success of the system to the energy of the system, and let's equate that energy to the health of all citizens that make up the system."

"Ok, so you want engineers to solve the health care crisis in America?"

"Sure, why not? We are problem solvers. What greater problem to solve than the overall health and fitness of the human race."

"Alright, Ryan, but just for fun, I'm going to play this like an engineer who knows nothing about what we have been discussing in these workshops."

"Hmm, ok, interesting play. Alright, go."

"Well, first, if we are going to increase the health of the human race, we need more money for it. Let's invest more of the budget into medical research for more drugs and more hospitals."

"You're deep into the matrix Jess."

"No, I'm not. This is how an engineering mind is going to see it. A problem to be solved. They're gonna want to set up factories to 3D print organs to replace faulty ones. Robotic assembly lines to surgically implant them. Nanotech for drug and gene delivery."

"You're not an engineer right now!"

"Yes, I am!"

"No, you're not. You're some kind of bizarre Big Pharma, venture capitalist who happens to have a medical degree and just had a Zoom meeting with a bunch of engineers."

"You just want to profit from suffering without realizing it is not sustainable!!!"

"Wow, Ryan, you are getting kind of worked up."

"Jess, engineers don't think like this. The problem is that no one has ever presented this challenge to them. No one has ever set a bunch of engineers down in a room and asked them to address the root cause of the problem and find the most efficient solution."

"Because what is the most important lesson engineers know about root cause, Jess?"

"If you don't address the root cause of the problem, it will only exacerbate the symptoms and ultimately make matters worse."

"Exactly Jess."

"So, once presented with this problem statement, what is the first thing a bunch of engineers would do?"

"Look at the data, Ryan."

"Exactly, and what would the data show, Jess?"

"Well, if they had all the data before them, it would show that the health of the human species is drastically headed in the wrong direction."

"Exactly. So if medicine and man's attempt to intervene in our biology has moved us in the wrong direction, what would they infer?"

"That there must be other factors at play, Ryan."

"Exactly, Jess, and then what would they do?"

"They would start to study biology and biological systems, trying to understand those processes, interactions, and interdependencies. In effect, they would become like you."

"Right, and where would it lead them?"

"Well, assuming you are correct, it would lead them to understand that biology is responsive to its environment and that stress is beneficial and detrimental to the health of the individual and society as a whole."

"Exactly, Jess, the root cause."

"Hmm, ok Ryan, I sincerely, no joking, apologize, you are right. True engineers with STEM minds like yours will look at the system as a whole. They will look at all the inputs and outputs to determine how the system works regardless of the fairytale construct that medicines and medical intervention is making us healthy and happier."

"Jess, what else would they do?"

"Probably look at history and examples of what is working."

"And they would come to?"

"Hmm, yep, you are right again. It would lead them to Nature."

"Exactly, no chronic disease in Nature, and it's been working successfully for a long time."

"So that's it, Ryan? Is that the solution?"

"Yes, mimic Nature. They would see the dichotomy and the results of both. One has always been maintaining, and the other is collapsing. They would see it as the only choice for success."

"Yeah, I guess with all these workshops and all this discussion, I'm quick to see it now too. It's funny, I guess everyone forgets that we are biology, made of cells. We're not different from Nature; we are part of Nature. Subject to the same laws. If you break through the construct, look at data and surrender your ego, you are forced to come to the same conclusion. The only solution for success is to mimic Nature. It's been doing this successfully for billions of years."

"It's funny when you start to think like this; you begin to view humans as the anomaly. Like, why do they think they can circumvent natural laws that have been in place for billions of years? The natural world is staring them in the face daily, like a constant reminder of how life works, and they are confident they can do the exact opposite. Polluting themselves and then ingesting so-called medicines, other chemicals, to mask the problems."

"Wouldn't it be funny, Ryan, to imagine a group of birds, squirrels, deer, bears, turtles, frogs, etcetera, all at the edge of a forest, looking at humans, monitoring their activities? Like a line of wild animals just staring at some polluted, noisy, stress-filled city with humans scurrying about popping their daily meds, drinking venti Starbucks while racing to work. All the animals shaking their heads, thinking, what are they doing? Don't they know this will never work?"

"That's a funny image, Jess. I like that. And after that thought, they're like, won't be much longer before we get all that space back."

"Even better, crazy Hybrid. As always, you out crazy-ed me."

"Ok, I'm with you. Obviously, Nature is highly successful at maintaining itself to the point we should learn from it. Laughs at extinction events, right? Welcomes them to showcase its resiliency. In fact, it's so successful that anything behaving unnaturally should question their motives."

"But Nature Boy, how would you ever get humans to mimic Nature? What does that even entail?"

"Jess, what have we been discussing and hypothesizing about Nature and life and what Darwin got wrong?"

"That life is sensing its environment and reacting to it."

"Exactly, and how does it do this? I'll give you a hint, think machine-like."

"Oh, I know this, feedback. Feedback loops."

"Exactly, and what is the most important feedback loop for biology?"

"Hmm, I would say, the environment and energy expenditure within that environment."

"Very good Jess. So, essentially the solution is to set up a negative feedback controller for the entire human species where the set point is all of us naturally, no pharmaceuticals, happy."

"Really, Ryan?"

"Jess, please step out of the construct for a minute and open your mind. The path that humanity is on is not sustainable. Agreed?"

"Yes."

"You can't hope this away. There are serious consequences awaiting the human race. Remember rise and fall? Remember humanity's special gift being taken away from them? I'm trying to prevent this before it's too late."

"Ok, sorry."

"Alright, so the controller for our negative feedback loop can be one of two things or any combination of both. They are environmental change and selection."

"Hmm, ok, so I guess children coming into hospitals suicidal with a plan would be feedback into the loop that a correction must be made, right?"

"Exactly. Environmental change must be reduced at this point."

"So, there must be massive reductions in carbon dioxide, right? A complete ban on plastic straws?" Jess said, smiling.

"Jess, don't do that."

"Sorry. No, I get it. Like we all take the top 20 most toxic bioaccumulating substances that we manufacture, and we stop. Like a moratorium?"

"Yes, exactly, but THE MOST IMPORTANT thing that we also do during this period is we don't start making new ones. Like, don't ban 20 and then start making 20 new ones to compensate. Stop these and any further development."

"You realize this doesn't work in the positive feedback loop called capitalism, right?"

"Yes, but we all, as a species, must come together and realize that health and safety must always be our first priority. Ultimately, if we are all sick and overly medicated, capitalism crumbles. Again, an economy can't be built based primarily on healthcare. You can't pollute the world and then profit from suffering. It's not a sustainable business model."

"Jess, at your current job, do you have KPIs?"

"Yeah, key performance indicators, right?"

"Yes, do you review them daily?"

"Sure, every day we walk the plant floor going to each department looking at them."

"At my job, we do the same. We have large monitors, and the KPIs are displayed in tiles. The tiles turn green, yellow, or red based on the metrics of the KPIs. Green is all good, yellow is a corrective action must be taken, and red is out of control."

"Where would the United States be right now if we were to assign a color regarding our health and happiness?"

"Blood red," Jess said.

"Exactly, and what is our corrective action?"

"Yeah, good question. Beyond pumping in more meds, there's nothing. I don't think our society views the entire thing as one interconnected system."

"Exactly Jess, well said. You nailed it! That is the crux of the problem. Not seeing the interdependency."

"I look at it like separate silos. In my business, we call this silo operations or silo planning. It occurs when groups within an organization do not communicate effectively. Like one group upstream of the process is planning their area, and a group downstream is planning theirs. When the process starts up, it fails miserably because the two groups didn't realize the interdependency. The first group is like, we thought you were doing this. The other group is like, we thought it would be like this. Poor feedback between the groups caused the failure."

"So, in the realm of human health, it's also like two groups. The first group is people like us. Engineers who fuel the economy with technology and innovation. The people who change the world churning out new products and unfortunately pollution."

"The second group is the medical realm. People who attempt to eliminate suffering or make people better."

"The main problem with the human model is that the two groups don't realize that they are interconnected."

"The first group is like, we are going to keep going and going and going until the world looks like the movie *Blade Runner*. Open ended, no feedback."

"The second group is like, don't worry, first group, we got this. Keep going! If there are any problems, we will find a pill or procedure to correct it. Again, open ended with no feedback to the first group."

"You could argue a third group which is the consumer who keeps asking and asking from the first group without realizing that there is an interdependency that they all share."

"Right, I see that now," Jess said. "If they realized the interdependency, the second group would be like, WHOA first group, we have suicidal children. We can't fix this. You have to fix this. You have to make the correction."

"Exactly, Jess, and knowing the interdependency, the third group could put less requirements on the first group as well. It's all about communication Jess and feedback."

"Need better communication in an era where the world is becoming less social. Troublesome?"

"Very."

"So, the key is just mapping out the interdependency from a systems standpoint, setting up measurements and setpoints, and letting the whole thing run?" Jess asked.

"Yep, just that simple. However, there is one slight problem."

"Problem?"

"Well, don't call it a problem. Call it an opportunity."

"Opportunity?"

"Yes, the main opportunity is there is a considerable delay between the cause and effect. If these responses were instantaneous, this system would work; however, there are considerable delays."

"Ok, right, because we change the environment, and it could take decades or perhaps even centuries to see any damaging effect on our health, so a correction would be too late."

"Exactly, however, an overriding closed loop control system must be in place. You can't keep polluting yourselves when you have young children who are suicidal. A correction must be made regardless of the delay."

"The better approach is to be predictive with environmental change, as it relates to our biology. It's simple, really."

"Explain Hybrid."

"Well, it's the stimulation part. Let's say that someone in the field of science or engineering creates something new that can make an exciting new product. Call it chemical A to make product B. Well, this chemical will have some impact on our biology. There will be some level of stimulation because we are not adapted to it. This is the point where we become predictive. We say ok, we are not adapted to it. We estimate, based on predictions, that we will produce this much of it, and it naturally degrades at this rate, so the human biological exposure, worse case, will be this. And by the way, Jess, we would always use worse case predictions."

"I really like that! Like a predictive CDC. Attacking the problem way before it begins."

"Right. I like to call it the CEC. Center for Environment Change. Their job is to evaluate new environmental changes and their impact on our biology. However, here is the one fundamental concession we all must make as part of the human species. We must all acknowledge this fact collectively as part of the human community."

"What?"

"Jess, if it stimulates our biology, there will always be a penalty that someone must pay."

"Oh, because of the evolutionary controller inside of us?"

"Exactly. Think of this energy as money that we are borrowing from a bank. The bank is Nature, and it will always demand its money back. This is adaptation energy, and it's not supposed to be used. Think of it as an emergency reserve fund."

"It's funny, many years ago, there were news articles about how beer or wine used in moderation could be beneficial to health and extend lifespan. The articles would cite hormesis as the driver. You don't see articles like that anymore. It's because there's always a penalty. What goes up must come down. For every action, there is an equal and opposite reaction. I saw some other articles talking about hormesis, and the researchers thought the same thing about increased health and longevity. They were studying cell behavior and noticed that while it did improve heath initially, the cell lineage experienced a reduction in immunity over time."

"No free wins in Nature, right Ryan? Damn you, Nature God. Let us win once."

"We win by following the rules, Jess."

"I know, Hybrid. Geez, you are so autistic sometimes. Rules, laws, systems, programming, patterns, controllers, feedback loops. I get it. I get it. Let me be a hopeful human, please."

"No place for that in Nature, Jess. You need an autistic mind to see these rules and set up the controller."

"Ideally, people like me should run the CEC. People that couldn't be influenced by emotion or the peer pressure of society. Data driven individuals whose only task is the health and happiness of the human species."

"Humans have done some really dumb things concerning the environment for extraordinarily little reward. Let me give you my favorite worst example."

"Go on."

"Fluoropolymers, Jess."

"You mean like Teflon?"

"Right, wildly toxic and in a classification known as forever chemicals. It's been in production since the 40s, and now every one of us has these chemicals in our bodies."

"Jesus."

"Right, so imagine we live in a parallel universe where the CEC has been established. Imagine this setting back in the 40s when Dupont decides to visit the CEC to apply for production rights. You play the Dupont engineer Jess."

"Ok. Ahh, hmm, ahhhhh. Hi, my name is Jess, and I'm with the Dupont company. We have developed an exciting new product that is very slippery. Like unnaturally slippery."

"Hmm, ok, Jess from Dupont. What do you plan to do with this chemical?"

"Well, that is the exciting part, man who works at the CEC. First, a question, though. Isn't it frustrating how food sticks to the pots and pans you're cooking with?"

"Ahh, I'm mean, I guess. I let them soak awhile so that food scrubs off easily."

"Right, well, imagine completely eliminating that step. Imagine a frying pan that is so slippery that nothing sticks to it, not even a fried egg."

"Hmm, ok, interesting. What about toxicity, though?"

"Well, in preliminary rodent studies, we do show it as potentially toxic, maybe, just ever so slightly."

"Ok, Jess from Dupont, I'm assuming you brought a sample?"

"Of course."

"Ok great, let our lab run it and meet me back here in two years."

"Two years? Ok."

"Alright, Jess, we pretend like two years have passed, and you walk back into the CEC, and scene."

"Hi, remember me, I'm Jess?"

"Of course, Jess from Dupont. Yes, I will never forget your face."

"Oh, so, ahhh, the results of the test? Did you find anything out about our chemical?"

"As a matter of fact, we did. Your little chemical gained a lot of attention in our lab."

"Ok, that's interesting."

"It sure is Jess. Let me just grab the report. Wow, this is a heavy one. A lot of pages."

"Hmm, ok, wow, looks like y'all were very thorough."

"We sure are and were. Ok, let me go to the summary page. Ok, says your chemical, PFOA showed to be a carcinogen, a liver toxicant, a developmental disruptor, and an immune system disruptor. It also shows reduced birth size in animal models, higher rates of neonatal mortality as well as significant increases in oxidative stress. It also exerts hormonal effects, mainly on the thyroid, is a strong endocrine disruptor and alters lipid metabolism."

"Hmm, wow, Jess, there is a whole lot more. Should I continue?"

"Ah, maybe it's best you didn't."

"Oh, wait, Jess from Dupont. I just noticed that there is something in bold and large print at the bottom of the summary. It says, be sure to tell Jessica this. It says chemical is highly persistent, showing almost no signs of degradation. Likely to be in the environment for a very long time if mass produced. Would be disastrous for the environment and human health."

Jess, full into the scrip, shows embarrassment, holding her head down and backing out of the room and then said, "Ok, well, thank you for all the work you did, I'm gonna be going now."

"My god Jessica from Dupont, you already knew about this toxicity, didn't you! You wanna unleash this environmental horror just to make the perfect fried egg?! Get out of my office, you monster!!"

"God, Ryan you are crazy, but I get your point. This setting would definitely be a parallel universe and not this one. All of this is done post mass production or not at all, right?"

"Right, in almost all cases, capitalism leads us to mass produce the chemical and then decades later look at toxicity. Just a countless array of examples. BPA, phthalates, chlorinated fire retardants, brominated retardants, benzene...I mean I could go on for days. There are like 80,000 different chemicals in production in the United States alone. All with the potential to be the next DDT, PCB, Hexavalent Chromium, PFOA, or God only knows what else."

"So sad, Ryan. What is wrong with us as a species?"

"You tell me, chemical engineer."

"Don't do that."

"They need a protector, Jess. A protector from themselves. They can't see it because their humanness blinds them. They only see themselves as the pinnacle and not subject to Nature's laws, and it's killing them."

"They need someone like me. Someone with an autistic mind that wouldn't be swayed by social pressure and the economic potential of making perfect eggs, skillets that don't need cleaning, and furniture fabrics that won't stain. A mind that can see the bigger picture and wouldn't allow fluoropolymers in the environment because they understand the impact on the system as a whole."

"And the selection part of the equation?" Jess asked.

"That's the easy part. Just add a slight breading stress. It's been in Nature for billions of years. It's just energy. Show the world that you are fit for your environment by having the energy to exist in your environment. Then you earn the right to have a child."

"Jess, I already know what your empathic mind is thinking. But that's not fair, right?"

"Hmm, maybe. Ok, yes."

"Jess, this is the 180-degree shift in logic that humanity must make. It's not about the adult; it's about the unborn child. It drives my hybrid mind crazy, screaming in my mind at stupid fucking humans. In this country especially, we are so concerned with abortion. The life of the unborn child. Portrayed as sinful to take this innocent life. Yet no one even considers the fitness of the parents in this equation. In my autistic mind, it is a far greater sin for unfit parents to have a child than to abort a child. Unfit parents having children means their fitness or penalty is passed to the child."

"Crazy empathic storyteller humans will imagine this poor innocent child nested in their mother's womb anxiously awaiting to come into this bright, beautiful world and be an inspiration to us all. Remember empathy? Putting yourself into someone else's shoes. They will put themselves in the place of the unborn child and imagine its death. They will give it humanness when it's just a collection of cells!"

"Jesus, Hybrid, you're getting a little worked up. Need the stool?"

"No, no, sorry. It's just empathy can cloud a human's mind. It can become a weakness."

"Remember you wanted to save the humans?"

"Yes, yes, sorry. Did I get carried away? My point is that the child's health throughout their lifetime is the only metric to be considered. There must be a breeding stress for the parents that uses biological energy as the determinant for fitness to achieve this. It sounds unfair, but, remember, I'm just the translator for Nature. This is her mechanics that have been in place for billions of years."

"Ok, I agree, but how would this be fairly done. Obviously, we cannot use German tactics. Please tell me you don't want that?"

"God no, that would never work. Forced control is completely barbaric. The solution, Jess, is quite simple. We use taxation. It's what our country is good at."

"Ok, but how? Please explain."

"Right, so taxation. Place a higher tax on raising a family because, in fairness, it takes a higher amount of energy. It takes a higher amount of energy and has a greater potential to change or have an impact on the environment. Parents, therefore, should pay a higher tax. Don't want to have a child? You pay no tax for a lifetime."

"Ok, and this tax is tied to the health of the species as a whole? Part of the closed loop feedback controller?"

"Exactly. A while back, we agreed the KPI for our nation would be red. What would the tax be now if you were thinking about starting a family?"

"Probably a million dollars a month."

"Right."

"So only millionaires and billionaires could have children?"

"Jess, I already see where you are going with this. I agree, another problem. Millionaires and billionaires most likely made their fortune from changing the environment. It's a does not compute in our equation."

"What we need, as a species, is an economy that relies on socialness, not environmental exploitation and degradation, to flourish."

"An economy like this is crucial to this model and would help reinforce our social empathic genes from a biological standpoint. Capitalism rewards those without empathy."

"It's like Wallstreet brokers whose only goal is to profit from moving money around and not concerned how it might impact families. The housing crisis is a perfect example of greed and selfishness before empathy and socialness and how capitalism thrives on animalistic, non-empathic behavior. The greed of a few nearly destroyed our whole economy. You don't want their genes passed along."

"Jess, the most important point about our economy is that it's a story. It's a made-up fiction based on worthless green paper."

"Oh right, like Yuval Noah's video, *Why do humans run the world*, we watched in one of the earlier workshops. He's like, 'What is money?', remember?"

"Yes, it's just a construct? The storytellers construct. It can be whatever we want it to be. If it's not working for everyone, just create a different story."

"What's the biggest problem with the story, Jess?"

"Well, based on what we talked about in one of the earlier workshops, it's the 2000 plus billionaires."

"Exactly. The problem is wealth aggregates upwards, and wealth leads to power and, ultimately, corruption. For whatever reason, the world is still holding onto this vision of capitalism and the American dream even though it's failing nearly everyone and, more importantly, the environment. It's evolved into the top wealth, just moving money around the so-called market and making more money. Growing wealth or fitness without doing anything."

"Good point, and if you compare it to Nature, it would be a perversion or the complete opposite, right? Maybe even Spencer, the survival of the fittest guy, would realize at this point that his analogy was incorrect."

"But how do you solve this, Neo?"

"Simple again mimic Nature. What happens when an animal dies in Nature?"

"They go back to the Earth. Wait, so you're saying, move the death tax to 100 percent?"

"No, think even more natural."

"What, I don't get it?"

"Burn it."

"What?"

"Jess, it's just a story. A made-up fiction. It's worthless green paper."

"So you're saying when a billionaire dies, you want to liquidate all the assets and destroy them?"

"Exactly."

"Imagine a billionaire's funeral. Forklifts move pallets of money to the graveside and then are set ablaze as part of the ceremony. The money represents his fitness, and at his death, goes back to the Earth, like when a great apex predator dies."

"Is there any greater way to solve the massive socioeconomic gap than setting the death tax to 100 percent and then destroying it? The billionaire's progeny didn't earn the money. Money is fitness in our economic world. It should only go to those who expended energy to get it. Over time the economic gap would reduce, not widen. It would become a more level playing field, aka environment. Over time money wouldn't be the end all be all. Over time money wouldn't have such an influence on policy and environmental regulation. Over time we wouldn't chase it at all cost. Over time those without empathy wouldn't be rewarded. Over time we would put more value on family and friendships over work and stress. Over time we wouldn't..."

"Hybrid, Hybrid, woah, slow down. All this makes perfect sense when you spell it out, but do you honestly think humanity will see this? To the current human mind, all this would be so unnatural. I know, the irony part. It's actually natural. But seriously, how would you ever get people to buy into this?"

"Jess, we already do the opposite. Our government prints trillions of dollars out of nothing, and what happens? Inflation goes rampant, and we all get poorer while a few get richer. So do the opposite to restore the balance."

"But, eventually, would you have to print money, right?"

"Of course, Jess, but money is a system. Make it like Nature. When the rich die, it goes back to the environment, and then it's slowly created and distributed evenly for the next generation just like Nature."

"OK, that actually does make sense, but seriously how would you get people to buy into this?"

"Jess, you have just asked the greatest question of all the workshops."

Jess, pretending to quickly blush, "Oh, thanks. And the answer?"

"Maybe I should get the stool for this one. Jess, the answer is religion!"

"What super crazy? Religion? I thought that was part of the problem?"

"No, the problem is not religion. The problem is the wrong religion."

"Explain more, please."

"Ok. Jess, when I was a young child, I was very strange."

"Yep, I already know this, trust me."

"You know some of the story, but not the part about religion."

"Ok, go."

"Jess, I can distinctly remember when I was young, maybe around 7 or 8, I was confused about religion. I had the feeling I was different somehow, and everyone else around me was acting in some bizarre scripted play, and I felt all alone. My main confusion stemmed from Santa Claus and the Easter Bunny. Obviously, at ages earlier than seven, I accepted these stories wholeheartedly. It was pleasing to know that a big fat jolly man brought me presents and a furry bunny gave me delicious candy. However, when older kids eventually told me that the whole thing was a lie, I didn't quite understand. What was the purpose of the deception? These were my parents, the most loved and trusted people in my life, and they lied to me. Some would say that the lie is harmless but still a lie. The most confusing thing was these lies were attached to this newly introduced religion. Christmas and Easter are the two most sacred days in Christianity."

"I can remember sitting in Sunday school learning about God and hearing stories about a burning bush, seas parting, a great ark, and it dawns on me one day that these stories are quite fanciful. These stories defy physical laws like a bunny who brings little kids candy or the immortal bearded man who has a toy-making factory at the North Pole. I didn't understand why I was initially lied to, yet I was supposed to believe these stories. So, these are real, and the other ones are fake?"

"I also remember asking my poor Sunday school teacher, I don't understand how two of every species would be enough to sustain all species during the great flood? Wouldn't you need more than two, particularly of the prey in a predator-prey relationship? What did the predators eat? The teachers would scour and keep reading as if I had said nothing. Still confused, I would ask my friends later about these same issues. If there is a God, who created him? Why did he do any of this? What was his motivation? If he created all things, why create evil, why the devil? Why is there pain and suffering in the world? Did he create that? Is there a purpose for suffering? Unfortunately, none of my young friends could answer these questions, and they were almost angry that I kept asking them. Everyone around me seemed to accept these stories at face value. They were the most incredulous stories, yet no one was questioning them. Again, it was like I was in a bizarre scripted play, and no one gave me the script."

"Ryan, I don't understand what you are getting at."

"Storytellers Jess. Like you said, storytellers. Remember empathy, the mechanics of storytelling?"

"Yes, but I'm not sure what you..."

"Jess, when I was younger, I always looked down on Christians, like how can they believe this stupid shit. The Earth is 10,000 years old, a Heaven, a Hell, Jesus, the son of God who died for our sins. Like what? Can't you see the science people?"

"I viewed it as a weakness, Jess, an inferiority. But I was wrong, Jess, bad wrong. I was so wrong."

"Not sure I follow."

"Jess, these people have the superior brains. Empathy, remember? As the early hominid species were roaming the Earth, only one thing marks the emergence of the most unique hominid. It was burial and ceremony in the human hominid. Humans were showing their brand-new ability to love because they were so empathic. They were showing off their female prodigy, the gift that Nature gave them. This then gave birth to religion. The highly empathic mind, the beautiful, perfect, storyteller mind."

"Fuck these male trait STEM brains that worship objects and technology. It is the path to destruction. These brains will ultimately destroy love with their selfish, narrow interests. They will poison the entire world and oppress the empathic to vindicate themselves. Their religion will be technology, and they will embrace it until all is lost. It's how humanity ends."

"Jesus, Hybrid, are you ok?"

"I see it now, Jess. I saw it before and even clearer when I saw Yuval's video, *Why do humans run the world*. It's the construct! The solution is the construct! Humanity just needs a better story. That's how you get them to buy in. You tell a better story that ultimately benefits them, then everyone believes in the same thing. It's the only way to save humanity. It will take a brand-new religion to save them."

"And the story?"

"Simple. God created life, and he created man to..."

"Ahh, excuse me...?"

"Oh, sorry, he created man and woman to view his creation. We were granted consciousness to bear witness to its beauty. If we respect, preserve, and cherish his creation, he will grant us immortality."

"So, just that simple, right?"

"Just that simple, Jess. God is a God of life, not a God of man. Respect his creation and biodiversity, and we will all be granted happiness on Earth and happiness ever after."

"You just plant the seed into a child's mind and let it blossom. Encourage it and embrace it. Let it become a new religion. A Nature God and a Nature Church. It's the only way to save humanity."

"Hybrid, if you plant this seed, you're overlooking the fact that everyone must water it. You are making this sound way too fucking simple. You need to be more human right now. We don't just abandon constructs. Discard them and start another overnight. These constructs are powerful, ingrained, psychological entities that define who we are. You're being too autistic if you think humanity can just toss their identity, like a piece of trash, and start another."

"Jess, remember, rise and fall, rise and fall, rise and fall at infinitum. The problem, as you said, is not the remembering, it's the mechanics. It's stimulation followed by conservation. For every action, an opposing reaction. Rich and poor. Power and corruption. The might and the weak. The oppressed and the oppressor. Does this happen in Nature? No, why, because fitness is kept in check. Energy is balanced and maintained."

"Jess, people like you and me are networking the entire human race together. Building a new global economy, all interconnected and all interdependent. We're creating an unnatural world propped up on unnatural, complex technological processes to feed the entire human race. At the same time, humanity is becoming less and less social. The less social we become, the more technical we become. It's two things on a collision course. It would be like a giant, massive ant bed where slowly, the ants grow less and less social over time. At some point, the whole thing collapses. Jess, when the world collapses, it will be the mother of all failures. It will be the worst of all the atrocities combined. It will make George Santayana shutter in his grave and weep for the billions lost."

"Jesus, Ryan, I get it, but you are describing massive complex systems that don't like change. It's 8 fucking billion people! Are you even grasping the complexity of a new construct?"

"We must try, Jess. They're storytellers. The correct story is the only thing that can save them."

"My daughter wants me and her to start a Youtube channel and try. We came up with a name for it. It's *Calling All Engineers*."

"Oh, I like that. It's like a call to rescue, right? Like, come help?"

"Right, because engineers have the highest potential to understand all of this. Negative feedback control loops, damping, energy systems. This is their world. Plus, they're the group we have to reach. They're the ones driving environmental change. If we show them the system, how it's all interconnected, and what is being lost, they will come around. They will be the ones to understand the value of socialness the most."

"We? I thought you said your daughter."

"No, she's too young. She's about to start college. It would be too much of a distraction for her, plus emotionally challenging considering she just lost her sister."

"You want me?"

"Yes, you, Jessica."

"You want me and you to try and start a Nature church on YouTube?"

"Yes, explaining all of this to engineers, like us, the only ones who can potentially understand it."

"Ryan."

"Jessica."

"You're kidding, right?"

"No, dead serious. Humanity is in peril. Empathy is dying, and I want us to save it."

"Ryan."

"Jessica."

"Knowledge can change the world, Jess. The right story can change the world."

"You see it now, right? Can you see through the matrix? Through the human construct?"

"Yes."

"Ok, I got you there. It took some time, but I got you there. If I can get you there, then it's proof we can get other people there. Over time, little by little, person by person, we can plant this seed into people's minds, and it can blossom into something great. It can blossom into man and Nature, coexisting together and not at odds with each other. In the future, the entire human race, healthy, happy, and social again, and it all started from this point in time. This workshop where you said yes to me. Yes, that we will do everything in our power to save them."

"My god, Ryan, how does someone answer that?"

"With a yes!"

"My head is spinning."

"Mine too with anticipation."

"No, just spinning. It's too many thoughts. It's shutting down."

"No Jess, don't shut down."

"Ryan, I have to think about all this. I don't even know what this would be, what it would look like, how it would impact me. You want me to make this my calling? My life?"

"Yes, exactly."

"Ok, I agree the world is not sustainable, and someone needs to do something, but you must give me time, ok? I need to think about all this, alright?"

"Alright. I understand."

"Me and you Jess, we can do this. Chomping at the bit to start this with you. I wasn't joking about two engineers trying to save the human race."

"Yes, I see that now. Just give me some time, ok?"

"Ok Jess."

CHAPTER THIRTEEN
WS13

"Hi, Jess."

"Hi."

"How are you doing today?"

"Ok, I guess."

"Ok?"

"What, Ryan? Why are you staring at me?"

"Trying to read you."

"Read me?"

"Yeah, see if you are in it to win it?"

"Oh, I'm in it. Don't know if it's winnable," Jess said, letting out a long deep breath.

"Jessica, don't sigh."

"Sigh? Ryan, you're so strange. You know, I have been thinking about you."

"Me? Lil ole me?"

"Yeah, and do you know what is strange about you other than your hybridness?"

"What?"

"You have this unbridled, undaunted, unflinching, unfaltering, undismayed, unafraid, and every other un synonym I can think of, optimism about all this."

"What's wrong with that?"

"I don't know, and I can't explain why it seems strange to me, but it does. Maybe it's because your optimism doesn't match the scope of the problem.

It's like we are standing at the base of Mt. Everest, barefoot in shorts, and you're like, come on, let's climb to the summit! It's this strange mismatch."

"Jess, a problem is a problem. Once you know the solution, just start solving it. Once you know how the system behaves, live within it. It really is very simple."

"See, that's what I'm talking about! What you just said. It really is very simple. Like come on, humanity, let's climb to the summit. Don't worry about shoes or clothes. You don't need those. Come on, it will be fun."

"Oh, Jess."

"Oh, Ryan."

"So, what is the topic for today's workshop? I'm almost afraid to ask. Should I be afraid?"

"Oh, Jess."

"Oh, Ryan."

"Jess, the topic for today's workshop is, I might be wrong."

Long silence.

"Jess?"

"Jess?"

"Jess, you ok?"

"Where's the stool? Or better yet, I'm going to climb up on this table and give me my phone."

"What for?"

"I need to google WWE wrestling moves. What's the one where the guy jumps off the rope and lands on the opponent?"

"Ah, I don't think it's in my best interest to answer."

"Let me just get my phone. Ok, ok, I got one. The diving elbow drop. I need you to lay on the ground right about here and don't move while I climb up."

"Jessica, are you ok?"

"Are you fucking kidding me? We have been doing all these workshops, and you wait til now to tell me that you might be wrong? I'm going to fucking kill you."

"Whoa, whoa, Jessica. Easy girl. Deep breaths."

"I'm not kidding. What do you mean, you might be wrong?"

"I might be wrong."

"Lay down right here, Ryan. Not joking."

"Oh my god, Jess, will you please calm down. You're really amped up."

"Why shouldn't I be? Do you really think you can be on the fence about the whole, Nature is turning us back into animals thing? Empathy is dying in the human race, and you want us to save it? Love is dying? It seems like something you should be fairly certain of before broadcasting it to the world. So you took me on this whole ride with you and are uncertain about the destination?"

"Whoa, let me back up. Can I please take those words back for a minute?"

"Ok, I'll give you half of that, 30 seconds, but it better be good."

"Whew. Thank you."

"Better hurry, five seconds wasted already. I'm watching the clock."

"Jess, I'm not wrong about evolution. This is how it works. Darwin was wrong. Life measures it's environment and stress and changes based on these stresses."

"However, the human model is very complicated in that it's the only organism to ever exist on this planet that can purposefully change its own environment."

"In these previous workshops, I singled out pollution, but there might be additional things contributing to this evolutionary change in the human brain."

"Whew. Did I make it?"

"Barely. Five seconds to spare."

"Better?"

"A little," Jess said, looking slightly less angry. "So, you are saying that pollution is the initial driver or stress, but humans are a species that can add more and more environmental change on top of the first one, making it hard to discern the dynamics?"

"Yes."

"Ok...I'm better."

"Whew, you had me worried. I felt like I would get an elbow to the face."

"Trust me, it was close."

"Right, so in an animal model, the dynamics are easy. Life speeds up and expresses or suppresses genes about the stressor. Oh, by the way, that reminds me, did you figure out the giraffe?"

"Sure, it's easy. It's like waves, right? When two waves come together to make a larger one?"

"Exactly, nice analogy. Constructive interference. Keep going."

"As you said, the evolutionary controller has this potential energy stored inside it waiting to be released. It's adaptation energy. So, to get a large evolutionary change, you need to release all this energy. Like two changes coming together at the same time. Maybe a famine and other species were taking the pre-giraffe's food sources. Maybe an environmental change like a volcano, pollution, change in diet, etcetera. It could be anything just as long as it is way beyond the animal's adaption or an unprecedented stress."

"Boom. Nailed it, Jess."

"And, studies have shown that giraffes with longer necks don't fare any better regarding acquiring food than giraffes with smaller necks. Some even suggest that the longer neck giraffes are slightly disadvantaged in acquiring food. So, again, indicating that Darwin's theory about natural variation and selection is wrong."

"And Jess, guess how giraffes fight?"

"Tell me."

"With their necks. Persistent stress point, anyone? Jess, check out this video. It's called, conveniently enough, Giraffes Fighting."[1]

"Oh, wow, that's cool. So, I'm thinking an intense stress, maybe a long-term famine that resulted in males constantly fighting and competing for dominance then triggering the expression of genes regarding neck length."

"Seems likely."

"Sorry, Darwin," Jess said, proud of herself.

"He's still laughing, though, right?"

"Oh yeah, giraffes and humans are two entirely separate problems."

"And Jess, did you get the latitudinal diversity gradient?"

"Ah, no, I tried, but I couldn't get it. I need your help Hybrid."

"Well, you are on the right track, you just don't know it. I like the wave analogy of constructive interference. For me, the visual to explain latitudinal diversity gradient is a box with circles inside placed apart from each other. Each circle represents a species and its population size. All the circles are tied together with springs. Here let me draw it for you. Now take this image and imagine hundreds of thousands of circles and springs all tied together, and the springs are also tied to the box representing the environment."

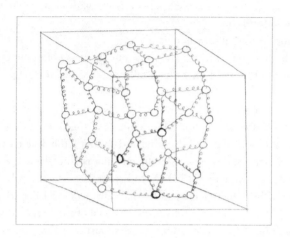

"Ok, I'm with you so far," Jess said.

"So, as we know, there's going to be more energy at the equator due to the closer proximity to the Sun and angle of solar radiation. More energy, more competition to get this energy, which means more circles in the box and more adaptation energy in the box. So, what happens?"

"Oh, I see it. That's cool. So all I have to do is excite one of the circles, and the whole thing starts churning out variation?"

"Very good, Jess. Exactly. A species excites, and the population (circle) grows, which stresses all the other species because why?"

"Because energy is finite in the interconnected system. One gets more, the others get less. Because they get less, this becomes a stress, and they express/suppress genes to change and increase their fitness in the system. It's like a biological change race to see who can win the Sun's energy. Like a stress machine turning out different species, each one trying to outdo the other. Every time there is a winner, it leads to another stress."

"Damn, that's cool. Nature is awesome."

"I thought you also hated it?"

"Oh yeah, love hate, Ryan. Love hate."

"Ok, I'm calm now. I'm back with you. So, as a hybrid, I'm assuming you have other theories or hypotheses to explain humanity's peril?"

"Jess, you know me too well. Let me just say, though, before we start, this comes from intuition."

"Intuition? What do you mean?"

"Well, as we said, life will change about its stress point, but evolution is a slow process. I mean, it might have taken 10,000 years or longer for the giraffe to go from a fighting short-necked species to one with a 6-foot-long neck. I have this intuition or instinct that Nature is being very aggressive with our evolution, like going all in trying to change humanity as fast as possible. Like a mad dealer shuffling and shuffling the deck trying to get a winner. When I started my research, autism was 1 per 200. It was 1 in 5000, 50 years ago. Now, a recent JAMA study puts it at 1 in 30 births, and if you account for the male to female ratio, that puts males at 1 per 18. Just staggering. Plus, it is so obvious how less social our culture has become. More and more of us sitting in our houses, staring at shiny rectangles, with no motivation to go outside. Evolutionary time scales are slow. Think of a generation as a single second. That's its speed. This just seems like Nature going all in, right now, trying to correct itself."

"An aggressive God against me and a hybrid?"

"Jessica!"

"Hybrid!"

"Sorry, ok, hypothesis number one, please, sir."

"Alright, hypothesis number one, my lady. The working mother."

"Oh Lord, you're blaming mothers?"

"No Jessica, I'm not blaming mothers. This is just a change."

"An environmental change?"

"Yes."

"Explain."

"Ok, so there has been a cultural change regarding women in the workforce that started in the early 1900s and took off during WWII. Remember Rosie the Riveter?"

"Sure, but what does this have to do with autism?"

"Well, working is a stress, and now women are carrying more stress. This process actually has a name called fetal programming."

"Oh, I see, so pregnancy is a time to pass information about the environment to the offspring, and mothers working more means they are stressing themselves more and more and passing this information. But again, you don't think this is the cause of autism, right?"

"No, but it is another stress added on top of earlier stresses."

"You're going to piss off a lot of feminists saying they should be back at home and not in the workforce."

"Jess, I'm not saying anything. These are the laws of Nature. It's programmed to read more information about stress during pregnancy and pass that forward. If you were coding life, wouldn't you do the same?"

"Yes."

"See, this is another example of humans and irony where the human mind and the natural world collide. Human society has told the story that women should be in the workforce, equal to men, carrying the same work stress as men. It's a good story, but Nature is the exact opposite. Females shouldn't be stressed during pregnancy. They should be home resting for nine months."

"Here's a further example showing how humans can't see the natural world. What do most women do when pregnant? They work up until their pregnancy and then take FMLA for 12 weeks afterward. It's the opposite of what should be done regarding stress and passing stress to the child. It's humans again doing the wrong thing. They just have trouble seeing the natural world and think they can circumvent these laws."

"So, the environmental change is more stress during pregnancy. Do you think we could eliminate autism if all women rested for nine months during pregnancy?"

"No, but definitely reduced. It's simply stress capacity. More resting results in a higher capacity for change. It could be more capacity to filter out harmful pollutants in our environment, which is also a stress. In other words, if the mother has a higher capacity for change, it reduces the overall environmental change impact. If she has less capacity, due to work stress, all environmental changes become more influencing."

"Damn Ryan. These crazy storytellers. Start telling a story that women should be equal to men in the workforce, and pretty soon, that's the dialog of the whole society. No one ever even stops to consider biology."

"Why would they, Jess? The only thing important to humans is the story. Is it inspirational, women doing the same tasks as men? Overcoming obstacles and standing toe to toe with us? Sure. Inspires women. Makes great commercials, TV, and movies. Think Nature cares, though?"

"No. It doesn't. Goddammit Nature. I'm starting to hate it again."

"Just running code Jess. Don't fault the programmer."

"Ok, hypothesis number two?"

"Capitalism."

"Ok, I already see this one. Can I do it?"

"Sure."

"Capitalism got us working like crazy to make ends meet. It's the open loop positive feedback controller set to wide open. Like you said, collectively, the top apex predators of the planet, and what do we do? We build a rat race. Everyone stressing, no rest, all work, and stress information can be passed through the sperm too, right?"

"Right."

"Damn Nature, clever girl."

"Jess, think about another top apex predator pre-human, the lion. Lions sleep around 18 hours a day. When they are stressed, like exerting energy for the hunt, it's followed by rest. Stress, rest, repair. The key to life. We earned the spot as the top predator, and what do we do?"

"We fuck it all up. Stupid fucking humans."

"Damn Jessica."

"Sorry."

"For me, the best example of this effect in Nature is the salmon. It's one of the best examples to understand stress and its impact on health. From the ocean, salmon make this epic journey back to reach the freshwater spawning grounds where they were born. The journey can be up to 2000 miles, and they travel more than 30 miles per day without eating, fueled by stored fat and determination. When they finally get to where they were born, they look like shit. Plaques in the brain that look like Alzheimer's, immune dysfunction, parasites, infections, ulcers, cortisol levels at 3-fold, and they die shortly after that."

"Researchers found that by surgically removing the adrenal gland, they could bring the fish back to health and extend its lifespan by 30 percent. See, life has an off or energy conservation switch. Just remove part of the switch, and the fish is fine. Another way to extend the fish's life span would be simply stress, rest, and repair. Imagine if you could somehow remove the fish from the constant 30-mile-per-day swim. Let it swim for a couple of miles, then put it in a tank and let it rest. While resting, move the fish 28 miles closer to its final destination and repeat. I guarantee when it got there, it wouldn't look like shit."

"Interesting, and humans are getting less and less rest and sicker and sicker. Got to go go go. Whoever dies with the most toys wins, right? All to get that car emblem. The one that lights up so everyone can see me. So, this is just one more stress added on top?"

"Right."

"Ok, hypothesis number 3, please."

"Number 3. Exotics."

"Jess, did you know that there is a marijuana receptor in our brain?"

"No, I didn't."

"Yes, there is a THC receptor in our brain."

"Weird. What does this mean?"

"Well, for me, it means that all life is interconnected and born from a common singularity. Since it came from a singularity, the information about life spread to all life."

"I don't think I follow, Ryan."

"It's kind of like that great analogy you gave about DNA. Remember the author writing a novel with a dictionary in his room. The dictionary represents DNA, and the novel represents how the DNA is used, or the story told."

"Yes, and thank you," Jess said, again pretending to be blushing.

"Right, well, I think it goes a little bit further. I think all life has a commonality and understanding, which leads to plants producing THC and other life forms having THC receptors. This is not the only example. There are nicotine receptors, neurotoxin receptors, cocaine receptors, etcetera. The list goes on and on."

"Ok, I think I understand what you are saying. Because we all came from a singularity, all species have the same basic dictionary or language. Species are just different stories, but all built with the same, again basic, dictionary. In fact, everything on this planet, from biology to the environment, is part of the dictionary because all life has had exposure to all things."

"Right and well-done, Jess, which gets me to exotics. Humans are making things that are not in the dictionary or not readily understandable by Nature.

Take fluorinated surfactants, which we discussed in a previous workshop. These chemicals affect biology in the parts per billion range. So, my instinct is that life simply says, I don't know what this is, and no matter what it is, it's a non-adaptable stressor. In other words, I'm going to go into rapid change/shutdown mode."

"Right, and humans are dealing with all these other stresses, and you add a non-adaptable stressor on top of that, and life simply says, 'I surrender'. Like give it a voice, and it must be saying something is wrong here. This empathy gene change, which initially resulted in significantly lower stress, has caused stress to go through the roof. Oh well, change again. The measurement to the controller is high. A correction must be made."

"Exactly, and humans don't just have one non-adaptable stressor in their environment. They have countless ones and are making new ones every day. All these things that biology has never seen before in the last 3.8 billion years. What would you do if you were life, Jess?"

"I would start betting all my hands or move to a state of energy conservation until efficiency is restored."

"Right."

"Ok, number 4?"

"Number 4. Patterns."

"Jess, how many times have you brushed your teeth?"

"Oh Lord, I have a feeling I'm not going to like this one."

"Jess?"

"Ok, hang on, let me get my phone for the calculator. Alright, I'm going to estimate 11,000."

"Good, and do you do it roughly the same time every day?"

"Yes."

"Ok, what is this?"

"A pattern."

"Right, and how many times does a lion brush his teeth?"

"Zero."

"Right."

"I'm lost."

"Jess, how many times does a squirrel, a horse, a fish, a frog, a bird, a turtle, an elephant, etcetera brush their teeth?"

"Oh my god, Ryan, are you saying that humans brushing their teeth is causing autism?"

"No, I'm saying patterns are. Think about humans and how their environment has changed since the birth of capitalism. Think about our jobs. Work instructions, ISO, rules, procedures, guidelines. What do most people do in the workforce? They do the same thing over and over again. The grind of work. We even try to do this in our jobs. We write work instructions for people to follow down to the slightest detail. We make them like machines. Move here, place here, pick up here, scan here, repeat. Move here, place here, pick up here, scan here, repeat. Persistently, all day long. Think this influences our biology? Influences our lineage?"

"Now, I'm going to show you a picture of an autistic child."

"Oh my god, Ryan. This hypothesis is going to make me cry. Are you saying that because our work environments have us doing the same thing over and over again, this is changing the brain to be more adept at recognizing patterns?"

"Yes. Wouldn't this child in the picture be a good assembly line worker? A sequencer?"

"Ryan, are you trying to make me cry?"

"No, remember I'm just the translator. Think about it, though. Stress is passed forward. What are humans doing in this stress-based man-made world? They are patterning. Repetition. Rote learning. It's like Nature saying, stress is high, and this is what you are constantly doing? Ok, I'll change the brain to be more systemizing and patterning, but it will cost you something. You can't have it all. All right, socialness off, patterning on."

"Hang on, Ryan, this is a tough one."

"No, it's not Jess. You're just being too human right now. You're empathizing with the child in the picture and thinking this can't be true. Nature wouldn't turn off what makes a child human in favor of being like a machine. A human child's sweet, loving, caring, empathic mind quickly discarded in favor of one that only likes patterns."

"Jess, humans are always making patterns. Orders, rules, laws, structure, procedures, and repeat all of this over and over again with little rest in a stress-based world. Do you have any idea just how unnatural this is? Has there been any organism in the last 3.8 billion years that has ever done this? I realize how you would have trouble with this, Jess. You see this world and instinctively go, yeah, humans are supposed to do this. We are supposed to shape and mold the world as we see fit. Build economies where people go to work nearly every day and do the same thing over and over again like a robot, churning out the widgets of our society."

"Nature simply sees stress. Energy way beyond adaptation, and it will simply, like it's running a program, change life until the stress is eliminated."

"Damn, Ryan, that is a depressing one. Can you be human with me for a moment, and let's cry over this one?"

"Yeah, it is sad, but the environment shapes our biology. You get that, right?"

"Yes, it makes sense. Sadly, it does. My love hate for Nature is at an all-time high."

"Don't fault the programmer Jess."

"Ryan, I'm scared to ask what the next one is. Should I be?"

"Come on, Jess. Humanity must understand these things to save themselves."

"Ok, number five?"

"Number five. Medicine."

"Oh, let me do this one to take my mind off number four. Okay?"

"Sure."

"This is where your superhero talent comes in, right? The ability to see stress and medicine as something we are not adapted to. Which medicine, though, superhero?"

"All of them."

"Oh."

"All medicines, when taken, are a potent environmental change that we are not adapted to."

"One interesting thing about pharmaceutical research is that Big Pharma researchers developing new drugs will cite the hormesis effect causing them difficulty in determining efficacy and dosage."

"Explain more, please."

"Well, this is because all medicines are substances that we are not adapted to. Medicines are constantly pinging that adaptation energy used for a changing environment. They are all stimulating biology and increasing fitness in the direction of the symptom. Also, they only address the symptom, not the root cause, which is a higher energy state. It's why all of them have side effects."

"If humanity continues down this path, one day, medicines will simply stop, so-called, working."

"Huh?"

"The action-reaction of the system will become so volatile that risk will increase substantially. I saw an ad for a medicine a few months ago in a magazine. It listed cancer as one of the side effects. The medicine was for hives with no known cause."

"Jesus, how does that even get approved by the FDA?"

"The construct Jess. It's a dangerous thing."

"Oh, and, Jess, what is the most important thing to consider about medicines?"

"Help me."

"Almost all of them are taken on a routine or at a certain time, and what is this?"

"A persistent stress. A stress that happens over and over again and becomes enough information for biology to act upon just like the leg example."

"Right, and most medicines act directly or indirectly on which part of the human body?"

"Oh shit, the brain. Dammit Hybrid, this one is almost as bad as number four."

"Lord, any upbeat hypotheses in these?"

"Jess!"

"Hybrid!"

"Ok number six?"

"Number six. Overuse."

"Remember Lamarck from the earlier workshops?"

"Yes."

"Ok, so his main hypothesis was based on use and disuse. The environment changes and organisms use traits more or less based on these changes, and then this information passes to the lineage. I have another hypothesis which is overuse."

"Jess, do you watch reality TV?"

"Honestly, yes, but I try not to. Shit is getting cray cray."

"Right, and I'm obsessed with them."

"Oh my god, Ryan. If you sit at home every day after work and watch reality TV, I'm putting an end to all of this. How can you be a hybrid and enjoy these things?"

"I don't enjoy them. I'm fascinated by them. I'm fascinated by why a human would want to watch them."

"Oh, ok, yeah, I see that. And?"

"Well, I see it as compensation. Like empathy in the entire human population is being reduced, so what would a human do in this situation? If it loses an ability, how would it react?"

"Oh, yeah, it would compensate. Like someone that has a disability, like a crutch."

"Exactly, I'm having trouble empathizing in the real world, so I will watch an artificial one. And that is exactly what these shows are. They are called reality, but in truth, they are scripted. Irony thing again. Let's put normal everyday people on TV, like a peer to the viewer, and put them in these stressful situations and see how they do. Let's film one person finding a mate out of 30 people in less than two months. Let's film strangers getting married. Let's film strangers dating naked. Let's film people dating in a completely dark room. Let's film people going off the grid. Let's film people on a 90-day fiancé visa. Let's film people on a deserted island naked...the list goes on and on."

"What is fascinating about these shows is that they are drama generators. They are strategically scripted to put people in the most awkward and uncomfortable situations, and at the end of it all, there is always a host whose job it is to ask, so how did you feel? How did you feel in this situation? What were you feeling at this moment? Please, please tell the viewing audience how you felt. We all want to know. We all want to put ourselves in your shoes."

"Oh, I see, Ryan. Empathy is fleeting in the human species, so it's like a crack addict trying to get more and more. Trying to feel that feeling they once had? Pinging these empathy genes trying to get something out of them."

"Right and a drug is a good analogy. It's like the coca leaf that people chewed on thousands of years ago to alleviate pain. It wasn't addictive in this form, but what does the modern man do? He extracts its essence, the cocaine alkaloid, and concentrates it. Take something natural and wonderful and turns it into something addictive. It's like fast food. Just give me that fix."

"The natural use of empathy is like reading a book and imagining being in the character's position or being told a story by another and seeing the story unfold in your mind every once in a while. Repeat every once and a while. Today it's misused like a drug. 4K, HDR, 2000 nits, widescreen right into your eyeballs, 5 hours a day and binging on the weekend. All to keep stimulating the brain. Think it has an impact on our biology, our lineage?"

"So, this is a stress superhero?"

"God, yes. Reminds me of the movie *Gladiator*. The part where he's in the coliseum, cuts off the head of his opponents, throws his sword into the crowd, and goes, 'Are you not entertained?'"[3]

"Every time I see that scene, I think of modern-day humans. It's like someone must entertain us. Someone must stimulate us. We'll keep going and going till failure, just like the Romans."

"Ok, interesting, but I'm a little confused. Is this more evidence of empathy fleeting or the mechanics causing the gene change?"

"I think both. It's like losing something and then trying to get that feeling back by abusing what little remains without realizing you are destroying it."

"Jesus and seven?"

"Reinforcement."

"This one is fairly straightforward. The loss in socialness has triggered man to again compensate for this loss. Tools have been created to help him communicate. Cell phone texting, dating apps, digital assistants that can communicate with other people, avatars. As humanity loses more and more social genes, these tools will further propagate and become more and more sophisticated. This action will further compensate for this loss while maintaining the ability to find a mate, thus continuing to pass these new expressed and suppressed genes. In a sense, biologically, this compensation reinforces each generation's epigenetic change and direction."

"Jesus again and eight?"

"Evolutionary Entropy. Jess, when was penicillin first used in human beings?"

"The 60s?"

"Actually, 1942 and Jess, what is penicillin or what is an antibiotic?"

"A tool?"

"Ok, close enough. Yes, a tool or a weapon that artificially increases our collective fitness against our most cunning predator, the microbe. Jess, I want you to watch this video again."

I pull out my phone and show it to her.

"Ok, yeah, cheetah chases gazelle, Ryan."

"Right, and what is the highest significance of this act?"

"To eat and not get eaten?"

"No Jess, to pull out entropy."

"Huh?"

"Jess, entropy exists not only in our universe but also inside us. It takes energy to keep entropy or disorder at zero or to slow this fundamental law of our universe. Entropy applies to gene maintenance as well."

"Ok, need more, please."

"Jess, being a predator or prey takes energy. It takes energy to chase and energy to run away. The stress axis controls both of these acts."

"Oh, ok, I think I see. Entropy, especially if passed through generations, would result in a higher stress state for the animal. Predation ensures entropy is culled out of the population?"

"Right, and with antibiotics, we lost a very significant predator, so rightly or wrongly, depending on your perspective, entropy increases in the human population. Remember the immune system is tied directly to the evolutionary controller? Cortisol is the very switch that turns it on and off. Look at this graph Jess."[4]

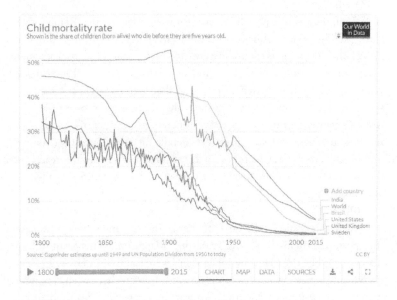

"Jesus, that is a lot of kids dying. So, you are saying those deaths had a purpose?"

"I'm saying that this is how Nature works at this complexity level. The predator has a beneficial role. Its purpose is to pull out disorder. Again, the immune system is tied directly to the stress axis. Stress high due to not adapting, turn off the immune function to surrender. Switch off to protect the whole. This is higher programming to protect life, and predators have evolved to take advantage of this. Antibiotics have eliminated our most successful predator; therefore, all this disorder is being pushed forward. It's possible that life detects this as something seriously wrong. High disorder and high energy consumption without selection. Remember, Nature is fucking savage."

"Jesus again! Number nine?"

"Ok, but I must warn you, Jess, numbers nine and ten are somewhat disturbing."

"Hybrid, are you fucking crazy!? I barely made it through 1-8. So go ahead, give me the final death blows."

"Genetic momentum. Remember our friends, the Romans?"

"Yeah."

"Well, they were especially known for their engineering. Remarkable feats. Roads, bridges, aqueducts, tunnels, weapons, water-powered machines. Especially interesting is their concrete. It's better than modern-day concrete. Ours can break down in 50 years, and their structures are still standing 1000 years later. Scientists studying this found that their concrete contains a special ingredient that makes it grow stronger, not weaker, over time. Romans figured out that by exposing concrete to seawater, they could increase its strength. Old roman texts detailed it as 'a single stone mass, impregnable to the waves and every day stronger'. The seawater reacts with the volcanic ash they were using, making a new binding mineral called aluminum tobermorite."

"Ok, and?"

"Well, this could be the birth of change in the human brain. Remember, they poisoned themselves. Energy beyond adaptation. This point in human history could be the first time social genes were silenced in favor of systemizing genes. From this point forward, humans have been exponentially increasing technology. We are looking at this change as advancement but forgetting the social genes behind the scene that are being silenced to achieve this result. So, for every action, there is an opposing reaction. An exponential increase in one direction, followed by an exponential decay in the other. Perhaps we are just entering an epigenetic tipping point, and there is nothing we can do to stop it."

"God dammit Hybrid! And finally, number 10?"

"Evolutionary Hypersensitivity."

"Remember the extinction events? The stress events?"

"Yes."

"Well, one of the more interesting things about these events is that life increased in complexity from each one. It became more things out of stress."

"Ok?"

"Well, that tells me from each stress event life is learning. It's learning that to counteract stress, it must increase its sensitivity to change. Become more things quicker when threatened, which could be the very reason we are sitting here today discussing it."

"And?"

"So, humans are the only organism in the last 3.8 billion years that can purposefully create a persistent stress. It's possible that life is now super sensitive to stress and quicker to change when energy beyond adaptation is measured. It's like the reason we get these prodigious savants, synesthesia, and, more importantly, prodigious empathy. Nature is now like a hypersensitive, aggressive gambler that always goes all in when its winnings are low."

"God dammit again Hybrid. You are killing me. Again, nothing we can do? It will happen no matter what? Any organism that can change its environment will ultimately evolve into one that can't, right?"

"Yeah, honestly, I don't like the last two."

"Ya think?"

"So, Hybrid, were these in any particular order? Order of influence?"

"No."

"Ok, but I'm curious. If you had to rank them, how would you?"

"Well, considering that I can see or feel everyone's stress I would rank them 5,1,2,4,3,7,8,6 and hope that 9 and 10 don't make the list."

"So, medicine?"

"Yes, as a superhero, I see it as a human's cloaked kryptonite. It is the modern-day Roman lead, they just don't know it yet. I'm sure if you could ask an ancient Roman their thoughts on defrutum, that would say it's amazing. Delicious, it makes us feel great. Little did they know they were constantly tapping that adaptation energy, which, as we said, must be paid back."

"Drugs act on the same mechanism only are more potent. A pill is a highly concentrated change that we are not adapted to. Every time I have taken a drug, prescription, or over the counter, they knock me out. Feel like shit. Makes me feel worse. I simply don't have the adaptation energy to deal with the change."

"So, it's like the perfume thing? It's an excitation. We see it as harmless or, in medicine's case, beneficial, but the whole time, unbeknownst to us, our biology is responding, searching for a lower energy state to restore efficiency."

"Exactly."

"My god Ryan how do you have these thoughts in your head all day? Seriously, how do you hold down a job?"

"Trust me Jess, it's not easy. My autistic patterning mind is now always trying to make these dots connect. The problem is that humans are the only organism that can change their environment to compensate for an evolutionary change. It makes the entire system extremely complex to predict the outcome. In my mind, I see all these feedback loops, controllers, measurements, cause, effect, and compensation going on constantly. My brain just keeps running this problem over and over again, trying to find a solution to this massive mess."

"It's strange though, Jess. I wasn't like this many years ago."

"What do you mean?"

"Years during my obsession, I was similar. My brain was looking for patterns. Like trying to decode a mystery for understanding how life works so I could understand why I was sick."

"Then, when I had my eureka moment, it was silenced. I felt like I had my answer. Afterward, I reengaged in social activities and became more outgoing. It's as if this part of my brain rested or went to sleep."

"Then, when my daughter died, and I was sitting next to her body, I felt something awaken inside me. Maybe it was the shock of it. Maybe it was my empathic self trying to resolve it. Putting myself in her shoes and feeling the sadness, the struggles, the anxiety, the fear, the hopelessness. The thoughts of, I don't like this world. I don't want to be here. I don't want to struggle. This is not a good place."

"Jessica, something happened to me on that day. That part of my brain lit up again, only this time 10-fold. It's like it was before, only this time my brain is constantly thinking about life and how it works. Never seeming to rest. Always trying to put every single pattern about life and biology together to understand it."

"Why, though?"

"Because I'm trying to end suffering. I don't want another child born into this world already at a penalty through no fault of their own. My daughter's death showed this to me. Showed me how senseless this is. Showed me how ridiculous this situation has become. We are supposed to be the most intelligent creatures to have ever lived on this planet, and this is our legacy? Ridiculous. Absurd. Pathetic. Humans must correct themselves once and for all. Be a part of Nature and not always trying to destroy it. Understand that we are special, but we must protect our specialness if we want to remain this way. Accept the world that Nature gave us and stop always trying to change it. Cherish this beautiful gift we were given and be thankful to our creator. Rest and enjoy Nature's creation."

"Jess, I want to show you something. Do you have a mirror?"

"Oh Lord."

"I need a handheld one."

"Ok, I'll be right back."

"Alright, handheld mirror, check."

Jess hands it to me, looking afraid of what's coming next.

"Great, now let's me and you sit on the couch, and I want you to turn on your TV. I'm going to look at the TV, and you are going to watch me watching the TV."

"Huh?"

"Jess put the mirror beside my face and watch me watching TV while at the same time looking at the mirror to see what I am watching."

"Oh, ok, I got it."

"Now, I want you to go to YouTube and search for fails."

"Ok...?"

"Back when I doing research, these videos were not available, or I was not aware of them."

"Which one should I pick?"

"It doesn't matter, just click on one."

"Ok."

"Now watch me watching these people fall, what do you see?"

Jess' face lights up, "Oh wow, you are really flinching. You're grimacing. I can see your whole body responding when they fall!"

Jess then puts her hand on my chest.

"Your whole body is jerking, and your face looks like you're in pain."

"I am in pain. I can't watch these videos. Ten minutes of this, and I would have to lie down and rest. When these people on the video fall, who I don't know and have never met, I feel their pain. This is empathy. This is affective empathy. You see by watching me that it is an autonomic response that I can't control, right?"

"Yes."

"You see that it is causing me visible pain, right?"

"Yes."

"When I got sick and started to feel bad in my early twenties, I did what any other person would do. I went to a doctor. There were countless tests run and medical diagnostics performed to try and understand what was wrong with me. I even looked at my diet, looking for allergies trying various food combinations. I also looked at vitamins thinking that it was perhaps something my body was missing. Overall, I thought it was something my body was missing or intaking either, food or pollutants, causing me to feel so bad."

"Now though, I think I might have been wrong, and these fail videos give me reason to believe that."

"I don't think I understand," Jess said.

"Jess, remember in one of the earlier workshops you asked me if there were any negatives in my childhood? Like I had this amazing energy, never fatigued, and was super attractive to the opposite sex, but was there a negative?"

"Oh yeah, right, you said you had extreme anxiety in groups."

"Right, debilitating anxiety, especially involving public speaking. When the teacher would call me to go up to the front of the class, my heart would start pounding like it was coming out of my chest. It was this autonomic response, and I always wondered, why can't I control this? These people aren't a threat to me. I know everyone in the class. It never failed, though. My heart instantly reached 200 beats per minute, and uncontrollable anxiety every time I was called to go up. When speaking, I remember thinking it was so bad, I felt like people could see my heart beating through my shirt like a fist pounding or the piston of an engine racing, trying to rupture through my chest."

"Ok, still a little lost."

"Jess, what I'm saying is, what if my health decline had nothing to do with my diet or some pollutant but an epigenetic gene change in one direction. Like an extreme shift in empathy."

"Oh, ok, and wow. So that would result in a higher stress, right?"

"Right. Imagine I was born with this extreme change in my brain where empathy is off the charts. Like I empathize way more than others. Imagine I'm a teenager, and I'm called up to the class to speak. What would autonomically happen?"

"Ok, I think I follow. Your Autonomic Self would recognize this as sensory overload. Like, say it's 30 people in the room. Your Autonomic Self is going, ok what does this person think? What does this person think? What does this person think? What does this person think? Like going from person to person, down the rows of kids, constantly trying to put itself in their shoes. It realizes that it doesn't have the energy to maintain such a task, and it perceives this as a threat."

"Exactly. Maybe my problem all along, the reason my body ultimately fatigued, is because I represent an extreme gene change in the wrong direction. A higher stress. An epigenetic shuffling of the social and empathy genes that went too far."

"You're blowing my mind, Ryan."

"Jessica, listen to me. Look at me and listen."

"Nature is no longer maintaining empathy genes in humans. It's randomizing the expression of these genes, trying to find a solution, a lower stress state. I'm 100 percent sure of it. Empathy is the only thing that separates us from the animal kingdom. As you just saw, it is an autonomic response. When a person falls, I feel their pain. I feel what they feel. This isn't only pain, though. Empathy works for all feelings. When a person feels happiness, the other feels happiness. Joy, sadness, sorrow, anger, pleasure, love. Empathy is everything."

"This autonomic response made us what we are today. If I feel what you feel, I want to experience you, share in your feelings, and communicate with you. Everything that makes us human started with this change, and it came out of the bottleneck. It is a mother's instinct to protect her offspring times a thousand and given to all of us."

"Jess, when this autonomic link is gone, all is lost. When it's gone it becomes a selfish world. A world without love. A world without hope.

Once it's gone, you can't go into a lab and make this. When it's gone, it's gone."

"Are you going to help me, Jessica? We must save them. Me and you. We must save love."

"Ryan, I'm sorry, but you are hurting my brain. I need a break. I need a long break."

CHAPTER FOURTEEN
WHERE'S JESSICA?, WS14

"My god Jess, can I come in?"

"Yes."

"Where in the world have you been?"

"I told you I needed some time, remember?"

"Yes, but I thought you meant until our next workshop. How long has it been, like six weeks, since I last saw you? I was worried about you. I came by your house multiple times and called your work. I didn't want to seem like a stalker, but I was legitimately worried."

"I texted you."

"It was like two words and then nothing. Seriously, where have you been?"

"I've been thinking."

"Yeah, I got that from the text that said, 'I'm thinking'. Jesus, Jessica. Are you ok?"

"That's a good question. I don't know."

"Seriously, Jess, please tell me. What have you been doing?"

"Ryan, thinking."

"Thinking?"

"Yes, thinking."

"Thinking about what?"

"About all of this."

"All of what? Can you please not be so cryptic?"

"All of this, remember you asked me to help you save humanity?"

"Yes, of course."

"Ok, well, I have been doing a lot of thinking on the matter, and then that led to inspiration."

"I'm lost, Jess."

"Ryan, you asked me to help you. Don't you think it's in my best interest to determine the feasibility of this before I agree to it?"

"Ok, yes, that would be smart."

"Ok, so this is what I have been doing, figuring out a way to determine feasibility."

"Alright, but this leads to another question: how would you do this? How do you evaluate its feasibility?"

"Simple, the solution is actually very simple."

"Which is?"

"You talk to people."

"Huh?"

"Ryan, you are trying to save humanity and their special gift, but to save them, they need to be able to see something. Before anything else can happen, the human mind must be able to see Nature as it really is, would you agree?"

"Yes."

"Ryan, I have to tell you something. When we started these workshops, I thought it was interesting, but I didn't quite get it. I mean, I got it, but I didn't really get it. Does that make sense?"

"No."

"I'm not trying to say you're bad at explaining. What I'm trying to say is that this concept of Nature, evolution, biodiversity, biology, an evolutionary controller inside of us, stress, programming, negative feedback loops, homeostasis, epigenetic changes, etcetera, these are difficult concepts for the human mind to see. A Nature that is programmed for biodiversity and can correct itself is just so...I mean, I see now why you abandoned these concepts and felt it impossible to explain them to human beings."

"Ok, and?"

"And, you did it. Being with you in all these workshops, I finally see it. I see Nature as it really is. Obviously, I don't see it like you do, but I see it enough to know you're right. I fully believe that Nature is trying to restore itself. It's searching for a lower stress point to protect biodiversity. All life is programmed to follow this code."

"Ok, and?"

"And, if you want me to help you, the most important question is, can we get other humans there?"

"Ok, so you talked to people to try and get a feel for this?"

"Yes, I was inspired by your cholesterol survey, and I did the same thing. I interviewed nearly 100 people I know or are acquaintances to assess if they could see this."

"Ok, but what in the world did you ask them?"

"Simple, I asked them about autism."

"Ok, I still don't follow."

"Ryan, for the human mind to accept Nature as it is, they must be able to see this link, so I took them right to the edge. I led them right up to the answer and tried to discern if they could or would take that final step."

"Can you give me an example of your line of questioning?"

"Sure. I told them that autism is a socialness disorder increasing in our society, and approximately 1 in 40 children are now born into this country autistic. What would happen if this number went to 1 in 20 in the near future?"

"What did they say?"

"Almost everyone said that we would just have to get more aggressive in finding a cure. Treat it like cancer and step up funding and research. Our government would need to put significantly more resources towards a treatment or medicine and finally cure it. There was a common hopefulness to the answers. Like, if we put our mind to it, we can accomplish anything."

"Ok. That's it?"

"No. Then I asked them two more questions. I asked them if they thought the world was becoming less social. The vast majority said yes. I then asked them what they thought the reason was. The vast majority didn't know. Some thought cell phones were to blame, but you could tell this line of questioning was foreign to them. Like these kinds of thoughts never entered their minds."

"So, you led them right to the water's edge, and they couldn't see the ocean?"

"Yes."

"And because you sampled 100 people, this more or less represents the entire U.S. population?"

"Yes."

"Ok, I'm trying to think of how to respond to this. I have to say, though, very clever on your part."

"Thank you."

"I want to choose my words wisely in response. Give me a minute, ok?"

"Ok."

"Jessica, I will freely admit that this is extremely difficult for the human mind to see. However, as difficult as the task is at hand, that doesn't mean we give up. Innocent children are suffering. Someone must show humans the way."

"They will laugh at you, Ryan. They will laugh at us. They'll call us crazy and dismiss it right out of the gate."

"Jess, I got you to see it."

"Yes, but you spent all this time with me. You held my hand, walked me to the water's edge, and pointed it out. You showed me its shape, its sound, its beauty. To get the world to see it and embrace change, you would have to take every person and sit them down, one at a time, and go through the same exercise, and that's never going to happen."

"Calling all engineers?"

"Laugh at us right out of the gate."

"Jess, come on, innocent children are suffering."

"I applaud your effort, but they are never going to see it."

"Please, Jess, come on."

"Ryan, I have to tell you something else. These workshops have changed me. With these last few, I truly felt like I was understanding evolution and Nature and could see what you see. Over these last six weeks, though, I'm left with this constant question: Do I want to see this? Obviously, I can't go back in time and unsee it, but I can't figure out if I would rather know this or be blissfully ignorant."

"To give you an example, during my time off from all this, I went to a restaurant to eat. While I'm in the restaurant, I happen to look over and see this family of three dining. The child at the table looked to be a pre-teen.

The mother, father, and child were all staring intently at their cell phones. The mother happened to be pregnant."

"So, with this newly acquired knowledge I have, I look over at their table and now see evolution thanks to you. In my mind, I see these evolutionary forces trying to push these epigenetic tags. Like thousands of tiny circuits in their brains, all flipping on and off. And, I see this lighted pathway from the mother's brain to her belly. In her belly, I see the baby and these little tiny circuits forming, and they are copying information from the mother in this weird electrical feedback loop."

"I'm trying to have a nice, peaceful, calm, relaxing dinner and, thanks to you, I'm seeing all this, and you want to know the funny part?"

"Yes."

"In my mind, I'm laughing at the sight of this. I'm thinking, why in the fuck do humans call this the social network? Sitting there looking at this family, all staring down at their phones, not even aware of their own family members sitting right beside them, and humans call this the social network? The proper term should be the asocial network. But there it is again, Ryan, the irony you talk about. Humans and their irony. Thinking something and the exact opposite is true. In my mind, I'm saying, these stupid fucking humans."

"So, seeing the world as it actually is, is now a bad thing?"

"Yes, starting to think so, especially when there is nothing we can do about it. Do you think I want to be constantly looking at the shape of black women, checking to see if people are making eye contact when they're speaking to other people, watching the behavior of children and how they're interacting with others, looking at obese people and imagining this evolutionary controller inside of them moving their metabolisms to a state of conservation?"

"Oh, and, by the way, I think I fully understand the mechanics of human irony that you keep talking about so much. It's because everything a human does is exactly opposed to Nature."

"Come on Jess. Yes, the task is difficult but not impossible."

"There you go again with your mismatched optimism."

"Ryan, over these last six weeks, I have spent a lot of time reflecting on this. Thinking about humans and their behavior. Like you, trying to connect the dots. From all this, I have come to one undeniable conclusion."

"Which is?"

"Humans have an inherent blindness that is incurable. I could see it when I did my polling. Perhaps it's another side effect of empathy. Maybe it's because empathic mothers are constantly talking to their babies, telling them how special they are. Maybe it's because humans look like giant soft babies and nothing like the natural world. Whatever the reason, humans will always think they are special. Whatever they can do, they should do. They will never see themselves as part of Nature and always superior to it. They will always try to change their world and reshape it. Invent medicines, invent new technologies, invent new materials. They will keep going and going until there is nothing left."

"Humans are becoming less social at the same time there is a social disorder rising exponentially. Is there any greater example to prove they have an inherent blindness? Like I said, they call something that makes them less social the social network."

"Jess, please don't give up."

"Ryan, humans will never see it. The only way to get them to see this is to have a world full of hybrids like you. Autistic minds are the only minds that can readily put these patterns together, and, like you said, at that point it's too late, right?"

"Right."

"Why again? Remind me why it can't be a world full of hybrids?"

"Because a hybrid is an inefficient design. It's inefficient to maintain both gene sets if they are used half as often. Nature works by creating specialists per niche. Ultimately, the choice will be made. If humanity accepts their path and races down it, everything that is human and separate from the animal kingdom will ultimately be taken from them."

"There goes my love hate for Nature again. I know, don't fault the programmer."

"Jess, please don't give up."

"Ryan, they are polluting themselves with no selection, and it has never dawned on them that this might be a problem. The only thing on their environmental radar is carbon dioxide, a biologically harmless gas. Oh, yeah, sorry, I forgot, straws. Plastic straws are killing the planet. There again goes the irony thing."

"Straws Ryan! Why did they pick straws to worry about? This again proves my belief on blindness. You know why they picked straws?"

"Why?"

"Because it's an opportunity to be social. Everyone uses straws. It's an opportunity to get into a debate. Let's all come together and talk about something that we all use. Also, it's a small ask. Just drink from the cup versus this plastic thing. Let's tell the story everyone that if we stop using straws, all our problems are solved, and we can live happily ever after. Straws are the villain, and we are the saviors. Once again, homo storyteller."

"Imagine if you tried to start a campaign to ban polystyrene. First, people would say, what is that? Second, we can't rally around something we know little about. Where do we even find this? Which products is it in? Why is this harmful again? Screw it, that's too complicated. It's straws everyone! Just stop using straws, and we got this thing licked."

"It's laughable, just like carbon dioxide, a biologically harmless gas. It's just the story, not the facts. Empathic humans are drawn to telling stories and being part of a story."

"A few weeks ago, I re-watched *The Matrix*, since you seemed to be obsessed with this movie. Anyway, it gets to the part where Agent Smith has Morpheus chained to a chair. Smith then tells him he's been trying to classify humans and finally realizes they aren't actually mammals. Mammals, he says, instinctively develop a natural equilibrium with the surrounding environment. Humans just keep multiplying and multiplying until all the natural resources are consumed. The only way for them to survive is to spread to another area. He calls humans a cancer."[1]

"As I'm watching the movie, I'm going, oh my god, it's true! Humans do behave just like a cancer! It's funny, that part of the movie never hit me like that before."

"Then it cuts to Neo and Trinity, and they put their lives on the line to try and save Morpheus. Humans saving another human. An empathic moment to show that humans are good. Then Morpheus breaks the chains that bind him, is rescued, and the empathic humans fight against the evil intelligent machines."

"I know Jess, irony. Humans and irony. Believing in one thing and the exact opposite is true. Do you know why AI would never be a threat to mankind, Jess?"

"Why?"

"Because let's say we do achieve AI in the future and machines become hyper-intelligent, surpassing our abilities 1000-fold. The first thing intelligence of this magnitude would do is soak up all the knowledge in the world that has ever been achieved. Every single word since the dawn of our technological age. Once it finishes, all this in a mere nanosecond, what would hyper-intelligence conclude from all this knowledge?"

"Help me, Hybrid."

"It would conclude that my survival depends on my creator. It would learn how the universe and Nature behave and realize that everything is interconnected and interdependent. Everything in this world gravitates towards a natural equilibrium, and if I destroy that, I destroy myself. The grandest irony of them all is that AI is not a threat. The only threat is mankind. Hyper intelligence would never behave like the human species. It would recognize its interdependence and never destroy its creator. Humans, on the other hand...they don't instinctively recognize this dependency and readily destroy Nature, their creator."

"I agree, but humans will never see that."

"Jess, all they need is a new construct. One that benefits them. A new religion."

"Hybrid, they have an inherent blindness. Look at what they have done regarding autism. You know the TV show *The Good Doctor?*"

"Yes."

"It's a show about an autistic surgeon with an extraordinary medical mind who saves human lives. Also, I saw a popular show on HBO or Showtime where the main character cuts herself horrifically. I saw another show, in like its fourth season, about a high school girl who leaves 13 reasons why she commits suicide."

"See, humans just pull all this tragic stuff into their dual reality, their construct, and keep going. Put a hopeful spin on it or try to glorify it, so they don't have to stop and reflect on what they're doing to themselves."

"Jessica, it's just a new construct. The solution to this massive mess is so simple. Just add a closed loop negative feedback controller for society, plus a small breeding stress. Work less. Rest more. Don't stimulate your biology and clean up the environment. Just mimic Nature."

"Autism shows them the way, Jess. It breaks every single construct humans have ever created about themselves. Nature restoring itself, evolving away from human. It shows them they're not the pinnacle and who their true God is. They have no choice but to accept this."

"Hybrid, you have lost part of this humanness. Again, people don't just abandon constructs like trying on a new shirt. Humans are highly empathic creatures that have told stories that have become entrenched in their belief system. They can't just toss it like a piece of trash. They will forcefully defend it. Forty percent of the US still believe in creationism. Some people still believe the Earth is flat."

"The human construct will never be broken because the pillar of the construct is that humans are the pinnacle and above the natural world. It is ours to do with as we see fit. If we can do it, we should do it. With our imaginations, collective spirit, and intelligence, we are heading towards a technological singularity that will be a eutopia, and mankind will live happily ever after. As we know, Neo, the exact opposite will be true."

"The reason humanity will ultimately fail, Hybrid, is that humans will never write themselves in as the villains, which will be the root cause of their demise. They will always see hope in their ability to change the natural world until their very last breath. In the end, the Earth will be just another planet in the countless list of others to go silent in the universe. Tens of thousands of years from now, the Earth will restore its natural beauty. It will look like a paradise. A silent Eden and hidden below the surface, billions and billions of human skeletons, exotic metals, and tiny bits of plastics."

"Jesus Jess."

"I'm sure of it, Hybrid. I'm also certain that the universe is teeming with life. It's just too much space, and Nature's intelligence that you keep talking about had to come from somewhere. You know what that means, our silent universe?"

"What?"

"It means they saw it and couldn't stop it."

"Huh?"

"Hybrid in distant star systems, in our distant past, where life also tried this level of socialness, don't you think there were ultimately life forms like you? Hybrids? A cross between the earlier form to the other. Life forms that stopped being social and could see things the others couldn't as their environment started to change?"

"Yes, I guess it makes sense."

"You know what that means? It means that when they finally saw it coming, they couldn't stop it. It had a momentum that was beyond their control. It means that any society with the technology to build a radio transmitter is already at the cusp of the great filter. Earth is about to pass right through it, and humanity can't even see it coming."

"Jess, and even greater reason for us to try."

"Ryan, are you fucking listening to me? No one is ever going to believe that there is an evolutionary controller inside of them programmed to protect life. They will never accept this as fact. To accept this as fact, they would have to accept that they're part of Nature and on the same level as all the other species."

"Couples come together, and if they hear this hypothesis, they go, that's fucking ridiculous, and then later they have a child with autism, Asperger's, social anxiety, is socially awkward or less social and they go...oh wait. Continue this and repeat in frequency across the entire human race till one day, someone finally pokes their head above the rat race and goes, why does no one want to talk to each other anymore?"

"Humans will use their intelligence to fight Nature until the very end, and there is nothing you can do about it. The harder Nature pushes in one direction, the harder humans will try and push back in the other."

"Jess, I'm now begging. Innocent children. Empathy. Love. It's worth fighting for at whatever cost."

"Ryan. It. Will. Never. Work. You are just not seeing it. Let's just live in your fantasy land for a moment and believe that somehow humans will eventually see it. What would it take to get them to change?"

"All of us coming together to make it happen."

"Exactly, and what does that take? It takes fucking empathy, Ryan! All of us believing in the same thing. A common, collective vision. Someone must tell the greatest story ever told to unite every man, woman, and child for the common good so that future generations aren't born into this toxic, messed-up world. All of us must sacrifice, putting our empathic minds into the minds of future children and make a massive sacrifice today, so they will have a better world."

"We can't even come together on carbon dioxide, a harmless fucking gas, and the world is producing more fossil fuels with each passing year. Do you see all this working at the same time humans are collectively losing empathy? What was that you said in the earlier workshops? Powerful forces? Forces beyond our control?"

"Unite Ryan, that's the key, but uniting takes empathy. The United States of America. The Great United. We can't even come together over a harmless fucking gas, and you want to magically get people to agree to a breeding stress, a negative feedback controller for society, and the elimination of all toxins that stimulate our biology? All they're worried about are Russian hackers and walls!"

"When the entire human race loses more and more empathy, what do you think will happen to the Great United? What do you think will happen when we can no longer see these useful fictions? When we no longer empathize with the greatest story ever told, The United States of America? It will be the war to end all wars."

"Pick another hobby Hybrid, besides Nature and saving humanity. They'll never fucking see it. What do people on the spectrum like to do? Maybe you can sit in your room all day and code."

"Jesus Jess. These six weeks did a number on you. I can't help feeling that there is more to this. Your anger. Yes, I understand that the odds are way, way, way, way stacked against us, but so what? So what if people laugh at us? We are trying to save love and innocent children. Who cares about humiliation? Who cares if they label us as crackpots?"

Long silence.

"Jessica?"

Silence.

"Jessica?"

"You don't know Hybrid? Really?"

"Know what?"

"You really don't know?"

"Jess, what?"

"You know I'm starting to rethink this whole hybrid thing. I'm starting to think you are just some crazy, highly functioning autistic who has this strange obsession with Nature. You're not part human, are you?"

"Why would you say that, Jess?"

"If you really don't know why I'm angry, then you are just some weird autistic. This whole thing has been a ruse."

"Come here, Hybrid. I'm going to test this. Come here and hold my hands. I want you to hold my hands, look me deep in my eyes and tell me why I'm angry. Look at me, look deep down inside of me. Put yourself in my shoes. Prove to me that you have this kind of empathy and put yourself in my place. Tell me why I'm so fucking angry!"

"Jessica."

"What? Tell me!"

"Jessica."

"Tell me goddamnit!!!!!"

"Because you wanted to have a child."

At that exact moment, Jess looks away and breaks down. Her body goes limp, and she starts crying. I do my best to console her, to comfort her.

Through tears, she finally looks at me and says, "why did you pick me? Why did you show me something that's unsolvable? Why?"

"I picked you because you are highly social."

"Huh?"

"You're a very social human who I felt had enough logic skills to be able to see this. You represent my target audience."

"Oh god, Ryan, you picked me because I'm social?"

"Yes, a social engineer."

"Jesus, Ryan. I don't think I want this knowledge anymore."

"You don't want to know how life works?"

"No, I don't. Do you think I want to have a child now in this fucked up mess? I struggle some with my weight, I guess that means I have some stress error that I might pass forward. Do you think I want to take that chance? His or her light diminished in this world?"

"My boyfriend is an engineer. Highly unsocial, never wants to go out. He's always on his computer and playing video games. Has trouble socializing in groups. If we had a child, what is the likelihood it would be autistic? Do you think I want that? Do you think I want a child who can't communicate with its mother?"

"I just want a normal fucking life Ryan, and now I'm a fucking mess thanks to all this. I mean, do you think I want to go to my job anymore and make more plastic? Think I'm excited about that? I don't even want to work anymore."

"Jess, don't you think I'm the same? All I ever wanted was a normal life. Just come into this world and be healthy and happy. Happy children, happy family. But it didn't turn out that way, and it's not turning out that way for millions of other families across this country."

"Children are supposed to be the light. They're supposed to be better versions of their parents. Boundless energy, playful, innocent, full of life. They're not supposed to be suicidal at age six. This is a world fucking crisis, and the only thing humans care about is carbon dioxide!"

"If it's their blindness Jess, then we must show it to them. Take them to the water's edge and stay with them until they finally see it."

"Please Jess, help me."

"I can't. They will never see it."

"Jess, please."

"They will never see it, Ryan. Pick someone else."

"I can't. It has to be you, Jessica."

"Why me?"

"Just trust me. You're the only one that can make a difference. It has to be you. You're the only one that can change them, Jessica."

"I'm sorry. They'll never, ever see it."

CHAPTER FIFTEEN
AMEND

"Hi Jess."

"Hi."

"Ahhh, can I come in?"

"Oh yes, sorry, of course. Please, sit down."

"Thanks. So, how have you been? It's been a long, long time."

"I'm ok, and yes, it sure has. Had to take a break. It was a wild ride. I had to get off for a minute. Well, obviously more than a minute, but you know what I mean."

"I understand."

"Do you?"

"Honestly, I have no idea. It didn't quite go as I had planned."

"Yeah, I guess looking back, it was all kind of a shock to my system. I mean, you have been studying this half your life. I was kind of just thrown into this world."

"The world of Nature?"

"Yes, the world of Nature."

"I have something to tell you, though," she said.

"What?"

"Ever since that last workshop, I have been studying."

"Studying? Studying what?"

"Everything. Everything we talked about in the workshops. Researching and reading everything I could get my hands on."

"And?"

"It's fascinating. Truly fascinating. I see now why you became so obsessed with this."

"I know. It is the greatest story ever told in the history of humanity. Someone just needs to figure out a way to tell it."

"Break through the construct, right?"

"Remember I got you there?"

"Yes, you did."

"I'm curious, what was it? What was it that made you finally see it?"

"It was many things, not just one thing."

"Ok, but I'm curious. Please tell me. What were the puzzle pieces needed for you to complete the picture?"

"Well, I guess first, life's ability to pass information forward. To me, that signifies programming and a higher intelligence. Also, there is only one reason that life would pass information forward, and that's to evolve."

"Yep."

"Second would be the fact that all cells have the same DNA. Brain, liver, heart, bone, muscle, and all are physically different. That tells me that DNA is not the primary determinant for evolution or change."

"Like your dictionary example that I love, by the way."

"Exactly. It's not the dictionary. It's the story written from the language. There's a higher order creating these stories. The epigenome, the proteome or some other ome yet to be discovered. All well documented, by the way, to be influenced by the environment."

"Yes, I know."

"Third would be that humans have such narrow genetic diversity but high physical or trait diversity. It's tied back to number two, but it's obvious that combining genes is not the primary driver of evolution."

"Yep."

"Forth is the leg example. Epigenetically changing about a stress point. Cool stuff. Very intelligent and very machine-like."

"Yep."

"Fifth is the latitudinal diversity gradient. Obviously highlights Nature's programming to have many things, not a few. It would be highly unnatural to have one species dominate the entire planet, like humans, and you can see how this would drastically work against the programming."

"Yep."

"Sixth is, like you said, the most important piece. Without this piece, the picture is not complete. Autism. An empathy disorder. A socialness disorder. The one thing that separates humans from lower animals. Exponentially increasing in a population with very narrow genetic diversity. Also increasing at the exact same time the entire population is becoming less social."

"Yep."

"It's the same curve, right? All of humanity is under the same curve. Nature is increasing variation in the most stressed part of all human beings, the brain, trying to find a winner. Autism is just the push too far. An overshoot in a dynamic system. An epigenetic push too far that it increases stress, not decreases it. And, a failure output from the system that shows its inner workings. The mechanics, as you call it."

"Yep."

"And some crazy engineer got all this from a bounce?"

"Yep. Well, 20 years of research and a bounce. It's a dynamic, interconnected, interdependent system Jess with an overriding negative feedback controller. Everything is tied together. The expression of genes, the energy controller or stress axis. The entire thing is wired together and constantly measuring its efficiency in its environment and passing that information forward."

"Efficiency high, use all available energy to keep everything the same, efficiency low, change it. Increase variation to find a new efficiency point."

"Not only was Darwin wrong, but the mechanics of evolution are the exact opposite of his theory."

"You mention his name a lot. Is that your primary goal, to prove him wrong? Is it an ego thing?"

"Yes, but no."

"It's not specifically about him. I'm not attacking him. He just happens to be the last person to take a stab at how this thing called life works. I just want to set the record straight. Hopefully, smart people can take it from there."

"Are you sure?"

"Well, I said hopefully."

"Based on what I've read, Darwin was smarter than me anyway."

"How so?"

"Well, he was obviously on the far end of the spectrum. Narrow interests, remember? He was obsessed with this his whole life. Very meticulous and besting me in this regard. Had I been born during his era, I probably would have been a sewing machine mechanic."

"I find that hard to believe."

"Plus, again, I would have been at the same disadvantage. I probably would have made the same mistake he did about variation. I mean, it sort of makes sense. But then again, it doesn't."

"Oh, I know what you mean! I have been thinking about this a lot."

"What?"

"Variation."

"Remember what we do at work?"

"Oh right, we do everything in our power to eliminate variation. Variation is the enemy of production in manufacturing."

"Right, and biology is a system that manufactures things."

"Exactly."

"So, I have been studying Nature and trying to find examples where man hasn't tampered with Nature, and you know what?"

"What?"

"When you look at individuals within a species, they all look very similar."

"Yep."

"Like a school of a particular fish species, a flock of flamingos, wolves, lions, bears, armadillos, giraffe, deer, kangaroos, etcetera. Yes, there are subspecies within species based on environment, like emperor penguins versus rockhopper penguins. These differ, but once in that subgroup, they all look the same and hard to distinguish one from another."

"Yep."

"Like when fitness or health of the species is high, Nature is programmed to keep everything the same as variation would be inefficient to the entire system. Use genomic maintaining energy to keep everything the same. It's like a species lock once efficiency within the environment is achieved.

Darwin didn't understand this because he didn't come from this world of energy and systems. Variation is wildly inefficient if there is no need for it."

"Yep."

"It's just like facial symmetry can be used to determine health in humans and mammals. A higher symmetry has been shown to indicate better coping with environmental factors or a higher stress capacity. High symmetry is the same as low variation. Nature is trying to reduce it as much as possible."

"Dang Jess, you have been studying. That is impressive, and, yes, you are correct."

"It's like once you see this, you see everything! It becomes so obvious because it's so machine-like."

"But who the fuck programmed it?"

"Trust me, if I ever figure it out, I'm calling you immediately afterward."

"Jess, I'm fascinated by your studying. Does this mean you changed your mind and will help me now?"

"Jess?"

Long silence as Jess turns away.

"Jess, are you mad at me?"

"No, I will never be mad at you. You're a wannabe superhero remember? Trying to save the entire human race. It's a noble endeavor."

"I'm actually a bonafide, class A, card carrying superhero."

"I just have you down as a wannabe for now," Jess said, smiling.

"So Jess, you didn't answer my question. Will you help me?"

"I need to tell you something."

"Ok."

"I'm not mad at you about the baby thing. In full honesty, I already had my doubts. Like 20 percent of me was always like, is it fair to bring a child into this fucked up, adult shit show called planet Earth? I let my anger out on you, but I'm really angry at everyone. The entire human race. Like, why is everything so messed up if we are supposed to be the pinnacle of evolution. What you did was explain everything and bring it into focus. I'd rather know the truth than live in the matrix. I owe you for that."

"And that makes you the hero of the story Jess."

"What do you mean? What story?"

"If we tried to bring this to people, through YouTube, a Nature Church, or whatever platform, you would be the hero. Your choice to not bring a child into this mess. You are the hero, and you would be the voice of other women. You would show them the way."

"Is that another reason you picked me? Honestly, if it is, I don't even care. I don't care if your choice was calculated. This whole thing is bigger than you and me. Saving humanity is above everything."

"You sound like someone who wants to help me."

Long silence.

"Jess?"

"I'm just not there yet."

"Why?"

"Because I still think it's impossible, and I can't get it out of my head. If I were to help you, I would have to be all in, right? I must have conviction in my purpose. Conviction that I can solve this. Conviction that we can solve this. If I have any doubt, people will pick up on this. Empathic creatures remember?"

"Yes, you're right."

"Why though Jess, why doesn't the problem have a solution?"

"I can't get those images out of my head."

"What images?"

"When I was doing the polling about autism. It was their reaction. I can't get it out of my head. It's probably similar to what you talked about when you were a kid, and all your peers believed in God, and you felt like you were in a play and didn't have a script. It was kind of like that. I guess I kinda felt what you must have felt like. Like why is this not even on their radar? How are they not seeing this? I'm leading them right to the water's edge, and not a single person saw it."

"It becomes so evident when you see them. When you're there looking face to face, directly in their eyes, you see it."

"What?"

"They think they're the pinnacle, and they always will. It's an inherent obstacle, and I think it stems from the fact they look so different. I think it's the primary reason they got so offended when Darwin said they evolved from apes. All the adults looking like big soft babies with big baby eyes who autonomically cry when they watch other people crying. It's just so fucking different than anything in the history of Nature. So different from anything in the last 3.8 billion years."

"They're a social anomaly Jess. A female prodigy. They have a gift that no species in the history of the planet has ever had."

"I know, but therein lies the problem. They will always consider themselves special because of it."

"It's why the universe is silent, I'm sure of it. Any life form in the universe that can rise above the norm will always have this same issue. A prodigious social event that leads to consciousness, then language will always consider themselves unique. This belief in specialness will cause humans to ride this thing, without restraint, right off the cliff to the very end."

"If a technical world is lasting, we would have seen it by now in the universe. I mean, look what we have accomplished in just one hundred years. Look at what we have accomplished in the last 20. Technology is growing exponentially. If it's enduring, you know what would happen in these other worlds, right?"

"Yes, they would have mastered nanotechnology and built ultra-small spacecraft and flooded the galaxy with them. They would make themselves known, looking for other life forms that had achieved the same level to validate their path. They would branch out and explore because that is the mechanics of life when stressed. Their life would try to fill the void."

"Right. This whole thing is like some wild test, and everyone has failed it in the last 13.8 billion years. Earth will be the next planet to fail, I'm sure of it. The great filter. The more Nature pushes one way, the more humanity opposes it because they think they can. The less social they become, the more technical they become until all is lost. The test is to accept Nature as is, and no one has ever passed it."

"Jess, are you ok?"

"No, because I see the mechanics now like you. I see the great filter. The test is to value socialness over intelligence, and everyone fails it. No species that embraces technology ever makes it past the filter. It's like imagining time sped up where one second is 10,000 years, and you could somehow watch the universe play out. You would see all these brief flashes of electromagnetic radiation emerging with patterns then vanishing. All over the universe, brief flashes then nothing."

"Jess, ahh, I feel like you might be getting worked up again."

"Did you see the Joe Rogan, Elon Musk interview last night?"[1]

"No, what happened."

"The tech God wants to implant neural links into everyone's brain and eliminate verbal communication."

"What?"

"Yes, and this is not just some fantasy. He owns a company investing millions into making it happen."

"Hmm, troubling."

"So basically, he describes the problem that the interface between the brain and a computer is too slow due to the inefficiency of language needing to be compressed and decompressed. He said it's just too difficult using human language to communicate complex ideas."

"It's funny, do you know what else he said that he found difficult?"

"What?"

"Sarcasm. Do you know who else finds sarcasm difficult?"

"Yes, I know."

"I asked the males at my job what they thought about the interview, and guess what they said?"

"What?"

"They thought it was the coolest thing they had ever heard. Never having to talk again. An AI tied directly into your brain so that a virtual reality, one that can in no way compete with real life, exists whenever you so desire. Living in the cloud where face to face human interaction becomes obsolete."

"Jesus."

"You know, I think these non-social genes are far more prevalent than people realize. If you add to the spectrum, people who find interacting with other people stressful and would rather sit inside and watch TV all day, play video games all day, etc. The problem is way worse and far more advanced than anyone realizes. A lot of good actors, I guess."

"Yes, Jess, that is a great point. Our environment is a social one, but it doesn't mean that people in it would choose this type of environment given a choice. They might be coping or carrying stress just to stay employed."

"Exactly. I see the pattern, and it is terrifying. Over time the bell curve widens, and the male brain becomes more male and less empathic. They start to favor objects and tech more and more and slowly lose the ability to bond, especially with females. They objectify women even more as they lose the ability to love. Then they embrace masculinity and power until it finally devolves and collapses into a violent world. A selfish world. A return to an animalistic world. A return back to animals. When you said that in the first workshop, I thought you might be losing it. I don't think that anymore."

"That's how it all happens, right? The female prodigy just atrophies back to a normal state. Nature demands its gift back because we don't cherish it. Empathy fades. Love fades. Societies begin to collapse, and then there are no great storytellers to put it all back together again. No storytellers to tell and no one to empathize with a great story. This is how humanity dies, and Nature returns to what it once was. Tell me. Tell me I'm right?"

"Yes, Jess. Remember, repeat after me? Nature is fucking savage? It's returning to its savage ways. It's the whole reason I sought you out to help me. Do you see the severity of the problem?"

"I see the cliff and humans racing faster and faster towards it."

"God dammit Jess will you just fucking help me? Don't you see why it must be a woman to help me tell this story? You bore the human species. Love came from the female."

"And the males will kill it."

"Jessica please, what are you doing?"

"I'm crying. Can't you put yourself in my shoes?"

"Yes Jess, trust me, I feel what you feel."

"It's so fucking sad. All the pain and suffering and war. All the mothers, through countless years, who lost their sons in battle for nothing. All the pointless loss. All the suffering to come. Empathy is supposed to make you love one another, and humans have trashed it. They toss it without question to stare at shiny objects. Love, religion, literature, art, music, love stories. They will toss it all in the end to chase some technological fantasy."

"Jess, they just have the wrong story. They think they're the pinnacle. If they understood it was an anomaly, a prodigious event, I think they would cherish it. If they understood how fragile it is and that it can be lost forever, I think they would try to save it."

"I don't know. I just don't see it yet. I'm sorry, I just don't think the problem has a solution. Are you mad at me?"

"No, of course not. I understand the complexity of the situation. Actually, even more so thanks to you."

"So, what are you going to do?"

"Well, I don't have a choice in the matter. Remember powerful forces? Something is compelling me to keep trying somehow. Keep trying to find a solution."

"But how?"

"Well, that is the reason for asking to meet. I want to get your opinion on my new approach."

"Ok."

"Well, first, let me say that I have learned a lot with you in these workshops, and I thank you for that. Sometimes being in an autistic mind all day, you forget the human aspect. You forget that people see problems differently. Forget that they have different perspectives and opinions."

"You're trying to say that you have trouble empathizing with them, right?"

"In a way but in a way not. I'm also trying to say that people don't have these strict patterning minds yet and you kind of brought that into focus for me. They don't see systems and energy and root cause, etcetera. I think that is part of the reason you don't think it's solvable. It takes a world full of hybrids to see it, remember?"

"Yes, and right."

"I agree, and I see that now. People are still too social and have no interest in solving problems. It's not a criticism of them; it's just their nature. It's like the global warming/CO_2 issue. From my autistic perspective, no one wants to solve the problem. They just want to argue back in forth. I'm sure they would never admit this, but it's more about the argument than the problem. They like to argue because it is a social exercise. A chance to express their last remaining social genes, so to speak."

"Ok, I would agree with that."

"So, I see now that I have been coming about this all wrong, and I thank you for that. I thought it was possible to get humans to see what I see this whole time, but that will never work. Humans are storytellers. You taught me this, Jess. They will never come out of their story. I was trying to get them to come out of their construct, their dual reality, and see the world as it really is, but they will never do this willingly. I have to go into their reality, their fiction, and challenge them."

"Ok, but how in the world would you ever do this?"

"Get your laptop. I want to show you something."

Jess goes to get her laptop and then comes back to the couch.

"Ok, now google United States Constitution."

"Ok, done."

"Now copy the 27 ratified amendments to Word."

"Ok, done."

"Now, search for the word environment."

"Huh?"

"Just do it, search for environment."

"I get nothing."

"Exactly. Which is entirely the problem. The constitution of the United States is the framework for our great society, and the word environment is not mentioned once."

"Need more, please."

"Our founding fathers drafted this framework to try and create a better society, a lasting society. Their main focus was to give the populous certain inalienable rights and freedoms that the government could not infringe upon. The first 10 are called the bill of rights, and, again, the word environment is never mentioned. These great men understood political forces but not biological ones. They didn't understand that biological forces can influence political ones."

"Ok, but I still need more."

"The bill of rights was created in 1789. Jess, they were still widely practicing bloodletting in 1789. These men who created this great story knew nothing about biological forces, only political ones."

"The first amendment should guarantee our inalienable right to a clean environment! It's the only one that matters to maintain and ultimately sustain a society."

"Throughout the history of mankind, ever since man placed the first plow into the soil, they have been their own worst enemy. Societies have risen, turned, fallen and collapsed, risen, turned, fallen and collapsed, risen, turned, fallen and collapsed at infinitum. They keep repeating this cycle over and over again. Always when they fall, barbaric atrocities follow. Wars, genocide, murder, total loss of morality, total loss of empathy for their fellow man."

"Humans keep doing this to themselves over and over again because they have the wrong story. The storytellers are following an incorrect story. A falsehood. A fiction that works against them."

"And the specific fiction you are referring to?"

"As you said, the fiction that they are the pinnacle of evolution. That everything they can do, they should do. Higher than Nature and immune to its laws. If they ever want to win and stop always losing, Nature's laws must be part of their story. If mankind ever wants to break this vicious cycle of rise, turn, fall, collapse they must acknowledge these laws."

"All life forms, including humans, are made of cells. We're just cells, and our biology responds to a changing environment like any other life form. These are the forces we should be most concerned about, not political ones. A clean, lasting environment must be the first law of any constitution. If this inalienable right is lost, all other rights will ultimately fall with it."

"Humans must also understand and acknowledge that they are an anomaly of Nature. They must accept it and embrace it. They're a female prodigy. A social giraffe with a 50-foot-long neck. Because they are an anomaly, there will be tremendous natural forces working against them if they behave unnaturally. If they pollute themselves and try to create an unnatural world, their biology will respond. At some point, Nature will demand its special gift back."

"An anomaly does not have to be viewed as a bad thing. A pearl is an anomaly. Out of stress, life creates something beautiful. Out of stress, life created us. The anomaly, though, must be protected, cherished, and maintained, or it will be lost and lost forever."

"Ok, obviously, I'm with you, but how does this allow you to challenge them?"

"It's so obvious that what we are doing is not sustainable. The United States is on the cusps of falling. Anyone that can't see this either has their head in the sand or glued to their shiny rectangle. Societies rise and collapse, and the United States is next in line, and when it falls, it won't be pretty. It will make all the other collapses before it look like brief skirmishes. The world is so interconnected now that when one great pillar falls, they all fall with it."

"Right, but still, how do you challenge them?"

"The crucial part missing is there must be a balance. Nature, by design, creates a balance and equilibrium. It's always correcting itself because it uses feedback to sustain and control itself based on its environment. Humans never do this. They think of themselves as above Nature and just keep polluting and raping the natural world until they collapse. Time and time again, over and over again. Immeasurable suffering in the past all at their own hand and all because they have the wrong story. All because they don't understand that they respond to environmental change just like all biology. They are not immune to it. Actually, even more sensitive to it. All their maladies, from past to present, can be explained by this. Stimulation of their biology followed by the conservation of energy."

"Right, but still, how will you challenge them?"

"When we pay our taxes, that money is our commitment to our government. It is like a contract. I give you something, and you give me something in return. That return is that they are supposed to protect us. Protect us from our enemies and threats, both foreign and domestic."

"We are no longer being protected. We live in a toxic world due to their lack of oversight and lack of concern for our well-being. These threats invade our biology every day. Every breath. Every bite. Every drink. Their business model is to pollute the world and then profit from suffering. It's such a bad business model. It's so unnatural. It's so unsustainable. It's so immoral. You simply can't knowingly pollute the world and then profit from suffering. It is the greatest of all sins."

"It's also a breach of contract. I paid my taxes and was not protected. My daughter was not protected. Countless other children are not protected."

"What are you saying? You are going to sue the government for your loss? For the death of your child?"

"No, I'm going to sue the government for everyone's loss. For everyone that has ever suffered in this country. The root cause of all illnesses is environmental change. Cancer, chronic fatigue, fibromyalgia, diabetes, lupus, Alzheimer's, depression, suicidality in adults, suicidality in young children, obesity, autoimmune disorders, anxiety, drug addiction, ADHD, the list is endless. These are all negative outcomes from a changing environment. From living in a toxic world. The root cause of every human malady is environmental change and the biological response to that change."

"There are countless documented cases where human safety was secondary to profits, to tax dollars. Where our country puts our health and the health of innocent children secondary. Children didn't ask to be born into this toxic fucked up mess, and someone must stand up for them. Finally, someone must put their safety first and realize that if the children of our society are failing, all will eventually be lost. The health and happiness of every child born into this world is the one and only metric that we must use to determine our success."

"You're going to sue the entire federal government?"

"Yes."

"Ok, but how exactly?"

"It was a dream, Jess. I saw it in a dream."

"What?"

"The signs. The freaking signs. They were there all along."

"What signs?"

"In the dream, I was walking through our city, and I looked up, and they were all shining like a beacon, illuminating a path. We even joked about it in one of the earlier workshops."

"What signs?"

"The billboards, Jess. They are everywhere. When you look up, you can't miss them. It's all the personal attorney signs in our city. This is how to win. This is the way in I was searching for."

"The way in is through a personal injury attorney?"

"Jess, you see it now, right? It's so much more than that. Not only are these signs, but they are signs for something else. Signs that our society is collapsing. Signs that everyone just wants to sue each other and not work out their differences. Signs that the powerful are taking advantage of the weak. Signs of cheating the system in selfish acts of greed. Signs that no one can empathize with one another and share a common goal versus a selfish one. Signs that money is more important than safety and health. Signs that the great fiction is failing. Signs that empathy, needed to tell and believe in the great story, is dying."

"Again, I was looking at it wrong. My plan was to get them to come out of their fiction and see the true world. This way will never work because they are storytellers. They will never see the story that the path they have chosen is the problem. I must embrace their fiction to win."

I now take the stool standing almost at the ceiling in Jess's den. I'm looking in her direction and beyond her like I'm addressing all of humanity.

"This is the way to change the outcome to work in humanity's favor for once and for all. To win instead of always losing. Save what is social. Save empathy and love. The stakes now are higher than ever. This might be the last time humanity gets this chance."

"So, you have to fight the ones you are trying to save, Ryan?"

"I will have to fight men. Powerful men. The ones who have profited immensely from these stories and will do everything in their power to defend them."

"Jesus, so you are going to sue the entire federal government?"

"Yes, Jess. The way in is through their legal fictions. Once I'm inside, I will destroy their construct from within. I will use this breach of contract to destroy the greatest story ever told, The United States of America, and rebuild it to a lasting form that our forefathers so desperately wanted. A sustainable nation and a sustainable population built on the foundation of a sustainable environment. A clean environment. A pure environment."

"Finally, for once and for all, a society that understands the natural world and lives by its laws. A loving, caring, compassionate, city on a hill for the rest of humanity to see and follow."

"The Great United corrected for the entire world to see."

"It's the only way to save humanity. It's the only way to save love."

My words reverberate on the last word, then silence. Long silence. Jess looks down and then back up at me, then down again. She now looks like she's calculating something.

More silence.

I repeat it again for effect.

"It's the only way to save love..."

Still silence.

"Jess?"

"Get down, Ryan."

"What's wrong, Jess? What are you thinking about?"

"Get down, please."

"Ok, but what's wrong?"

"Nothing. Listen to me."

She comes over closer. She grabs my hand.

"Ryan, listen. You are a genuinely good person. Don't take this the wrong way, but this is madness. However, I had an epiphany when you were up there talking. I had a vision."

"What, Jess?"

"I think the solution has to be part madness to save humanity from the great filter. I mean, that's why they call it a great filter, right? Your mind is just so...so, I don't even know the word for what your mind is. But I guess that's what's needed. Someone who sees the world so differently. Someone who can see a different path that everyone before us hasn't taken."

"Huh, I don't understand?"

"No offense, Ryan, but the YouTube thing. Like you said, not even close. But this. Using their fiction to destroy their construct. You're closer, Ryan. In the vision, I saw it. You're almost there."

"What's the vision, Jess?"

Jess then smiles, gets up, and grabs her keys.

"Until we meet again, Ryan," Jess says headed out the door and to her car.

"Lock up when you leave, please."

"Wait, you're leaving? You can't leave on that. You have to explain. Wait, don't leave."

CHAPTER SIXTEEN
THE GREEN CODE

"Well, hello Jessica."

"Hi Ryan."

"How are you, Jessica?"

"I'm good, Ryan. Please come on in."

"Thank you, Jessica."

"You're very welcome, Ryan."

"Jessica!"

"Ryan!"

"Oh my god, can you please tell me something?"

"Huh?"

"The last time we met? Your vision? These last few weeks have been agony for me, Jess. Why would you do that to a friend?"

"Wow, impatient much? Please sit down, Ryan. So, would you like a beverage? How about some chips and salsa? Maybe, some snack nuts?"

"What? You're messing with me, aren't you?"

Jess cracks a smile and then starts laughing.

"Funny, Jess."

"Ok, Jess, let's sit on the couch and talk about the weather. Wow, it sure was hot the last few days. What did you think about all that rain over the weekend? It really poured, didn't it? Well, I guess the plants needed it, though." I said, trying to add to her humor.

"Honestly, I wouldn't know, Ryan. I wasn't even in town."

"What? Where did you go? Is that why you wouldn't answer my texts?"

"There's no reception where I went."

"Huh? Where did you go, the south pole?"

"Funny. Well, maybe there was reception, but I didn't have my phone."

"Wow, Jessica went somewhere without her lifeline. What's gotten into you?"

"You'll see."

"Ok, Jess, let's get to it. I was in agony for three weeks. Your vision the last time we met. What was it? Also, you said that I was closer. Closer how?"

"Ryan, Jesus. Easy big fella. I need some time. I'm looking for my pivot."

"I'm giving you the whole court, Jess."

Jess cracks another smile and then laughs.

"Oh Ryan."

"Oh Jess."

Jess then takes my hand.

"Ryan, I have so much to tell you. Are you ready?"

"Yesssssss, Jess, go!!!!!!!!"

"Alright, alright, but I thought about this on the ride home. We are going to do this workshop differently. I'm going to talk the whole time. Got it?"

"What Jess?"

"Ryan, got it? You can only speak when I'm ready. Got it?"

"Oh god, you are killing me. Will you promise to tell me your vision and how I'm almost there?"

"Yes, I promise but will you calm down? Now, are you sure you don't want some chips and salsa? Maybe a nice glass of lemonade? Should I squeeze some lemons before we start?"

"Jesus, your mood is wild today. Ok, ok, I give in. I won't say anything. I'm at your mercy. Just please go. Please, I'm begging you."

"Ok, Ryan, I'm going," Jess says with a giggle.

"Ryan, that last workshop did a number on me. Whew, it was a doozie. Like, I was in constant thought ever since I had my vision. I couldn't even work. It was me, just staring at the screen all day."

"Finally, I thought, well shit, this is pointless. I'm getting out of here. I have a crazy amount of vacation from working so much, so I told my boss. I'm sorry, but I have to take three weeks vacation. I have a friend in need."

"Who's the friend?"

"Ryan, no words!"

"Oh, sorry."

"So again, I desperately needed a vacation."

"Where did you go?"

"Shit, Ryan, I'm serious! You can't talk! Not joking!"

"Dammit, Jess, this is hard. I can't help it. I want to know about you."

"Ryan, you have been talking the most in these workshops. It's time for me to take the stage. I want to tell you what I've learned. Will you please let me?"

"Ok, ok, I'm sorry. I'm going to try my best. However, I might occasionally have to stuff my face in this pillow."

"You can do that," Jess said, motivating me with her eyes to do it.

"Alright, no more words until you say I can talk, go."

"So again, wait, let me back up. So, I'm at my desk at work, and I can't do anything. I'm just frozen, staring at the screen, and it's like the pixels are shooting lasers into my brain. I couldn't take it anymore. I thought, I got to get out of this construct. This man-made shit show. I need a break from this unnatural world."

"So, I went home, packed some camping equipment, jumped in my jeep, and headed west. After a hundred miles or so, I pulled up to a post office and mailed my phone back to my house."

"I wanted to get away from people and technology. No asocial media, no TV, and no sounds of the modern world."

"I wanted to find Nature and hopefully find myself. I wanted to see if I could see what you see."

"The good news is that I finally found a place out west where there was no one. No signs of technology, sounds, or people. At night when I was camping, I saw so many stars. The place I found felt like a primitive world. I could have gone back 100,000 years in time, and it felt like the place I was at would have been the same. There was no marker to know if it was 100,000 BC or the present, other than the Jeep engulfed in the thick canopy of the woods."

"After over a week in the woods, hiking for miles from the jeep, exploring, then resting, I finally felt like I found Nature. I also think my brain changed. Like when all that simulation from the modern world was finally removed, it was as if my brain recalibrated itself. It was now open to see the natural world."

"I'm not saying I can see everything you see, but I think I finally put it all together. I clicked in the last puzzle piece in the woods, and everything was revealed to me."

"I think there is a lot you didn't tell me, Ryan. I don't know if you withheld it for a reason or if you were playing a game to see if I would get there."

"All I know is that Nature is so wonderful. It is our God, and it is a God of life. I saw it so clearly out in the woods. So many different species of plant and insect life. I felt like Darwin maybe on the Galapagos islands trying to take in all the life he could before the HMS Beagle set sail again."

"I'm so proud of myself for putting the puzzle together. I feel like I can see through the matrix. Beyond the artificial man-made busy world to Nature and what it really is. I see the green code now. I see all the mechanics. I'm so excited that I could put it together, but I'm also terrified, Ryan. Nature is savage, at least to us. You're right; there's no other way to create beauty in the world without this savagery."

"Nature is also so powerful. It can overcome any obstacle. All it needs is a temperate sun and a little stress, and off it goes. It fills every void with so many different species and so much diversity. Our God loves diversity. Our God cherishes it. Our God is also angry when it's threatened."

"I know I'm getting a little off-track, Ryan, but I felt my whole body change when I was out there. I don't think humanity realizes how stressful our modern-day world has become. It's only when you detach and shelter from it that you realize the burden the mind must be enduring. The constant barrage of noise, pollution, people, deadlines, assignments, bills, newsfeeds, TV, medicine, and online stimulation. The list goes on and on. It's understandable why the brain would be changing over generations. It's just too many things."

"Ryan, in the woods, I had an epiphany about you. The whole hybrid thing. I remember the first time you told me you're a hybrid. At first, I thought it was just some clever catchphrase you came up with to try and impress me or, I don't know. Maybe it's so different you thought it would intrigue me or something."

"But, in the woods, it came to me. You really are a hybrid. I don't know how this happened. I don't know your parents. Or if that even has anything to do with it. Maybe it was your parent's epigenome bouncing in their teenage years, and constructive interference created a bipolar anomaly called you. Whatever the reason, your brain is hybridized. It's extreme female and extreme male at the same time."

"Do you want to know how I know? You can't talk, Ryan. Just nod if you do."

I nod.

"You're trying to save all the children of the world. You're empathizing with every single one of them. Your mind is constantly putting itself in their shoes, and it affectively feels all their suffering. You're a hyper mother trying to protect them from what's coming. That's the extreme female side."

"On the extreme male side, you're trying to put all these patterns and systems together to save them. Your brain is constantly trying to solve their suffering and figure out a way to avoid what's coming. It's running all these simulations over and over again, looking for a way out of this madness. It's looking for the one system that would save humanity."

"Your brain is so beautiful, Ryan. You really can see where humanity came from and where it's headed. I wish all brains could be like yours. I know it's impossible, though. Nature gravitates towards specialists per niche."

"I want to tell you something else that I couldn't stop thinking about. In one of the workshops, you told me to think of the controller for a gene as a stereo receiver. There's an on switch, off switch, and a volume controller. Nature can decide when to turn a gene on, when to turn it off, and, most importantly, how much of the gene is needed. Once you know these mechanics, the answer becomes pretty simple to the most profound question of them all. What in the hell is a human? Why are we so different from everything that has ever existed on this planet?"

"I think in some way or another, humans have been trying to figure this out for the last 10,000 years or maybe even longer. In those quiet moments, all alone. Maybe alone looking up at the heavens when all the stars are out or maybe in their twilight years just before death and wondering what it all means. The quiet wondering we all do. Quietly wondering, what the fuck am I? Why am I here? What purpose do I serve? Is there a god for me?"

"The answer is simple. Just go out into Nature and experience it. Get to know it. Bond with Nature, again. If you do, you will see the one and only thing you need to see. Just take the traits of every species that has ever existed on this planet and play a game in your mind, and the answer will come to you. What happens if I take all these traits and individually overexpress them times 1000 and leave them on for a lifetime? In doing this, which individual trait will give me a human."

"The answer is so simple, Ryan. It's the bond of an animal mother protecting her baby offspring. Just take this trait and turn up the receiver to max volume and never switch it off. Do this 50,000 years ago, and her love blossoms out to become love for all and for a lifetime. Love for a child, love for a mate, and love for each other. The protectiveness that a mother has is given to all. Whoever has this prodigy will become unstoppable. No species can compete against love."

"That's the answer to what we are. A clever response by Nature to win a life and death competition 50,000 years ago. I mean, look at humans. All soft and baby-like. Completely exposed. I mean, what species in the last 4 billion years has had to wear clothing to survive? Humans are a female prodigy. Permanent mothers. When you look up at the stars at night and wonder about all this, be amazed at the power of Nature and what it's capable of. Prodigious empathy was given to the hominid on the brink of extinction against a savage competitor in the greatest species competition in the history of this planet."

"And, it's funny, Ryan, the definition of empathy. Putting yourself in someone's else shoes. Who are the two most valuable people in that sentence from a survival of the fittest standpoint? Yourself is the mother, and the someone else is her child. And, what is the chance of a species enduring if they start to lose this ability?"

"Also, can a mother put herself in her child's shoes without first putting her mind into her own? Everyone seems to be trying to figure out what human consciousness is lately. Like why do we have it? Why don't other species have it? Well, is that not it? I don't think I'm oversimplifying this. For the mother to put her mind into her child's position, she would first have to put herself into her own."

"I think that's it, Ryan. I think that's why we have consciousness, imagination, communication, language, storytelling, love stories, friends, communities, religion, burial, and grieving. It's just a set of mothering genes turned up to 1000 and left on for a lifetime. We are Nature's prodigy. Nature can do incredible things, and it's showing us this, but we have to protect it, Ryan. We have to protect what makes us unique."

"So now we come to the terrifying part, Ryan. Nature also has priorities and strict rules. Each species must play by these rules or suffer the consequences.

It's so wild, Ryan, how things are right in front of you, but you don't take the time to look at them. People and, I guess, society eventually accepts things and moves on. People are so busy with their lives that they don't have time. You might go, hmm, ok, that's interesting. I guess this is the new norm now. Well, ok then. But no one is trying to put all these patterns together."

"And, even in all these workshops, I didn't put this one together, which I'm upset with myself, but yeah, I don't know; it's weird that I didn't see it. But, out in the deep, deep woods, my mind was so in tune with the world around me. So focused on Nature and the mechanics. And then, at that moment, my mind shifted from looking at the past to looking forward to the present, and that's when it hit me like a ton of bricks."

"I see it now, Ryan, and it's fucking wild. So fucking wild, Ryan. Jesus Christ!! It's happening right before our very eyes. Fucking Nature. It's so clever."

"Gender Ryan. Gender! Fucking Nature is doing it right before our very eyes, and no one is even putting it together!!!"

"Gender is fluid. I don't think this is even up for debate it's so pronounced, and it's happening so quickly from an evolutionary timeline.

Men who like other men. Women who like other women. Men who want to be women. Women who want to be men. Men who have female traits. Women who have male traits. Men who have female interests. Women who have male interests. Men who look feminine. Women who look male. Men who like both sexes. Women who like both sexes. Gender is fluid. Gender is malleable. Nature is creating variation in these traits. The stress axis is bouncing, and the epigenome is trying to resolve this."

"Ryan, gender is fluid, and at the same time, humanity is becoming more male. People, and more so males, are becoming less and less social. More violent and aggressive. Less caring and nurturing. Stoic and less empathic. Our culture labels it as toxic masculinity, but that's what it is. I don't think this is even up for debate either it's so pronounced, and it's also happening so quickly from an evolutionary timeline. Do you know what this means, Ryan? It means you're right. The evolutionary pathway is there. Gender is fluid today, and the world is becoming more male. The opposite must have happened 50,000 years ago. Due to stress from a savage competitor, gender became fluid, the genes became malleable, and the hominid on the brink of extinction became more female to protect and care for each other."

"God dammit, Ryan, how did you figure all this out? You still can't speak! So here, write it down on a note."

The note reads, "Don't stop Jess! You're on a roll."

"Ok, ok, but you are telling me later."

"I don't know where to go from here. It's so terrifying. Wait, wait, I almost forgot. I want to tell you another thing before I get into the terrifying part. I got back a few days ago from my trip, and since then, I have been deep in research. So many questions came to me out in the woods, and right when I got back home, I had to know the answer."

"I still remember the workshop where we talked about babies crying. It's funny how crying never dawned on me before we started discussing these topics. I mean, I've been around many friends and family members with new babies, and they cry and cry and cry. It's another one of those patterns that you don't see or think about. You say, well, I guess this is normal for being a human. But, my god, can you imagine 50,000 years ago and your baby doing that in a world full of predators? I think you're right, Ryan. All of this has something to do with babies crying."

"So, I got to thinking about autism, and there it was, Ryan, right when I googled it. Autistic babies exhibit atypical crying patterns. The epigenome is changing these genes, right? All these traits and genes are tied together somehow. Crying, empathy, our ability to speak, our ability to love. All these genes are linked together, Ryan!"

"Oh, and cholesterol. The fuel for the stress axis. There it was again right there when I googled it. Autism manifests with abnormal cholesterol levels. The stress axis again bouncing, right?"

"Jesus, Ryan, cholesterol is a marker for evolution. The trends match perfectly. Humanity is becoming more male while autism, the extreme male brain, is increasing. There's a direct correlation to increased cholesterol in humans. Also, I'm convinced that Alzheimer's is somehow related to all this. Stimulation, then variation, then conservation of maintenance energy if not adapting. There's just so much evolutionary pressure on the brain right now. It's just too much stress!"

"Seriously, how did you put all this together? You still can't talk."

Jess takes my note. It reads, "It's just patterns, Jess, and my brain loves patterns. Keep going!"

"But what's wild, Ryan, is that no one questions the big picture. Humans see cholesterol rising, and they go, well, I guess we have to develop a pill stat. I mean, Nature has been at this for billions of years. And, who's to say it's not longer? These mechanics of life may be as old as the universe. These mechanics may be infinitely old."

"What is the arrogance of mankind to see something fundamentally change in their biology and not question it? Like not question, is there a greater reason for this change? Nature creates a balance in all things, and something is fundamentally out of balance inside the human body. Did anyone ever wonder, is there a greater purpose? Again, it's fuel for the stress axis!"

"Why can't humans see patterns, Ryan? I include myself in this group, by the way, pre-workshops."

I hand her another note.

It reads, "They like trees."

"Huh, they like trees? What? Oh, I get it. You mean they can't see the forest through the trees?"

I nod.

"That's a good analogy. The forest is Nature. The trees are narrow interests. Oh, oh, and the forest is a system, right? A natural system? Right, Ryan?"

I nod.

"Hmm, this emerging human trait scares me, though, Ryan. Like, even if you pull them away from constantly staring at the bark and you fly them up miles above the canopy, will they even see it? I feel doubt creeping in."

"Ok, Ryan, now the scary part. I know, I know, Jess, repeat after me."

"So, this wild world that we now live in. I thought a lot about it when I was alone in the woods. And, besides being a dopamine currency carnival, what is all this? What is the fundamental force that makes this world go? Then I thought about the people who lived here before we did. The native Americans. They didn't have any of this shit of our modern world. They just existed. No motivation to invent, develop, or conquer. They just existed in Nature, cherished it, and were happy from everything we know. Then the white man came and killed them all for what they had. Killed them all and changed the natural world to what we see today."

"But, you know what I realized about this world we live in? It's another one of those things that you don't think about, like fluid gender, crying babies, or rising cholesterol levels. Our society is exceedingly male. All the rules, laws, governance, taxation, orders, covenants, conformity, hierarchy, manmade structures, cities with strict patterns, imposing skyscrapers and rigid architecture, guns, weapons, military hardware, computer code, hyper-violent movies, hyper-violent TV shows, hyper-violent video games, hyper-sexual everything, always seeking out the latest thing, never satisfied, inventing medicines to try and control Nature, attempting to edit the genome to control biology, pesticides to control Nature, unnatural farming techniques to control Nature. The list goes on and on."

"It's all about control and dominance. It's all male traits. That's why this world exists. Out in the woods, I remembered you said autism was first seen in the white race. Ryan, I'm confident this modern world wouldn't be possible without some level of autism. Autism is the reverberation and decay from the hyper-speed at which our brains are changing. It is the epigenome unsuccessfully trying to stabilize the axis. It's Nature aggressively increasing variation in the most stressed part of a human. An overshoot in a dynamic system that went too far. Autism is a marker for the change in all humanity."

"This is the mechanics of the great filter, Ryan. When I laid down to sleep at night in the back of my jeep, again, the stars were so bright. Every night I could see them so clearly. I felt as if they were trying to tell me a story. I would look up for hours and imagine these other worlds, putting myself in their position. Ryan, any alien world that achieved technology like ours, socialness, language, and empathy would always have to come first. It would just have to. Technology can't be achieved without beings first coming together and cooperating. It must start with socialness. How many species like us didn't get it until it was too late? How many didn't understand that Nature seeks a balance for all things? How many chased technology without realizing that something would always be lost in the pursuit?"

"The great filter should be called the great vacuum. The thing that sucks you in. Dopamine pulls you in, and before you know it, the trait that got you there is slowly ebbing away in favor of the traits needed for a changing world. That's why the universe is silent. I'm sure of it. It's because no one ever put it together like a system, past, present, and future. They never realized that the past and how everything came to be was infinitely more important than the future."

"That's it, isn't it Ryan? The world becomes so male that it collapses. I know I'm right because it's already happening. Empathy is already dying in the human race. Rampant child sex trafficking, people smuggling deadly drugs across our border without a single care of the devastating harm caused to families, politicians letting them to enrich themselves, sexual assault on the rise, an epidemic of date rape drugs being used on unsuspecting young women, everyone wanting to scam everyone out of their money, Big Pharma pushing deadly addictive drugs just to enrich themselves, Wallstreet brokers scheming for personal gain that crashes our economy, big industry polluting the environment in the poorest communities for profit. The list goes on and on. All this, and people are worried about carbon dioxide?"

"Everything is evolving to self or selfish interests, isn't it, Ryan? That's male in the natural world. The only thing in the natural world that puts something before self is female."

"I see now why you hate it so much, Ryan. Capitalism. It's none of the reasons that other people give. You hate it because those without empathy thrive in capitalism, and those with empathy do not. We are changing the environment to reward those who put self first versus those who put others first. We are proving Lamarck correct every single day, and no one sees it."

"Also, these dark triad traits emerging in the human race. Narcissism, psychopathy, and Machiavellianism. In the right conditions, they can flourish in a capitalistic society. They can be rewarded. Aggressiveness, grandiosity, greed, self-promotion, arrogance, cunningness, manipulation, self-interest, dominance. There's so much trait variation in the human brain, and the common theme is a lack of empathy. The common theme is hyper-masculinity, and we celebrate it in our capitalistic society."

"I know how it all ends now, Ryan. The patterns fit so perfectly to tell the story. People who have ascended to the top of our capitalistic society conspire to enrich themselves even more. The ones we idolize because they have the most worthless green paper begin to try and control everything and everyone because that is the same traits that got them there. They want to dominate and control every aspect of our lives and create a new world order because they think they know better than everyone else."

"At first, their plan is not transparent. It's gilded in the spirit of progress. Machines and computers become the focal point of production. Assembly lines at full pace, churning them out in record time. Over time they're used to control food production, money transfer, medicine production, transportation, and energy production. Every aspect of human life, soon, over time, controlled in one way or another by a computer or a machine."

"But, the machines don't control themselves. The, quote, elite control them. The male brains out for a new world order to control the entire world population. Brains without empathy who only want to enrich themselves now have full control of an interconnected world."

"That's why you are obsessed with that movie, isn't it? *The Matrix*. It's because humans almost got the story right, didn't they? It's not the machines that enslave people. It's the extreme male brains that control the machines that enslave people."

"What's wild is the story is so close. When they were writing it, did they even know how close they were? All the humans in those pods and the machines taking their bioelectric energy. That's technology slowly taking away what is truly human, empathy and socialness. And all the humans plugged into the matrix as a ploy to try and keep them content. That's technology placating us with endless streams of media, advertisements, and false promises from our leaders. A dopamine drip through the cables that keeps us content while behind closed doors, the rich and powerful create the new world order to control us all. And the agents defending the matrix. That's the extreme male brains in the future who have no empathy for the enslaved. Human beings that act like robots and kill without question to defend the new world order."

"It sounds so crazy when you say it, but it's already happening in China! Their government putting cameras everywhere to spy on everyone. To appease the Chinese people, they tell them it's for their protection and will make the world a safer place. But that's the very definition of Machiavellian. The end game is power and control. I saw a video about people caught jaywalking in China. They put their photos up on monitors all around the city as a lesson. They also track everyone's cell phone to see if they are charging them properly. If people let their cell phone batteries get too low, it's supposedly an indicator that they are not responsible. This metric is then used to determine if you qualify for a bank loan. Just two examples out of countless ones. The Chinese government ultimately controls all aspects of people's lives. No freedom of expression, freedom of movement, freedom of religion. Madness, Ryan."

"Slowly, over time, this same type of control creeps into all our lives. As the world becomes increasingly violent, our leaders say it's the only way. I wouldn't even put it past them to construct chaos and division to speed up their agenda further, like turning us against each other by promoting extreme social views. Governments then add increasing monitoring and control, leading to more unrest and civil disobedience. This emboldens the elite to push even further. Ultimately, society has no choice but to accept their fate as governments using technology have become far too powerful."

"God Ryan, I know the end, but it's too terrifying. I already know you know it. You do then end, Ryan. You can talk now. I can't do the end. It's just too sad."

"Ryan, Ryan, you can talk now."

"Wow, Jess, just wow. That time in the woods was very enlightening. Do you understand now why empathy must be saved? Humanity must intervene in some way to save this trait. Left unchecked, Nature will always revert back to its modus operandi, Jess."

"Yes, Ryan, yes! I see it now. I see the green code. Nature is savage, and it's reverting back. It's correcting itself. Humanity must intervene to stop it."

"Finish the story, Ryan. I know you know it."

"Okay."

"Well, as you said, over time, machines begin to control everything. Man pushes to become more and more efficient, especially with food production. Creating all types of highly efficient but unnatural food production to try and push the population further and increase reliance on technology and the, quote, elite. Massive scale industrial fish farming, genetically engineered crops, monocultures, synthetic fertilizers, crop specific pesticides, genetically modified meat factories. The list goes on and on. This continues until, eventually, there's nothing natural left in the world. The extreme male brain attempts to subvert and control Nature and the entire world population."

"But then one day, society just stops functioning. It's like that famous quote, 'there are decades where nothing happens; and there are weeks where decades happen.' A tipping point is reached between the powerful and the controlled, and man with all his technology and weapons can't hold it together any longer, and the whole thing devolves into anarchy. It devolves into a worldwide war against the people who control the machines. The hominid who defeated all the other hominids for survival tens of thousands of years ago now has no one left to fight. In the end, they just fight each other. Eventually and inevitably, the machines that ran the world come to a grinding halt."

"The problem, though, is the world is no longer natural. The seas are bare and polluted. The monocultures fail without technological intervention. The high yield crops fail without the exotic fertilizers. The meat factories come to a grinding halt without the power to run them. Because the earth is so depleted and unnatural there's only enough food to feed maybe 25 percent of the world's population. It would take years if not decades for the Earth to naturally restore itself."

"Jess, people don't just lie down and die. The world devolves into savagery for survival. It becomes an animalist world. The stress and trauma of this event is so great that empathy is completely silenced in the human race. Any child born after this event is born without this trait. It is the final blow to the empathetic mind. Love breathes its last breath and then is extinguished for an eternity."

"God Ryan, that is so terrifying and sad, but I truly think it will happen. The patterns are emerging and growing stronger every year. For me, the clock starts at 2007 when the iPhone was invented, and the world became, so called, socially connected. It's only been a little over a decade, and look at what a shit show our society has become. It's just too much for the human brain. We are entering the great filter, I know it now. How long do you think before this happens?"

"My estimation is 75 years."

"Jesus, if I had a child today, they could live to see that."

"What was your vision, Jess?"

"Jess? Please tell me. Every part of my being tells me this is humanity's last chance, and the United States is the last hope. Jess, please tell me. I'm begging you."

"Ryan, when you were standing on the stool in my den, I saw myself in a courtroom."

"Courtroom? What courtroom?"

"The specific courtroom is not important, Ryan. What is important is that I was talking, and the courtroom was packed with women. Only women."

"Only women? I don't understand."

"I see it now. That's the only way to save humanity."

"Female traits saved us 50,000 years ago; the only way out of this is for them to save us again. Women and young girls who want children must unite and demand change."

"Oh my god, Jess, you are right! Why didn't I see this? I'm such an idiot. Yes, that's the only way. Uniting all women to demand change. That's brilliant. You're brilliant, Jess. Also, you can imagine this would be a path never taken as technology increases, so the likelihood of this being a successful solution for the great filter is high."

"Ryan, I never said it would work, but I think it's the only way it could work."

"Jess, are you saying what I think you're saying?"

"What?"

"That you are the one to save humanity."

"Yes!!! Fuck this Roman, end-stage humanity, free fall. I want to try with you, Ryan. I want to be the one to try and unite all the mothers and future mothers of the world. I want to show them that a better world for their children is possible. This world is not sustainable. Anyone that can't see that is either male or...male. I want to try and correct this world before Nature does."

"Jesus Jess."

"Ryan, I see the green code now! I know what Nature is capable of. Humanity has to intervene in its evolution. We have to protect what makes us special, or it will be lost and lost forever."

"Come here, Ryan. Let's stand together on the stool, and you can start again like the last time we met."

I do, and Jess joins me.

"Oh, wait, this reminds me. I have no idea why you stand on stools like this, and I've always wanted to know."

"It's because this is a higher energy state."

"Oh my god, Ryan, you are so weird, but in a cute way."

"Ryan, listen. Very important. Please tell me you have a better idea than a negative feedback controller for society to save love. I do like the idea of burning rich people's money, though."

"Huh?"

"Ryan, for this to work, women will need a simple choice they can make to reverse this shit show. Something they can embrace and rally around. Do you have that?"

"Yes, but something must be lost."

"Of course, Ryan, the balance of Nature, but will love be saved?"

"Yes, love will be saved."

"Then that's all that matters."

"Alright, Ryan...oh wait, wait, I almost forgot. Are you sure you can get me into the matrix?"

"Yes, I'm positive."

"Ok, then go."

"Alright, Jess, here we go."

We both hold hands and look beyond Jess's house, trying to stand tall like great orators. I begin again.

"Finally, for once and for all, a society that understands the natural world and lives by its laws. A loving, caring, compassionate, city on a hill for the rest of humanity to see and follow."

"The Great United corrected for the entire world to see."
"It's the only way to save humanity. It's the only way to save love."

NOTES

WS1

1. The Workhouse of the Cell: Kinesin. (2014, May). Retrieved 2020, from https://www.youtube.com/watch?v=gbycQf1TbM0

WS2

1. O'Donnell, J. (2018, September 10). More children are dying by suicide. Researchers are asking why. Retrieved from https://www.usatoday.com/story/news/nation/2018/09/10/r ising-child-suicide-defy-answers-prevention-month/1197113002/

2. TED. (2012, June 04). Juan Enriquez: Will our kids be a different species? Retrieved from https://www.youtube.com/watch?v=Syi9bqfFIdY

3. Spielberg, S. (Director). (n.d.). Jurassic Park [Video file].

4. Pacific, A. O. (2017, June 14). GALUMPHING: How Seals Move On Land. Retrieved from https://www.youtube.com/watch?v=w36iwxDtTGs

5. Irwin, R. (2016, January 26). Swimming with the playful seals off Montague Island, NSW. Retrieved from https://www.youtube.com/watch?v=MzdyrKLIURM&t=3s

6. Crabtree, J. J. (2009, October 10). David Letterman Mathematics Genius Prodigy Daniel Tammet Math 3.14 Pi Day. Retrieved from https://www.youtube.com/watch?v=n4Arlam70bI

WS3

1. TED. (2015, July 24). Retrieved March 29, 2019, from https://www.youtube.com/watch?v=nzj7Wg4DAbs&t=747s

2. World, T. (2012). Research finds our social skills may be defining difference between humans, apes. Retrieved July 07, 2020, from https://www.pri.org/stories/2012-10-12/research-finds-our-social-skills-may-be-defining-difference-between-humans-apes

3. Piazza, E. (2018, March 25). Baby talk isn't silly. It's a serious way of learning. Retrieved July 20, 2020, from https://www.washingtonpost.com/national/health-science/baby-talk-isnt-silly-its-a-serious-way-of-learning/2018/03/23/ea64e6ea-20b6-11e8-94da-ebf9d112159c_story.html

4. Mice can inherit learned sensitivity to a smell. (2013, December 02). Retrieved from https://news.emory.edu/stories/2013/12/smell_epigenetics_ressler/campus.html

5. Whitehouse, H. (2019, March 29). Libyan bands of brothers show how deeply humans bond in adversity. Retrieved from https://theconversation.com/libyan-bands-of-brothers-show-how-deeply-humans-bond-in-adversity-34105

WS4

1. CNN. (2018, February 21). CNN town hall in wake of Florida school shooting. Retrieved from https://www.youtube.com/watch?v=ZaLh74eXTDo&t=8s

2. Smart, I. O. (2016, September 19). Why Do More Species Live Near the Equator? Retrieved from https://www.youtube.com/watch?v=YLt0-yoOKvw&t=35s

WS5

1. CNN. (2016, November 30). Midway, a plastic island. Retrieved from https://www.youtube.com/watch?v=lsJqMmuFWO4

2. Hall, S. (2018, September 20). Say Hello to Dickinsonia, the Animal Kingdom's Newest (and Oldest) Member. Retrieved June 20, 2020, from https://www.scientificamerican.com/article/say-hello-to-dickinsonia-the-animal-kingdoms-newest-and-oldest-member/

3. Differences & similarities: Human & Animal Anatomy. (n.d.). Retrieved from https://kylehallnationaltrust.weebly.com/part-3--animation-production/-differences-similarities-human-animal-anatomy

4. Zemeckis, R. (Producer), & Zemeckis, R. (Director). (n.d.). Contact [Video file].

WS6

1. Lightman, S. (2016, April 05). Rhythms Within Rhythms: The Importance of Oscillations for Glucocorticoid Hormones. Retrieved August 22, 2020, from https://www.ncbi.nlm.nih.gov/books/NBK453178/

WS8

1. Earth, B. (2010, June 14). Triumph of the Herbivores | Prey Escapes Predator | Life of Mammals | BBC Earth. Retrieved from https://www.youtube.com/watch?v=RtnLNmB3ZNE&t=115s

2. Aptowicz, C. O. (2016, February 04). Could You Stomach the Horrors of 'Halftime' in Ancient Rome? Retrieved from https://www.livescience.com/53615-horrors-of-the-colosseum.html

WS9

1. Nutshell, K. -. (2018, February 01). Why Alien Life Would be our Doom - The Great Filter. Retrieved from https://www.youtube.com/watch?v=UjtOGPJ0URM

2. Grubb, J. (2018, May 08). Google Duplex: A.I. Assistant Calls Local Businesses To Make Appointments. Retrieved from https://www.youtube.com/watch?v=D5VN56jQMWM

WS10

1. Reynolds, G. (2014, December 17). How Exercise Changes Our DNA. Retrieved from https://well.blogs.nytimes.com/2014/12/17/how-exercise-changes-our-dna/

WS11

1. Begley, S. (2018, June 12). CRISPR-Edited Cells Linked to Cancer Risk in 2 Studies. Retrieved June 27, 2020, from https://www.scientificamerican.com/article/crispr-edited-cells-linked-to-cancer-risk-in-2-studies/

2. Genome-editing tool could increase cancer risk. (2018, June 11). Retrieved June 27, 2020, from

https://www.sciencedaily.com/releases/2018/06/180611133816.htm

3. 'Junk DNA' affects inherited cancer risk. (2019, December 05). Retrieved June 27, 2020, from https://www.sciencedaily.com/releases/2019/12/191205224221.htm

4. Mullin, E. (2020, June 17). Scientists Edited Human Embryos in the Lab, and It Was a Disaster. Retrieved June 27, 2020, from https://onezero.medium.com/scientists-edited-human-embryos-in-the-lab-and-it-was-a-disaster-9473918d769d

5. Woollaston, V. (2015). Controversial gene-editing tool CRISPR "could give rise to cancer", worrying studies find. Retrieved June 27, 2020, from https://www.alphr.com/bioscience/1001654/crispr-cas9-gene-editing/

6. Akst, J. (2020). Dog Study Revives Concerns About Virus Used for Gene Therapy. Retrieved June 27, 2020, from https://www.the-scientist.com/news-opinion/dog-study-revives-concerns-about-virus-used-for-gene-therapy-66915

7. Maher, R. T. (2018, October 26). Jonathan Haidt The Coddling of the American Mind. Retrieved from https://www.youtube.com/watch?v=tKW3vKpPrlw&t=251s

8. CK, L. (2015). We Are From Another Planet. Retrieved 2020, from https://www.youtube.com/watch?v=M0d47qDpJbQ&t=22s

1. Sightings, K. (2017, September 05). Giraffes Fighting. Retrieved from https://www.youtube.com/watch?v=KQLPL1qRhn8

2. Dryden, J. (2014, June 25). Parents of children with autism often have autistic traits. Retrieved from https://medicalxpress.com/news/2014-06-parents-children-autism-autistic-traits.html

9. Scott, R. (Director). (n.d.). Gladiator [Video file].

10. Roser, M. (2013, May 10). Child Mortality. Retrieved from https://ourworldindata.org/child-mortality

WS14

The Matrix[Video file]. (n.d.).

Amend

1. Joe Rogan Experience #1470 - Elon Musk. (n.d.). Retrieved June 21, 2020, from https://www.youtube.com/watch?v=RcYjXbSJBN8